CAT BREEDS
of the WORLD

A COMPLETE ILLUSTRATED ENCYCLOPEDIA

CAT BREEDS
of the WORLD

DESMOND MORRIS

VIKING

VIKING
Published by the Penguin Group
Penguin Putnam Inc., 375 Hudson Street,
New York, New York 10014, U.S.A.
Penguin Books Ltd, 27 Wrights Lane, London W8 5TZ, England
Penguin Books Australia Ltd, Ringwood, Victoria, Australia
Penguin Books Canada Ltd, 10 Alcorn Avenue,
Toronto, Ontario, Canada M4V 3B2
Penguin Books (N.Z.) Ltd, 182–190 Wairau Road,
Auckland 10, New Zealand

Penguin Books Ltd, Registered Offices:
Harmondsworth, Middlesex, England

First American edition
Published in 1999 by Viking Penguin,
a member of Penguin Putnam Inc.

1 3 5 7 9 10 8 6 4 2

Portions of this work appeared in different form
in Mr. Morris's *Catworld* published in the
United States by Viking Penguin.

CIP data available

This book is printed on acid-free paper.

Printed in Singapore by Tien Wah Press

CONTENTS

INTRODUCTION

Cat breeds of the world is a feline reference work, covering all the 100 breeds of domestic cat from the earliest to the most recent. It also includes general information about cat breeds, cat shows, feline anatomy, and coat colours and patterns. As much detail as possible is given on the origins of the various pedigree cat breeds. With many breeds there are often several conflicting ideas concerning how and where they began. In such instances, all the rival theories are presented, from the most outlandish to the most acceptable, to provide as complete a picture as possible of the history of the breed and the myths and legends that surround it, as well as the more modern, factual interpretations of its development.

THE DOMESTICATION OF THE CAT

We know for certain that 3,500 years ago the cat was already fully domesticated. We have records from ancient Egypt to prove this. But we do not know when the process began. The remains of cats have been found at a Neolithic site at Jericho dating from 9,000 years ago, but there is no proof that those felines were domesticated ones. The difficulty arises from the fact that the cat's skeleton changed very little during its shift from wild to tame. In countries where wild cats were common, we can only be sure that the transformation from wild cat to domestic animal had taken place when we have specific records and detailed pictures – as we do from ancient Egypt. Ancient bones alone can be misleading and may reflect no more than wild-cat eating rather than tame-cat keeping.

Luckily, however, we do have one intriguing feline record from a country where there were no wild cats – the island of Cyprus. In 1983, excavations at the ancient site of Khirokitia on the south coast of Cyprus unearthed a feline jawbone. The only possible explanation for its presence there, in that early human settlement, is that it belonged to a tame cat taken over to the island from the nearby mainland. It is unthinkable that settlers would have taken a savage wild cat with them. A spitting, scratching, panic-stricken wild feline would have been the last

THE HYPNOTICALLY APPEALING FACE of the domestic cat *(opposite)*, the modern descendant of the wild cat of North Africa.

kind of boat companion they would have wanted. Only tame, domesticated animals could possibly have been part of the goods and chattels of that early band of pioneers.

This slender piece of evidence from Cyprus dates from 6,000 BC, which means that we can hazard a guess that the cat had been domesticated at the very least by 8,000 years ago. How much earlier we cannot say, until future excavations bring more evidence to light.

One thing is clear: there would have been no taming of the cat before the Agricultural Revolution (in the Neolithic period, or New Stone Age). In this respect the cat differed from the dog. Dogs had a significant role to play even before the advent of farming. Back in the Palaeolithic period (or Old Stone Age) prehistoric human hunters were able to make good use of a four-legged hunting companion with superior scenting abilities and hearing. But cats were of little value to early man until he had progressed to the agricultural phase and was starting to store large quantities of food. The grain stores, in particular, must have attracted a teeming population of rats and mice almost from the moment that the human hunter settled down to become a farmer. In the early cities, where stores were great, it would have become an impossible task for human guards to ambush the mice and kill them in sufficient numbers to stamp them out or even to prevent them from multiplying. Any carnivore that preyed on these rats and mice would have been a godsend to the harassed food-storers.

It is easy to visualize how one day somebody made the casual observation that a few wild cats were approaching the grain stores and picking off the mice. For these cats, the scene must have been hard to believe. There, all around them, was a scurrying feast on a scale they had never encountered before. Gone were the interminable waits in the undergrowth. All that was needed now was a leisurely stroll in the vicinity of the vast grain stores and a gourmet supermarket of plump, grain-fed rodents awaited them. From this stage to the keeping and breeding of cats for increased vermin destruction must have been a simple step, since it benefited both sides.

With modern methods of pest control available to us, it is difficult for us to imagine the significance of the cat to those early civilizations. In ancient Egypt it rapidly rose to become, not merely a highly valued pet, but a feline deity, a sacred animal to be adored and worshipped. From there, it spread out across the Middle East, the Mediterranean and eventually, thanks to the Romans, to the whole of Europe. Everywhere it was highly esteemed for its role as a pest controller. As the centuries passed, it spread further and further, wherever mankind voyaged, working as a ship's cat to control the rodents that infested the early sailing vessels. Jumping ship in faraway places it soon established itself worldwide.

It has retained its role as an important pest-killer right down to the present day, most farmers, worldwide, still giving homes to working cats around their barns and stores. The domestication of the cat has been one of the great animal success stories. Their numbers now outstrip those of all the wild cats put together and, in their new, additional role of house-pets, their popularity is soaring to even greater heights.

How has this long domestication process changed the cat? The simple answer is: very little. Unlike the domestic dog, the modern cat has remained close to its ancestral form. Both in anatomy and behaviour it is still remarkably like its ancestor – the African Wild Cat.

Most of the changes have been superficial. Coat colour and hair length have been altered, but beneath the surface even the most pampered of pedigree cats is still the same predatory pest-killer that protected the food stores in ancient Egypt.

One of the few significant alterations has been a stepping up of the breeding cycles of the domesticated breeds. Modern pet cats can easily go through three reproductive cycles in a year, whereas the wild type will only breed once, in the spring. This tripling of the breeding rate accounts to a large extent for the dramatic way in which cat populations can explode in modern urban areas.

A second change is towards a slightly smaller body size than is found among the wild specimens. Whether this was a deliberate step taken by early cat-keepers in ancient times to make their new-found animal partners easier to handle, or whether it was the result of a great deal of inbreeding, is hard to say, but it is nevertheless a significant feature of feline domestication.

Third, modern domestic cats are slightly more 'juvenile' than their wild ancestors. This is the result, almost certainly, of unplanned selection by centuries of cat-owners. Animals that remain playful even as adults suit us better, so we favour them. They are the ones that we are the most likely to breed. They have the advantage that they look upon their human owners as pseudo-parents. This means that they will also look upon the human home as their 'nest' long after they have ceased to be kittens. And this means that they will be more likely to return home repeatedly for parental reassurance after each of their territorial forays. Less juvenile cats would be more inclined to wander off, abandon the parental site, and seek an entirely new territory to call their own. This is what wild kittens do when they become mature. But the domestic kitten must stay put and live out its life as a split personality, part-breeder and mouse-killer, and part pseudo-kitten towards its human family. This process has gone further and further in recent years as cats have become more important as house pets than as pest destroyers. The new, man-handled cat must be prepared for a great deal of interference. Human hands will repeatedly reach out to stroke and cuddle it. Only the kitten inside the adult cat will tolerate this. It is therefore perhaps true to say that the most important change in the 8,000 years of feline domestication is the creation of this infantile–adult feline.

The cat remains, nevertheless, highly adaptable and can switch to being a full-blooded wild cat with great speed. If kittens are born to a domestic cat that has turned her back on human protection, they will grow up as untame as any truly wild ones. A farm kitten that has never seen a human being during its formative weeks will become a ball of spitting fury if cornered when it is half-grown. Great patience is needed then to convert it into a friendly adult. So the cat has it both ways: it has the capacity to be a domestic kitten-cat and has retained the option of becoming a wild killer-cat if its circumstances change. No wonder it has been so successful during the past few thousand years.

FELINE GENETICS

Genetically, cats are far less variable than dogs. There are no feline equivalents of Great Danes or Chihuahuas, Mastiffs or Whippets. There is a historical reason for this. Dogs have been required to carry out a whole variety of tasks in their long partnership with mankind. Among their many roles they have been hunting partners, dogs of war, fighting dogs, guard dogs, herders, retrievers, setters, pointers, terriers, sight-hounds, scent-hounds, racers and lap dogs. By contrast, the cat has had only one official role, namely that of pest-controller.

To be a good rodent-destroyer required little or no modification of the wild cat's anatomy. A supreme carnivore, it has evolved as a highly efficient, specialized hunter. That was all that was being asked of it, so there was no pressure to change its shape. All that was needed for the domestication process to be successful was to reduce its natural shyness. Wild cats are notoriously retiring and secretive and, when cornered, become highly aggressive. In ancient

Egypt, these qualities had to be removed for the cat to become a bold and friendly participant in human affairs. This must have been achieved by repeatedly hand-rearing wild kittens and by genetically selecting for those individuals that were more juvenile in their behaviour, even when they became adult. This would have created a cat that was a perpetual kitten towards its new, human companions, while at the same time remaining a savage predator towards rodents.

This modified kitten-cat must soon have become an animal very similar to the one with which millions share their homes today. But the changes involved were only behavioural. The visual images we have of domestic felines from the arts of ancient Egypt show us a cat that is physically almost indistinguishable from the North African Wild Cat. It would probably have stayed that way, but humans have always liked to vary the colours and markings of their domestic livestock – for individual identification and to distinguish them from their wild relatives. So, over the centuries, colour variations were favoured and retained for breeding. Gradually the domestic cat became a cat of many coats and colours. As it spread into colder regions, longer fur and stockier bodies must have developed as a natural response to the freezing winters.

In the 19th century, when high-status cat-keeping became a popular new pursuit, and cat shows began, there were already several types of pet cat available for competitive exhibition. There were tough, heavily built European short-haired cats, exotic long-haired cats from further East, and delicate, slender, hot-country cats from the Orient. And they came in a variety of attractive colours and coat patterns. There were no extremes of shape or size, but there was enough variation already present to create a number of separate pedigree types and classes. And so began a century of competitive genetic manipulation which saw the few early types blossom into a hundred or so breeds, and the thousands of colour combinations that exist today.

Even so, despite strong pressure to find exciting new breeds, the cat has nearly always resisted any dramatic genetic alterations. Furthermore, on the rare occasions when these have occurred, they have encountered widespread hostility. Part of the reason for this is that the basic design of the cat is so graceful and so beautifully balanced that it seems almost sacrilegious to interfere with it. The body-design of the primitive dog is, by comparison, much more 'general purpose', and specialized breeding often seems to improve on the original shape in a way that is difficult to achieve in the world of felines. As a result, the efforts of breeders have been largely confined to creating more exquisite colour-tones or coat patterns, with dramatic alterations in body-shape very much in the minority.

CAT BREEDS

Although there are large numbers of colour forms, there are only about a hundred recorded cat breeds. Some of them appeared briefly and then vanished before they could become established. Others developed into major exhibition breeds with histories covering many years. They are listed here and set out on pages 28–226 in approximate historical order, with the date of their creation indicated where this is known. With the early breeds the dates are, inevitably, somewhat speculative. With the later breeds greater accuracy is often possible.

1 BIRMAN (Burma: early)
2 MANX (Isle of Man: early)
3 NORWEGIAN FOREST (Norway: early)
4 PERSIAN (Iran: early)
5 RUSSIAN BLUE (Russia: early)
6 SIBERIAN FOREST (Russia: early)
7 TURKISH VAN (Turkey: early)
8 JAPANESE BOBTAIL (Japan: 6th–10th century)

 9 CHARTREUX (France: 1300s)
10 SIAMESE (Siam: 1350–1767)
11 KORAT (Siam: 1350–1767)
12 BURMESE (Siam: 1350–1767)
13 ANGORA (Turkey: 1400s)
14 MAINE COON (USA: 1860s)
15 ABYSSINIAN (Ethiopia: 1868)
16 BRITISH SHORTHAIR (Britain: 1870s)
17 MEXICAN HAIRLESS (USA: 1902)
18 HIMALAYAN (USA: 1930s)
19 KARAKUL (USA: 1930s)
20 PEKE-FACED (USA: 1930s)
21 PRUSSIAN REX (East Prussia: 1930s)
22 BALINESE (USA: 1940s)
23 OHIO REX (USA: 1944)
24 AUSTRALIAN (Australia: 1946)
25 GERMAN REX (East Germany: 1946)
26 COLOURPOINT SHORTHAIR (Britain: 1947)
27 KASHMIR (USA: 1950s)
28 ORIENTAL SHORTHAIR (Britain: 1950s)
29 TONKINESE (USA: 1950s)
30 CORNISH REX (Britain: 1950)
31 ITALIAN REX (Italy: 1950)
32 HAVANA BROWN (Britain: 1952)
33 EGYPTIAN MAU (Egypt: 1953)
34 JAPANESE BOBTAIL LONGHAIR (Japan: 1954)
35 BOMBAY (USA: 1958)
36 CALIFORNIA REX (Marcel) (USA: 1959)
37 OREGON REX (USA: 1959)
38 AMERICAN BOBTAIL (USA: 1960s)
39 BRITISH ANGORA (Britain: 1960s)
40 CYMRIC (Canada: 1960s)
41 JAVANESE (Britain & USA: 1960s)
42 RAGDOLL (USA: 1960s)
43 SNOWSHOE (USA: 1960s)
44 DEVON REX (Britain: 1960)
45 SCOTTISH FOLD (Scotland: 1961)

46 BENGAL (USA: 1963)
47 OCICAT (USA: 1964)
48 AMERICAN SHORTHAIR (USA: 1966)
49 AMERICAN WIREHAIR (USA: 1966)
50 EXOTIC SHORTHAIR (USA: 1966)
51 SPHYNX (Canada: 1966)
52 SOMALI (USA: 1967)
53 TIFFANY (USA: 1967)
54 CALIFORNIA SPANGLED (USA: 1971)
55 SINGAPURA (Singapore: 1971)
56 SPOTTED MIST (Australia: 1976)
57 SOKOKE FOREST (Kenya: 1977)
58 AMERICAN LYNX (USA: 1980s)
59 COLOURPOINT BRITISH SHORTHAIR
    (Britain: 1980s)
60 COUPARI (Britain 1980s)
61 TIFFANIE (Britain: 1980s)
62 WILD ABYSSINIAN (Singapore: 1980s)
63 MALAYAN (USA: 1980)
64 AMERICAN CURL (USA: 1981)
65 BURMILLA (Britain: 1981)
66 COLOURPOINT EUROPEAN SHORTHAIR
    (Italy: 1982)
67 EUROPEAN SHORTHAIR (Italy: 1982)
68 YORK CHOCOLATE (USA: 1983)
69 OJOS AZULES (USA: 1984)
70 SEYCHELLOIS (Britain: 1984)
71 DUTCH REX (Holland: 1985)
72 LA PERM (USA: 1986)
73 SI-REX (USA:1986)
74 SELKIRK REX (USA: 1987)
75 REXED MAINE COON (Britain: 1988)
76 NEBELUNG (USA: 1990s)
77 SUQUTRANESE (Britain: 1990)
78 MUNCHKIN (USA: 1991)
79 URALS REX (Russia: 1991)
80 RAGAMUFFIN (USA: 1994)

In addition there are a number of obscure, unrecognized or experimental breeds, including the following: Asian Smoke (or Burmoiré), Bristol, Ceylon, Cherubim, Chinese Harlequin, Cornelian, Himbur, Honeybear, Karelian Bobtail, Khmer, Longhair Rex, Oriental Longhair, Palomino, Poodle, Racekatte or Rugkatt, Safari, Snow, Sterling, Traditional Siamese and Victoria Rex, bringing the total to 100 without taking into account all the colour variations of each breed.

GEOGRAPHY OF DOMESTIC BREEDS

DOMESTIC BREEDS. The 80 recognized breeds of pedigree domestic cat originated in the following countries:

AUSTRALIA: (1) Australian; (2) Spotted Mist.

BRITAIN: (1) British Shorthair; (2) Colourpoint Shorthair; (3) Oriental Shorthair; (4) Cornish Rex; (5) Havana Brown; (6) British Angora; (7) Javanese (also in USA); (8) Devon Rex; (9) Scottish Fold; (10) Colourpoint British Shorthair; (11) Coupari; (12) Tiffanie; (13) Burmilla; (14) Seychellois; (15) Rexed Maine Coon; (16) Suqutranese.

BURMA: (1) Birman.

CANADA: (1) Cymric; (2) Sphynx.

EGYPT: (1) Egyptian Mau.

ETHIOPIA: (1) Abyssinian.

FRANCE: (1) Chartreux.

GERMANY: (1) Prussian Rex; (2) German Rex.

HOLLAND: (1) Dutch Rex.

IRAN: (1) Persian.

ISLE OF MAN: (1) Manx.

ITALY: (1) Italian Rex; (2) Colourpoint European Shorthair; (3) European Shorthair.

JAPAN: (1) Japanese Bobtail; (2) Japanese Bobtail Longhair.

KENYA: (1) Sokoke Forest.

NORWAY: (1) Norwegian Forest.

RUSSIA: (1) Siberian Forest; (2) Russian Blue; (3) Urals Rex.

SINGAPORE: (1) Singapura; (2) Wild Abyssinian.

THAILAND: (1) Burmese; (2) Korat; (3) Siamese.

TURKEY: (1) Angora; (2) Turkish Van.

USA: (1) Maine Coon; (2) Mexican Hairless; (3) Himalayan; (4) Karakul; (5) Peke-faced Persian; (6) Balinese; (7) Ohio Rex; (8) Kashmir; (9) Tonkinese; (10) Bombay; (11) California Rex (Marcel); (12) Oregon Rex; (13) American Bobtail; (14) Javanese (also in Britain); (15) Ragdoll; (16) Snowshoe; (17) Bengal; (18) Ocicat; (19) American Shorthair; (20) American Wirehair; (21) Exotic Shorthair; (22) Somali; (23) Tiffany; (24) California Spangled; (25) American Lynx; (26) Malayan; (27) American Curl; (28) York Chocolate; (29) Ojos Azules; (30) La Perm; (31) Si-Rex; (32) Selkirk Rex; (33) Nebelung; (34) Munchkin; (35) Ragamuffin.

BREED POPULARITY

The most popular cats have always been the moggies, the non-pedigrees, the ordinary common-or-garden house pets. They are the rough, tough survivors whose parents have somehow managed to avoid being neutered by kindly feline welfare workers. Despite endless trips to the vet for 'altering' sessions, moggies are still the most common and the most widespread of all kinds of cats today, right across the globe. Their tenacity and their ability to infiltrate their way into the homes and the hearts of the public is second to none. Pedigree cats are everywhere rare by comparison.

But among those pure-bred individuals, which are the most popular breeds? In the very beginning, in the cat shows of the Victorian era, it was the short-haired cats (the aristocratic cousins of the moggies) that were originally the most favoured. Then, the long-haired cats, the Angoras and the Persians, arrived, and they quickly rose to dominate the exhibition scene. The Angoras were soon swamped out by the Persians, who were then joined by the exotic Siamese. As the years passed, more and more breeds were introduced, each finding followers and fanatical supporters.

Today a pedigree cat show is fascinatingly complex, with new breeds appearing each year and with new colours of old breeds being developed. But which, today, are the 'top cats'? After all the changes that have occurred in over a century of pedigree cat exhibitions, which are the breeds that have finally won through to become the most popular pedigree breeds at the end of the 20th century?

The best way of finding out is to check the number of registrations for each breed at one of the major cat societies. One of the biggest registration organizations in the world is the CFA (The Cat Fanciers' Association), and here are the 'top ten' breeds, as reflected by their registration records at the start of the 1990s. Although the dominance of the Persian was to be expected, its extent is perhaps surprising:

CFA 'Top Ten' Breeds

RANK	BREED	REGISTRATIONS	RANK	BREED	REGISTRATIONS
1	Persian	79.4%	6	Oriental Shorthair	1.6%
2	Siamese	5.5%	7	American Shorthair	1.6%
3	Abyssinian	3.6%	8	Exotic Shorthair	1.3%
4	Maine Coon	2.8%	9	Scottish Fold	1.2%
5	Burmese	1.9%	10	Colourpoint Shorthair	1.1%

Cat Shows

The first cat show took place in Winchester, in southern England, in the year 1598. It was no more than a side-show at the annual St. Giles Fair, but it was nevertheless a competitive event, since it is recorded that prizes were given for the best ratter and the best mouser.

Similar small shows were staged at similar fairs, but these were of little significance and had no official status. The breeding of pedigreed cats had little meaning at this time.

In was not until the second half of the 19th century that serious, competitive cat showing was staged. The earliest example was at a London house in 1861, but this was still not a true public exhibition.

In the 1860s minor cat shows were held in both England and the United States. In America there had already been annual livestock shows for many years. In New England, these started in earnest in 1832, and by the 1860s it is thought they must have included cat competitions because, by the 1870s, the Maine Coon, for example, was already considered as a separate and established breed for competition.

The first major cat show in the world took place on Thursday, 13th July 1871, at the Crystal Palace in London. There were so many visitors that the cats themselves were barely visible in the dense throng. A total of 170 cats were entered, and cats were, for the very first time, given specific standards and classes. These form the basis of the system still employed at modern cat shows all over the world.

This show was so successful that a second one was staged later in the same year and, although it was only open for one day, it attracted 19,310 visitors. Two more shows were held in the following year, after which it became an annual event. The enormous popularity of these cat shows saw the idea spread rapidly to other cities in the British Isles and eventually around the world.

In 1887 the National Cat Club was formed to rule this new competitive world. By 1893 the first official cat stud book had been started, and pedigree cat breeding had begun in earnest.

The first major American cat shows also took place in the 1870s. As early as 1878, for instance, there was a six-day National Cat Show in Boston. During that decade there were others in most of the Eastern cities, and as far west as Chicago. Later, in 1895, the biggest of all these early American shows was held at Madison Square Garden in New York. Due to its success, other shows quickly followed and were soon established as annual fixtures.

Today there are no fewer than 65 annual shows in Britain and 400 in the United States. Unfortunately, the world of cat-show organizers has become increasingly competitive within its ranks, and there have been splits and divisions since the earliest days. The result is that there is no single authority in either Great Britain or the United States, and each club or society has its own slightly different rules and classes.

All of this can be confusing to the outsider, but for the cats it does not make a great deal of difference. The survival of pedigree competition is the important thing, maintaining the serious attitude towards pure-bred felines and preventing cats from losing status in 20th-century society. With more than 94 per cent of cats today being non-pedigree, the cats of the show world constitute only a tiny minority of the general feline population, but this does not matter. As long as the elite pedigrees exist to be photographed and exhibited, they will lend an aura of importance to domestic cats in general. They are the ambassadors of the feline world, and when over 2,000 of them gather each December for the biggest cat show in the world – the National Cat Show in London – the interest they arouse is an admirable advertisement for the value we place on our feline companions.

ABNORMAL BREEDS

There is a great deal of argument about what constitutes an abnormality in the world of pedigree cats. A new colour form creates no problems, but when a mutation occurs that alters the anatomy of the cat in some way, there is often a heated debate as to whether the new variant should be encouraged or allowed to die out. If it puts the cat at a major disadvantage then the answer is obvious, but if it is only a minor disadvantage then cat breeders split into two warring camps. The result is that one official feline organization will recognize the new mutation as an additional breed, while another official body outlaws it and refuses to allow it to enter its cat shows.

At the present time there are several unusual breeds that fall into this category – accepted by some, rejected by others – and they include the Scottish Fold Cat, the Sphynx Cat, the Ragdoll Cat, the Peke-faced Cat and the Munchkin.

The Peke-faced Cat was known back in the 1930s, but the Scottish Fold, Sphynx and Ragdoll Cats were discovered in the 1960s and were quickly established by enthusiastic local breeders, delighted to be founding new lines of pedigree cats. As there is not a huge number of anatomically distinctive breeds, the discovery of new types was extremely exciting, and the intense interest aroused by them is easy to understand. But some authorities argue that, in the euphoria of the moment, the local breeders were blinding themselves to the fact that what they were really doing was preserving freaks.

In the case of the Scottish Fold, where the ears are permanently folded downwards and forwards, opponents of the breed have suggested that it might suffer from ear mites or deafness. Supporters of the breed have replied that there is no evidence for this. Critics have pointed out that if a Scottish Fold Cat is mated with another Scottish Fold Cat this may lead to skeletal abnormalities. Supporters counter that they always avoid this by mating Scottish Folds with normal Shorthairs.

From the cat's point of view, the folded ears have the slight disadvantage that they do not communicate the usual mood signals seen when a cat, becoming angry or scared, starts to flatten its ears ready for fighting. It is the shift from fully erect to fully flattened ones that transmits the all-important social signal. The Scottish Fold appears as though it is permanently in the act of lowering its ears. This should make it look like a cat that is about to fight, but strangely it does not. The reason is that the folding of the ears brings them forward and this places them in a posture that is not part of the usual ear-lowering signal. In a normal cat, ears flattened to this degree would already be twisted round to the rear. So the Scottish Fold has a unique 'squashed' ear, as distinct from a 'flattened' posture. Whether the cats themselves make this distinction is not clear. If they do, then there is no reason why this breed should not take its place among other pedigree types.

In the case of the Sphynx Cat, where the skin is naked, opponents of the breed have pointed out that the breed could suffer considerably in cold weather, without adequate protection. Supporters of the breed point out that these rare, valuable cats are always going to be looked after with extreme care by their owners and that because of this there is no problem.

Apart from its lack of fur, the Sphynx is a normal cat with a charming personality. If its owners can afford central heating, or live in a hot climate, there is little serious risk for the animal. The fact that the Sphinx appears ugly to many cat enthusiasts is irrelevant as far as the cat itself is concerned.

The Ragdoll Cat is reputed to lack sensitivity to pain and to go limp when held. Opponents argue that this means it can be abused and hurt by children who might think of it as a toy rather than as a living animal. Supporters of the breed argue that it is simply an unusually relaxed cat that, in the right hands, is ideal for an indoor environment.

The Peke-faced Cat, a flat-faced version of the Persian, is a different matter. This breed has been shown to suffer from difficulties with its eyes, its teeth and its breathing. To some owners, it may have the most appealing face in the feline world, but it also happens to suffer frequently from blocked tear-ducts, a poor bite when its mouth is closed, and problems with its respiration as it grows older, due to its reduced nasal cavities. Because of its facial appeal, the Peke-faced Cat has survived as a popular breed for over half a century, but whether it should be encouraged is another matter.

The Munchkin, a very new breed, is a cat with short legs like a dachshund. It also has strong opponents, but largely on aesthetic grounds rather than medical ones. Its supporters claim that, like the Ragdoll, it is ideally suited to a life indoors.

These 'abnormal' breeds are all comparatively recent and still have an uphill struggle to gain worldwide recognition. The long-established Manx Cat is as abnormal as any of them, with its strangely abbreviated backbone, but its presence at cat shows is taken for granted. The breed is hallowed by tradition as part of feline history. The new breeds lack this historical advantage.

Of the five new breeds mentioned, four are in no trouble providing they are well looked after. If the Scottish Fold is out-crossed and has its ears cleaned, the Sphynx is kept warm, the Ragdoll is kept away from juvenile tormentors, and the Munchkin is protected from any situation in which it would have to leap high to protect itself, then they can all lead contented and fulfilled lives. Only the Peke-faced Cat seems inevitably doomed to difficulties. No matter how much love and attention is lavished upon it, there will always be a danger that its respiration will suffer. A slight reduction in the extreme flattening of its face is probably all that is necessary to solve its problem.

Controversial bureaucratic interference in the affairs of the pedigree cat world has recently surfaced in new recommendations made by the Council of Europe. As part of their Multi-Lateral Convention for the Protection of Pet Animals, they are suggesting the future banning of blue-eyed white cats and breeds such as the Manx, the Scottish Fold and the Sphynx.

Britain has rejected these suggestions, but in January 1995 the German government did respond positively and introduced laws banning these breeds. It is also considering adding the most extreme forms of Persian and Siamese Cats to the prohibited list. It remains to be seen whether any of the other European member states will follow suit.

Whatever one may feel about the appearance of some of the more extreme and unusual breeds, there is no justification for this type of government intervention unless it can be proved beyond doubt that the animals concerned are suffering undue pain or health risks. To ban a breed simply because, to bureaucrats, it looks 'odd' is unjustified.

TERMINOLOGY

ASIAN CATS

The term 'Asian' has been introduced to cover the group of breeds that can best be described as 'unusually coloured Burmese'. During recent years a number of specialists have created new breeds that are based on the traditional Burmese type, but which have new colouring or coat-type. Some cat societies refuse to recognize these new forms as distinct breeds and call them all 'Burmese'. Others only accept the traditional, dark brown Burmese as 'Burmese' and call the modern colour-variants by other, separate breed names. This causes some confusion for the non-specialist.

In the broadest sense, the category 'Asian Cats' includes breeds such as the Burmilla, the Asian Smoke (also known as Burmoiré), the Asian Tabby, the Bombay, the Tiffanie (or Asian Longhair) and the Singapura. In the narrow sense it includes only Burmese types which are Smokes or Tabbies.

LONG-HAIRED CATS

Long-haired breeds of domestic cat have been known for centuries, but their popularity did not reach a peak until the Victorian era when Queen Victoria herself owned two, and they became the star attractions at the earliest cat shows.

Writing on the subject of Long-haired Cats in 1889, Harrison Weir, the organizer of the very first cat show in 1871, comments: 'There are several varieties – the Russian, the Angora, the Persian, and Indian. Forty or fifty years ago they used all to be called French cats, as they were mostly imported from Paris.'

A few years later, in 1893, John Jennings slightly increased this list of long-haired varieties: 'The several varieties which range under *Long-hair* embrace Persian, Angora, Chinese, Indian, French, and Russian.'

Of these six early forms of Long-haired Cats, little is known about the Chinese, Indian or Russian. The Chinese was said to be similar to the better-known Persian, except that it had pendulous ears (which seems highly unlikely). The Indian was also said to be close to the Persian, but with striped markings of red and black. In India it was said to be called the domestic 'Tiger cat', not to be confused with the wild Tiger Cat. The Russian was described as 'by far the most woolly of cats' with a comparatively coarse and very thick coat. As designated breeds, these three types soon vanished, although much later it was thought that perhaps the early Russian type was the ancestor of all the others, its long fur having developed as an adaptation to the intense cold of the Russian winter. This would certainly make more sense than suggesting that our modern long-haired breeds have originated from hot countries such as Turkey and Iran.

Of the other three forms, the Angora, with its lithe, long-bodied look and its plumed tail and exaggerated ruff, was the earliest of the long-haired breeds to be seen in Western Europe, where it first appeared in the 16th century. Later, in the 17th century and especially at the end of the 18th century, it was joined by the much more rounded and fluffy-coated Persian, which quickly became the top favourite. The type referred to as the 'French cat' was not a true breed, but was simply a name given to all long-haired cats in the middle of the 19th century because so many of them at that time were being imported into England from France, where they had gained considerable popularity. By the end of the 19th century, English and American breeders had become so serious in their interest in these breeds that they were no longer thought of as 'French Cats', and the name was dropped.

At the turn of the century, when cat shows were gaining in strength, there was great competition to produce the most exaggerated of long-haired specimens. Little attempt was made to keep the different long-haired breeds apart as pure lines. They were mixed together to create the softest, heaviest coats obtainable. Inevitably, this meant that the Persian breed became the most dominant element in the mixing, because its fur was thicker than that of the Angora and softer than that of the Russian.

By the early part of the 20th century, the Angora and Russian had been swamped out and the preferred long-haired type was predominantly Persian. For most people, this was a good-enough reason to refer to all long-haired cats simply as 'Persians'. The pedigree-cat authorities in England, however, took a different view. Because these cats were the result of a mixture of early types, they took the purist view that long-haired cats should be called simply that, and the name 'Persian' was eliminated from official documents. The rest of the cat world ignored this somewhat academic decision and has persisted in using the term 'Persian'. Even in England, ordinary cat-owners still use the term Persian Cat rather than Long-haired Cat, when talking about these animals.

In recent decades, new breeds of cat with long hair have been discovered or developed and today the official use of the name 'Long-haired Cat' to refer to a Persian Cat is not merely confusing, it is now also misleading, especially as both the Angora and the Russian have been 'rediscovered' and re-introduced (as the Turkish Angora and Siberian Forest Cat respectively).

At the present time, there are the following distinct long-haired breeds:

1 PERSIAN ('Longhair' in GB)

2 HIMALAYAN ('Colourpoint Longhair' in GB)

3 PEKE-FACED (Flat-faced Persian developed in America in the 1930s)

4 BALINESE (Long-haired Siamese, developed in the 1940s)

5 JAPANESE BOBTAIL LONGHAIR (Long-haired version, developed in the 1950s)

6 KASHMIR (Persian variant developed in America in the 1950s)

7 MAINE COON (Long-haired American breed, popularized in the 1950s)

8 TURKISH VAN (Related to the Angora and developed in the 1950s)

9 AMERICAN BOBTAIL (New American breed discovered in the 1960s)

10 BIRMAN (Long-haired Burma breed, popularized in the 1960s)

11 BRITISH ANGORA (Reconstituted Angora created in GB in the 1960s)

12 CYMRIC (Long-haired Manx Cat, developed in the 1960s)

13 RAGDOLL (New American breed developed in the 1960s)

14 SOMALI (Long-haired Abyssinian, developed in the 1960s)

15 TIFFANY (Long-haired American breed, discovered in the 1960s)

16 TURKISH ANGORA (Rediscovered in Turkey in the 1960s)

17 JAVANESE (Long-haired breed developed in the 1970s)

18 NORWEGIAN FOREST (Long-haired Scandinavian breed, popularized in 1970s)

19 AMERICAN CURL (New American breed discovered in the 1980s)

20 COUPARI (Long-haired Scottish Fold, developed in the 1980s)

21 LA PERM LONGHAIR (New American breed discovered in the 1980s)

22 SIBERIAN FOREST (Russian Long-haired Cat, rediscovered in the 1980s)

23 TIFFANIE (Long-haired Burmese, developed in the 1980s)

24 LONGHAIR REX (New Eastern European breed, reported in the 1990s)

25 NEBELUNG (Long-haired Russian Blue, developed in the 1990s)

26 RAGAMUFFIN (New American breed developed in the 1990s)

27 SUQUTRANESE (White long-haired Abyssinian, developed in the 1990s)

Clearly, the term 'Long-haired Cat' is now only appropriate in its broad, descriptive sense, as a term to embrace all these breeds. Its continued use in the narrow sense, in Britain, is increasingly difficult to justify.

NON-PEDIGREE CATS

This is the official name given to all cross-bred, moggie, or mongrel cats. To encourage non-specialists to participate in major cat shows, it is the custom to include special classes for Non-pedigree Longhair and Non-pedigree Shorthair Cats. To quote a recent show catalogue: 'The essential qualities of these non-pedigree pets are that they are happy, much loved examples of the non-pedigree cat being shown in sparkling, tip-top condition . . . they are all beautiful in the eyes of their owners.'

REX CATS

Rex cats have been reported from many places at different times, but in most cases the individual animals with the sparse, wavy 'Rex coat' have not been used for breeding and their genetic properties have died with them. In several cases, however, they have been developed systematically to start new 'pure-breeds'. The following are cases that have been specifically recorded. (See also separate entries.)

1930/1931. PRUSSIAN REX CAT: Discovered in East Prussia, but not developed.

1930s. KARAKUL CAT: Recorded in America, but not developed.

1946. GERMAN REX CAT: Discovered in the ruins of East Berlin after World War II. Used in successful crosses with the Cornish Rex, but apparently no longer preserved as a distinct breed.

1950. ITALIAN REX CAT: Not developed as a breed. Vanished in one generation.

1950. CORNISH REX CAT: Discovered in a litter of farm cats in Cornwall and carefully in-bred to develop the breed. Remains a popular Rex breed today.

1953. OHIO REX CAT: Born in an otherwise normal litter, but not developed as a breed.

1959. OREGON REX CAT: An American strain which seems to have been overshadowed by the popular Cornish Rex.

1959. CALIFORNIA REX CAT: Found in an animal shelter. Because of its longer, wavy coat it was called a 'Marcel Cat'.

1960. DEVON REX CAT: Discovered in Devon and developed into a popular breed. Although geographically close to the Cornish Rex, the Devon Rex depends on a different gene for its curly coat.

1972. VICTORIA REX CAT: Cat carrying curly-coated Rex gene found in Victoria, London, the offspring of feral cats in that district.

1985. DUTCH REX CAT: A recent addition to the Rex breeds, the Dutch version has a coarser wavy coat, with a more bristly texture.

1987. SELKIRK REX CAT: Another American Rex strain, this one was discovered in Wyoming. Its curly coat is thicker than typical rex breeds.

1988. REXED MAINE COON CAT: Rare cases of Maine Coon Cats with wavy, Rex hair have recently been reported by British breeders.

1991. URALS REX CAT: Discovered in Russia.

1990s. LONGHAIR REX: Eastern European breeders are reported to have crossed Rex Cats with Persians to create a long-haired Rex.

1990s. POODLE CAT: A new breed of Rex Cat with folded ears, created by crossing Devon Rex with Scottish Fold.

1990s. MISSOURI REX: The latest Rex discovery from the United States.

History: The genes for the sparse, short, curly hair of all the Rex breeds are recessives that seem to crop up as random mutations in different parts of the world. If left alone, they soon vanish, but if carefully inbred to intensify them, can be used to start a new form of pedigree cat. Most of the 'founding felines' of the various Rex breeds have been local strays or farm cats, spotted by enthusiasts, rescued and employed as foundation breeding stock. At least two genes appear to be involved: Gene 1. Rex. No. 33 (the Cornish and German); Gene 2. Rex. No. 33A (the Devon only). The new Selkirk Rex appears to be a third, and the Rex gene observed in Maine Coons may also be a different one.

Unusual Features: The wavy fur of these cats, lacking the usual guard hairs (which make up the topcoat) of other breeds, gives them a strange, unsleek appearance which is exaggerated by their slender, leggy bodies. In the world of show cats, the Rex breeds have caused heated arguments and divided experts into two rival groups. The pro-Rex faction sing the praises of Rex Cats because of their delightful personalities. They remain more affectionate, playful and inquisitive than other cats, the adults behaving more like kittens. The anti-Rex faction claim that the wavy coats are 'imperfect' and that they give the animals a diseased look even when they are healthy. They also feel that the thinness of the coats of most Rex breeds makes the cats look unduly angular, awkward and lacking in typical feline grace. Despite these criticisms, some of the Rex breeds, at least, appear to have a strong enough following to ensure their future in the realm of pedigree cats and cat shows.

SHORTHAIR CATS

At the earliest cat shows, in the final decades of the 19th century, all cats with short coats were lumped together as 'Short-haired Cats'. Some were named simply by their fur colour, while others were distinctive breeds, such as the Siamese or Manx. As time passed, the distinctive breeds were more strongly recognized as such and this left a mixed bag of short-haired cats, separated from one another purely by their coat colour. These cats then needed a more precise name to establish them as a particular breed. In Britain they acquired the title of the British Shorthair. On the Continent, they became the European Shorthair and in the United States, the American Shorthair. (See separate entries.)

SPOTTED CATS

Because so many wild cat species have spotted coats, breeders of domestic cats have several times attempted to develop a spotted pet cat that looks like its natural relatives. At present there are six different, exclusively spotted domestic breeds (see individual entries for each breed):

1 EGYPTIAN MAU (Natalie Troubetskoy, Egypt, 1953)
2 ORIENTAL SPOTTED TABBY (Angela Sayer, 1960s)
3 BENGAL (Jean Mill, USA, 1963)
4 OCICAT (Virginia Daly, USA, 1964)
5 CALIFORNIA SPANGLED (Paul Casey, USA, 1971)
6 SPOTTED MIST (Australia, 1980)

In addition to the foregoing breeds, in which spotted individuals *only* are allowed, there is also a 'Spotted Tabby' variant in a number of other breeds, including the American Curl, the British Shorthair, the Norwegian Forest, the Devon Rex and the Scottish Fold. Spotted Tabby Cats were recorded as early as the 19th century.

TAILLESS CATS

There are currently seven breeds of domestic cat with abbreviated tails: the Manx, the Cymric, the Japanese Bobtail, the Japanese Bobtail Longhair, the Karelian Bobtail, the American Bobtail and the American Lynx.

FELINE ANATOMY

EARS

The cat's ears are much more sensitive that those of its owners, which is why cats hate noisy homes. Loud music and shouting are torture to its delicate hearing apparatus.

It is the specialized hunting behaviour of cats that has resulted in their improved hearing. Although dogs have a much greater acoustic range than humans, cats exceed even dogs in their ability to hear high-pitched sounds. This is because humans and dogs rely most on chasing and trapping their prey, whereas cats prefer to lurk in ambush and listen very carefully for the tiniest sound. If they are to succeed as stealthy hunters, they must be able to detect the most minute rustlings and squeaks and must be able to distinguish precise direction and distance to pinpoint their intended victims. This requires much more sensitivity than we possess, and laboratory tests have confirmed that domestic cats do, indeed, possess a very fine tuning ability.

At the lower level of sounds, there is little difference between humans, dogs and cats – this is not where it counts if you are a hunter of small rodents and birds. At the higher levels, humans in the prime of life can hear noises up to about 20,000 cycles per second. This sinks to around 12,000 cycles per second in humans of retirement age. Dogs can manage up to 35,000 or 40,000 cycles per second, so that they are able to detect sounds that we cannot. Cats, on the other hand, can hears sounds up to an astonishing 100,000 cycles per second. This corresponds well to the high pitch of mouse sounds, which can be emitted up to this same level. So no mouse is safe from the alert ears of the predatory cat.

This acoustic ability of pet cats explains why they sometimes appear to have supernatural powers. They hear and understand the ultrasonic sounds that precede a noisy activity and respond appropriately before we have even realized that something unusual is going to happen. Even while taking a nap, the cat's ears are in operation. If something exciting is detected, the cat is awake and responding in a split second.

Deafness in cats is not uncommon, especially among very old animals. Also, kittens are deaf for the first few weeks of life, because their ear canals do not open immediately after birth. In addition, there is a genetic deafness in the majority of blue-eyed white cats, caused by a malformation of the inner ear. This condition is irreversible, but many blue-eyed white cats manage to survive well enough by becoming extra alert in other ways. Cats in which only one eye is blue are only deaf in one ear.

EYES

The cat has magnificent eyes which are very large in relation to its skull. They provide the animal with a wider visual field than ours (295 degrees instead of only 210). They also give it a slightly wider binocular field (130 degrees instead of 120). This frontal, three-dimensional vision is important for a hunter, which must be able to judge distances with great accuracy.

The cat's greatest visual asset, however, is its ability to see well in very dim light. This ability is made possible by an image-intensifying device at the rear of the eyes. It is a complex, light-reflecting layer called the *tapidum lucidum* (meaning literally 'bright carpet'), which acts rather like a mirror behind the retina, reflecting light back to the retinal cells. It is this that makes the cat's eyes 'glow' in the dark and gives them what, to some, is a sinister nocturnal appearance.

With this special layer, the cat can utilize every scrap of light that enters its eyes. With our eyes we absorb far less of the light that enters them. Because of this difference cats can make out movements and objects in the semi-darkness which would be quite invisible to us.

Despite this efficient nocturnal ability, it is not true that cats can see in complete darkness, as some people seem to believe. On a pitch black night they must navigate by sound, smell and the sensitivity of their amazing whiskers.

Another major difference between human and feline eyes is the way in which cats reduce their pupils to vertical slits. This gives them a more refined control over how much light enters the eyes. For an animal with eyes sensitive enough to see in very dim light, it is important not to be dazzled by bright sunlight, and the narrowing of the pupils to tight slits gives a greater control over light input. The reason cats have vertical slits rather than horizontal ones is that they can use the closing of the lids to reduce the light input even further. With these two slits working at right angles to one another, the feline eye has the possibility of making the most delicate adjustment of any animal, when faced with what would otherwise be a blinding light.

One way in which cats' eyes are inferior to ours is in their ability to see colours. In the first half of the 20th century scientists were convinced that cats were totally colour-blind and one authority reworked a popular saying with the words: 'Day and night, all cats see grey.' That was the prevailing attitude as late as the 1940s, but since then more careful research has been carried out and it is now known that cats can distinguish between certain colours, but not, apparently, with much finesse.

The reason earlier experiments failed to reveal the existence of feline colour vision was that in discrimination tests cats quickly latched on to subtle differences in the degree of greyness of colours; they then refused to abandon these clues when presented with two colours of exactly the same degree of greyness, so the tests gave negative results. Using more sophisticated methods, recent studies have been able to prove that cats can distinguish between red and green, red and blue, red and grey, green and blue, green and grey, blue and grey, yellow and blue, and yellow and grey. Whether they can distinguish between other pairs of colours is still in dispute.

One thing is certain, at any rate: colour is not as important in the lives of cats as it is in our own lives. Their eyes are much more attuned to seeing in dim light, where they need only one-sixth of the light that we do to make out the same details of movement and shape.

HAWS

The haw is the cat's third eyelid. It is situated at the inner corner of the eye and comes into action to protect the delicate organ from damage or to lubricate the corneal surface by spreading the cat's tears evenly across it. When the haws are activated, they move sideways across the eye and then return to their resting position. In this respect the cat has an advantage over the human species, for we are unable to move our third eyelids, which exist only as small pink lumps at the inner point of each eye.

The cat's haw – or nictitating membrane, to give it its technical name – is not normally conspicuous, but if the cat is in ill health, undernourished, or about to succumb to a major disease, it may become permanently visible, giving the cat's eye a 'half-shuttered' look. When this happens, it is an important clue that the animal is in need of veterinary assistance. The appearance of the haws in these circumstances is caused by the fact that there are shock absorber pads of fat behind the eyeballs which start to shrink if the animal's health is below par. This shrinkage means that the eyes sink into the head slightly, and this in turn causes the haws to move forward and half cover the corneal surfaces. When the cat returns to full health, the fat pads are replenished and the eyes pushed forward again, hiding the haws once more.

NOSE

Like most mammals, the cat has a good nose, well equipped to detect minute changes in fragrance. Internally, it is a maze of complex nasal cavities. One section of these cavities is covered with a nasal lining called the olfactory mucosa, which contains 200 million special olfactory cells. This mucosa is twice as large as the one inside the human nose and this reflects the huge importance of fragrance-detection in the feline world. It has been estimated that the cat's sense of smell is roughly 30 times better than that of a human being, and a great deal of feline communication is carried out through the medium of scent-marks. Cats leave their scent signals in their environment by means of spraying urine, depositing faeces, rubbing against objects with their scent glands and scratching at surfaces with their feet in such a way as to deposit scent from their paw-pads. They renew these scents at regular intervals, keeping them fresh and 'announcing' any changes that may have occurred in their condition since the last time.

This explains why house-cats are always asking to go out, and then soon asking to come back in again. Each visit is a 'scent-check' to see who and what has been entering their territory. They feel a strong urge to keep up to date with this information.

The visible patch of naked skin around the nostrils of the cat is known as the 'nose leather'. In the world of pedigree cats, the precise colour of this patch of skin is considered to be aesthetically significant, and many subtle distinctions are made between one shade and another. Nose leather colours given in modern breed standards include the following: black, seal, brown, chestnut, chocolate, brick red, tile red, cinnamon pink, deep rose, old rose, rose, rosy pink, salmon, flesh, pink, coral pink, lavender pink, lavender, pale fawn, blue, slate blue.

TEETH

The adult cat has 30 teeth: 12 incisors, four canines, ten premolars and four molars. It uses them to attack, to defend itself and to kill food. A tom-cat also uses his teeth to grasp the neck of the female when he is mating. And a mother cat will use them, with great care, to grasp the neck of her kittens when transporting them.

The large, curved, pointed canines (or should they be felines?) are important stabbing and clasping weapons. The premolars are shearing implements used to cut the prey into pieces that are small enough to swallow. Cats do not chew their food. They chop it up and swallow it. One of the problems they face when given nothing but prepared pet foods is that they never have to face the challenge of slicing up a large, tough food object. The soft food from the can or packet does not make them work hard enough and their teeth may suffer as a result.

TONGUE

The long, flat, flexible tongue of the cat is smooth underneath and rough on top. On its upper surface there are four kinds of papillae: (1) *Conical* papillae are the most common form and are the large ones that point backwards, giving the cat's tongue its rasping quality. (2) *Flattened* papillae are found at the very root of the tongue. (3) *Fungiform* papillae are arranged along the sides of the tongue. (4) *Circumvallate* papillae, which are few in number, are found at the back of the tongue.

The cat's tongue has many uses. Apart from (1) tasting food, it is also employed (2) to move food into the mouth; (3) to rasp clinging morsels of meat from the bones of its prey; (4) to greet the cat's companions with a licking 'kiss'; (5) to wash and clean the animal's fur; (6) to smooth the fur when ruffled; (7) to dry the fur when wet; (8) to pant when the cat is hot; (9) to lap up liquid when the cat is drinking; and (10) to cool the animal when it is seriously overheating, by covering its fur in wet saliva which will then evaporate and cool the cat in the process.

WHISKERS

In addition to their obvious role as feelers sensitive to touch, the whiskers also operate as air-current detectors. As the cat moves along in the dark it needs to manoeuvre past solid objects without touching them. Each solid object it approaches causes slight eddies in the air (minute disturbances in the currents of air movement) and the cat's whiskers are so amazingly sensitive that they can read these air changes and respond to the presence of solid obstacles even without touching them.

The whiskers are especially important – indeed vital – when the cat hunts at night. We know this from the following observations: a cat with perfect whiskers can kill cleanly both in the light and in the dark. A cat with damaged whiskers can kill cleanly only in the light; in the dark it misjudges its killing-bite and plunges its teeth into the wrong part of the prey's body. This means that in the dark, where accurate vision is impeded, healthy whiskers are capable of acting as a highly sensitive guidance system. They have an astonishing, split-second ability to check the body outline of the victim and direct the cat's bite to the nape of the unfortunate animal's neck. Somehow the tips of the whiskers must read off the details of the shape of the prey, like a blind man reading Braille, and in an instant tell the cat how to react. Photographs of cats carrying mice in their jaws after catching them reveal that the whiskers are almost wrapped around the rodent's body, continuing to transmit information about the slightest movement, should the prey still be alive. Since the cat is by nature predominantly a nocturnal hunter, its whiskers are clearly crucial to its survival.

Anatomically the whiskers are greatly enlarged and stiffened hairs more than twice the thickness of ordinary hairs. Technically they are known as vibrissae. They are embedded in the tissue of the cat's upper lip to a depth three times greater than that of other hairs, and they are supplied with a mass of nerve-endings which transmit the information about any contact they make or any changes of air pressure.

On average, a cat has 24 whiskers, 12 on each side of the nose, arranged in four horizontal rows. They are capable of moving both forwards, when the cat is inquisitive, threatening, or testing something, and backwards, when it is defensive or deliberately avoiding touching something. The top two rows can be moved independently of the bottom two, and the strongest whiskers are in rows two and three.

Paws

The feline paw, sharp and savage when tensed for action, smooth and rounded when relaxed, lives a double life. Claws out, it is a lethal hunting weapon, an acrobatic climbing device and a fighting tool; claws in, it is a padded, silent shock-absorber.

Beneath each front paw there lie seven small pads, separated by tufts of fur. There are five *digital pads,* one per claw. The first of these is the pad for the rudimentary thumb, which carries a dew claw. The others lie beneath the four, sharp retractile claws. In the centre of the underside of the foot is the largest of the seven pads, called the *plantar pad.* This has three lobes and is the main support-point for the animal's leg, protecting the weight-bearing leg-bones. Finally there is a small wrist-pad called the *pisiform pad* ('pisiform' means 'pea-shaped', and refers to the shape of the wrist-bone beneath the pad).

On each hind foot there are only five pads – the four main digital pads and the one large, central plantar pad. The hind foot is much stronger and stiffer than the front foot and must bear the greater burden during locomotion, especially when the cat is jumping.

All these pads are soft, smooth and spongy in indoor cats. By contrast, in outdoor, roaming cats, they are tough and leathery, echoing the difference between the hands of office-workers and farmers.

Cats' paws exhibit one rather common form of genetic abnormality, a condition known as *polydactylism,* in which extra toes are present. Biologists in Boston, Massachusetts, have discovered that their city has been the centre for the spread of many-toed domestic cats in North America. In Boston, of 311 cats examined, 39 had extra toes. This is a higher percentage than anywhere else in America. When cats in other cities were studied, it emerged that those locations which had received most (human) ex-Bostonians into their population during their past history also had the biggest percentage of many-toed cats. By their distribution, these cats were, in effect, acting as a measure of human cultural movements. Cities where there has been very little influx of Bostonians had only very small percentages. For example: Boston: 12 per cent; New York: 0.5 per cent; Chicago: 0.4 per cent; Columbus, Ohio: 0.4 per cent; Philadelphia: 0.2 per cent.

A final point of interest about cats' paws: although we are all aware that human beings are either left-handed or right-handed, it is not generally known that many cats are also either left-pawed or right-pawed. Careful tests have revealed that, of every hundred cats, approximately 40 are left-pawed, 20 are right-pawed and 40 are ambidextrous. These findings contrast strikingly with the human situation, where only 10 individuals are left-handed for every 90 who are right-handed.

Claws

The powerful, curved claws of cats are valuable when the animals are climbing, digging, defending themselves, fighting rivals or attacking prey. Each of the claws is attached to a final toe-bone and is movable. The advantage of this system is that the cat can keep its claws pin-prick sharp at all times. Many other kinds of animals, with fixed claws, have them worn down and blunted by constant wear and tear. The claws of the cat are as fresh and sharp as sheathed daggers.

Feline claws are usually referred to as retractile, but this gives a false impression of the way they operate. It is when they are relaxed that they are retracted. To bring them into operation they must be extended. In other words, they are normally sheathed and are only displayed when the cat tightens special muscles by a voluntary action. To put it another way, the claws of a cat are *protractile,* rather than retractile. This may be a small, anatomical quibble, but it is important for the cat. If the claws had to be actively retracted every time the animal wished to hide them, it would have to keep the muscles tensed for hour after hour, because the condition of 'hidden claws' is the usual one. The 'claws out' condition only occurs briefly, when there is some kind of emergency.

Some house-proud cat-owners today have the claws of their pets surgically removed by a veterinary surgeon. This is usually done to prevent the animals from scratching valuable furnishings. It is not a major operation, but it robs the cat of a vital part of its anatomy. A de-clawed cat is a maimed cat. To remove a cat's claws is far worse than to deprive cat owners of their finger-nails. This is because the claws have so many important functions in the life of a cat, including repeated scratching, which is a crucial part of the cleaning routine; climbing; self defence; and hunting.

TAIL

In a typical cat, the long, flexible feline tail contains between 21 and 23 caudal vertebrae. In exceptional cases, a fully tailed cat may have as few as 18 or as many as 28 of these bones. In the three stump-tailed domestic breeds – the Manx, the Japanese Bobtail and the American Bobtail – the number of tail-bones is drastically reduced.

In a normal tail, the tail-bones decrease in size gradually to the last one. Towards the tip they become reduced to slender rods of bone, slightly enlarged at each end. The final one, at the very tip of the tail, has a small conical 'cap', a mere rudiment of the last vertebra that finishes off the spinal column. The tails of domestic cats vary slightly in length, according to breed, but are nearly always more than 20 cm (8 inches) and less than 30 cm (12 inches), with 25 cm (10 inches) being the average.

Because of the numerous tail-bones and the longer, more flexible spine, the cat has a greater total number of bones in its body than we do – usually 244, compared with only 204 in the human being.

When Siamese Cats first appeared in the West it was noticed that many of them had kinks in their tails. This has now been bred out of them, but in the Orient, where the gene for kinky tail is widespread, a large percentage of the local cats exhibit this feature. Surveys have revealed that, in Hong Kong, about one-third of the cats have tail kinks; in the more northerly Malay states this rises to two-thirds; and in Singapore, it is at its highest, with 69 per cent of the local cats showing it.

The kink itself is caused by a twisting and often a fusing of several of the tail-bones. Clearly it causes no serious disadvantage, or it would have disappeared from the Eastern populations, or at the very least become extremely rare. Whether it carries some hidden, associated advantage for the cats concerned is not yet known.

HAIR

A wild cat has four kinds of hairs: down hairs, awn hairs, guard hairs and vibrissae. There may be as many as 200 hairs per millimetre, giving the cat an excellent fur coat that can protect it from even the most severe night air.

The *down hairs* are the ones closest to the skin and it is their primary task to keep the animal warm and to conserve its precious body heat. These are the shortest, thinnest and softest of the hairs. They have roughly the same diameter down their whole length, but instead of being straight they have many short undulations, making them appear crimped or crinkled when viewed under a magnifying lens. It is the soft and curly quality of this undercoat, or underfur, that gives it its excellent heat-retaining property.

The *awn hairs* form the middle-coat. They are intermediate between the soft underfur and the guard hairs of the topcoat. Their task is partly insulatory and partly protective. They are bristly with a slight swelling towards the tip, before the final tapering-off. Some authorities subdivide them into three types – the down-awn hairs, the awn hairs and the guard-awn hairs – but these subtle distinctions are of little value.

The *guard hairs* form the protective topcoat. They are the longest and thickest of the ordinary body hairs and serve to protect the underfur from the outside elements, keeping it dry and snug. These hairs are straight and evenly tapered along their length.

The *vibrissae* are the greatly enlarged and toughened hairs employed as sensitive organs of touch. These specialized tactile hairs form the whiskers of the upper lips, and are also found on the cheeks and the chin, over the eyes and on the wrists of the forelegs. Compared with the other types of hair there are very few of them, but they play a vital role when the cat is exploring in poor light, or is hunting.

Of the three types of general body fur on the wild cat, the down hairs are the most numerous. For every 1,000 down hairs there will only be about 300 awn hairs and 20 guard hairs. But these ratios vary enormously with the different breeds of pedigree cats. This is because these felines have been carefully selected for their special kinds of coats. Some are fine and thin, others short and coarse, or long and fluffy. The differences are due to exaggerations and reductions of the different types of hair. Pedigree long-haired cats, for example, have excessively lengthy guard hairs, measuring up to 13 cm (5 inches), and greatly elongated down hairs, but no awn hairs. Some short-haired breeds have guard hairs that are less than 5 cm (2 inches) in length, sparse awn hairs and no down hairs. Wirehair cats have all three types of body hair, but they are all short and curly. The strange Cornish Rex Cat has no guard hairs and only very short, curly awn and down hairs. The Devon Rex has all three types of body hair, but they are all reduced to the quality of down hairs. The amazing naked cat – the Sphynx – lacks both guard hairs and awn hairs and has only a soft fuzz of down hairs on its extremities.

So selective breeding has played havoc with the natural coat of the cat, producing types of animals that would not all thrive in the wild today. Some would suffer from the cold, others from the heat, and still others would become badly matted and tangled without their daily grooming. Fortunately for these pedigree breeds there are usually plenty of human helpers to tend to their needs and, should the worst happen, and the animals be forced to fend for themselves as strays, changes would soon take place. They themselves might suffer from the climate, but if they managed to survive and interbreed, the chances are that in a few generations their offspring would have reverted to wild-type coats once again, as a result of the inevitable mixing that would occur among the stray cat colonies.

1

Birman Cat

An ancient Burmese breed looking rather like a heavily built, long-haired Siamese, but with a unique paw-colouring. Also known as 'The Sacred Cat of Burma'. In France, where it has its strongest following, it is known as the 'Burman', or the *Chat Sacré de Birmanie*. In Germany it is called the *Birmakatze;* in Holland the *Heilige Birmann*. This breed has no connection with the Burmese Cat.

Appearance: The diagnostic feature of this breed is its pure white paws, giving the impression that it is wearing white gloves. The rest of the long, silky coat is essentially golden-fawn in colour, with the addition of the dark points typical of a Siamese. It is the combination of this dark-pointed pattern with the white paw colour that gives the breed its extraordinary, kid-gloved appearance. The gene that causes the white markings obviously clashes with the typical 'Siamese' colouring and overrides it, so that the darkening of the legs has to stop short of the paws, creating a sharp margin. The eyes are a vivid blue, again like the Siamese. The body, however, is long and stocky, with short, powerful legs and a large rounded head.

In the cat show world, the white front paws are referred to as 'gloves' and the back paws as 'socks'. The white markings underneath the back paws are called 'gauntlets'.

Legendary History: The legend of the Birman tells the story of the hundred pure white cats with yellow eyes who were the guardians of the sacred Khmer temple at Lao-Tsun on the side of Mount Lugh in Burma, many centuries ago, before the time of Buddha. The temple housed a golden image of the blue-eyed goddess called Tsun-Kyan-Kse, who was able to order the reincarnation of priests in the bodies of holy animals. Once the soul of a priest had been transferred to the body of one of the sacred cats it was then possible for it to pass on from the innocent feline to a heavenly state in the afterlife. In other words, for the priests, the cats were seen as the spiritual pathway to paradise, which explains why they were so carefully protected.

The high priest, Mun-Ha, had a favourite cat known as Sinh. One day they were sitting together in front of the idol when the temple was attacked by raiders from Siam. Elderly Mun-Ha suffered a heart attack as he prayed. Sinh reacted by placing his paws on the body of the

A YOUNG BIRMAN CAT *(opposite)*, showing its elegantly marked, white feet.
According to the famous legend, this special colouring was magically acquired
as the ancestral Birman placed his paws on the white hair of his dying master.

dying priest. As he did so, he was facing the golden, blue-eyed idol and in the moment of his master's death he was transformed, his eyes turning blue and his fur golden. Then the extremities of his body darkened to the colour of the earth, except for his paws which, where they were in contact with his master's snowy white hair, retained their original, pure white colouring. As these changes occurred, the soul of the dead priest passed into Sinh's body.

Witnessing this amazing metamorphosis, the other priests sprung into action and drove their attackers from the temple. Sinh never ate again and died a few days later, dutifully taking his master's soul to paradise. The other cats then reappeared in the temple, and it was soon obvious that every one of them had changed into the new, sacred colours – golden fur with dark points, white paws and blue eyes. They encircled a young priest called Lioa, indicating that he was chosen to become the new high priest. From that day onward the Sacred Cats of Burma retained their colouring and the Birman breed was fixed for all time.

Factual History: The truth about the origin of this breed is difficult to ascertain. If a colony of long-haired white cats really did exist in the ancient temple, the chances are that it was the sudden arrival of a virile Siamese Cat that caused the transformation rather than any supernatural occurrence.

Whatever their ancient origin, it remains to explain their recent history – how they came to be in the hands of French breeders just after the end of World War I. There are four different versions of this story:

1 In 1898 there was a large colony of these cats living in the Burmese temple of Lao-Tsun, where they were revered and cared for by the priests. There was a Brahmin invasion in the region and an English Officer by the name of The Hon. Russell Gordon, who had been active locally in the Third Burmese War in 1885, came to the rescue of the priests and saved them from certain massacre. He was received at the temple, situated east of Lake Incaougji, between Magaoung and Sembo, where the Lama-kittah (the head priest) showed him the sacred cats and presented him with a plaque depicting one of them at the feet of a bizarre deity, whose eyes were made of two long sapphires. As a result of his actions, he was later to be presented with a pair of the sacred cats, which were sent to France.

2 There is a variation of this tale, as follows: There was a rebellion in the region of the Lao-Tsun temple in 1916. Two Europeans, a British officer, Major Gordon Russell, and a Frenchman called Auguste Pavie, came to the aid of the priests during this crisis and helped some of them to flee to the mountains of Tibet. They took some of their sacred cats with them to perpetuate the breed and established a new temple of Lao-Tsun. The holy men were later to show their gratitude. In 1919 they sent a pair of their precious cats to France as a special gift.

On the surface, either of these stories sounds plausible enough, but on close examination they have many flaws and appear to be as fictitious as the original, legendary tale.

First, the Hon. Russell Gordon did not exist. According to Brian Vesey-Fitzgerald, Vice-president of the National Cat Club, writing in 1969, neither of the noble families to which he could have belonged had ever heard of him. Nor does he appear in any of the appropriate works of reference listing 'Honourables'. But supposing his name was, in reality, 'Russell, Gordon'? Could he have been the Hon. Gordon Russell? Apparently not. Once again, the noble families of that surname knew nothing of him. Supposing, then, that he was not an 'Hon.', but simply a Major? Unfortunately, neither a Major Russell Gordon, nor a Major Gordon Russell appears in any Army List for the period.

Not only is the Birman's saviour a mystery figure, but the Brahmin invasion is also in doubt. Vesey-Fitzgerald will have none of it: 'There could not . . . have been a Brahmin invasion of Burma. A Brahmin is a member of a Hindu priestly caste: and Burma and India were united under British rule. It would be better if the "Hon. Russell Gordon" and his fairy tales were forgotten.' In addition, the large discrepancies in the dates in the two versions of the 'attacked temple' story do not exactly enhance their reliability.

3 An alternative version of how these cats came to the West suggests that, in reality, an American millionaire travelling in the Far East – the name of Vanderbilt is mentioned – managed to purchase two Birmans in 1918, by bribing a disloyal temple servant to release them against the wishes of the priests. If the sacred temple cats were thought to harbour the souls of departed brethren, a reluctance to disposing of them as gifts would not be surprising.

A slight weakness in this story is that, if an American millionaire was involved, one would have expected the first exported Birman cats to end up in the United States, when in reality they arrived in France. According to one rumour, Mr Vanderbilt sent them to a Mme Thadde Hadisch in Nice.

Once we reach the stage in these three stories where the pair of sacred cats is on the high seas, heading for France, all three versions begin to agree with one another. In each case, the

THE BIRMAN CAT, also known as the Sacred Cat of Burma, has a mysterious, controversial origin, but nobody can deny that it is one of the most beautifully marked of all domestic cats.

pair of 'founding cats' is recorded as consisting of a male called Madalpour and a female called Sita. The male is said to have died during the long journey, but the female was more resilient and managed to survive. By a stroke of luck, she was pregnant and, on arrival, produced a litter in which there was one perfectly marked female kitten that was given the name of Poupée. Poupée was then bred either to a Persian or a Siamese, and the modern history of the Birman Cat began.

4 All three of the foregoing 'histories' of the Birman Cat have been questioned by certain authorities. They suspect that, not only the fanciful legend of Mun-Ha, but the whole Burma story is a complete fiction. It is their contention that the breed was artificially created by French breeders who carefully cross-bred a variety of Siamese and Long-haired Cats. Once they had created a delightful hybrid they then invented an exotic background for it, to make it more appealing and to add to its pedigree status. There may, of course, have been a real cat that was given to a real Monsieur Pavie, or a real Mr Vanderbilt, but it may not have looked anything like the present day Birman. It could have been a rather ordinary feline, which, with a little judicious help in French catteries was converted into the enchanting cat that the Birman undoubtedly is today.

One fact of which we can be certain is that, in France, the Birman became a great favourite and was quickly established as a pedigree breed. It was recognized as such as early as 1925 by the French Feline Federation and remained popular in that country in the decades that followed. As late as 1946, two American authors were labelling this cat, rather confusingly, as the 'French Burmese', confirming at least that France was the centre of the breed's development.

Despite its growing popularity there, however, it is said that during World War II, the population of Birmans in France was decimated and that eventually, at the end of the war, there were only a few left.

In Germany only two breeders managed to keep their Birmans alive. Although it was hanging by such a slender thread, the breed was saved and after the war the numbers were soon increasing again. The first of the Continental Birmans to be exported were sent to the United States in 1959. The breed first arrived in Britain in 1964.

In 1966 the Birman was recognized as a pedigree cat for competition purposes in the UK and in 1967 the United States followed suit.

There is an intriguing footnote to the confusing history of the Birman Cat. It is reported that in 1960 an American breeder, Mrs G. Griswold, acquired a pair of 'Tibetan Temple Cats' which, on inspection, turned out to be Birmans. To some, the conclusion was obvious: these cats must be descended from the few that were rescued from the temple and taken into exile with the priests.

Just at the point when many people were beginning to believe the criticisms of the Burmese origin of the breed, the importation of these Tibetan Temple Cats created a dilemma. If they are genuine, the Birman must, after all, have an ancient temple history, and the whole story of its historical beginnings must be re-examined.

Personality. Terms that have been used to describe this breed include the following: gentle, faithful, even-tempered, civilized, amenable, affectionate, intelligent, outgoing, robust and hardy. One Birman judge has referred to the breed as 'puppy-dogs in cats' bodies', because they are so responsive to their owners. Another commented: 'Birmans are really very polite cats . . . They speak in very soft, sweet voices, if at all.'

Colour Forms:

GCCF: Seal Point; Blue Point; Chocolate Point; Lilac Point; Red Point; Cream Point; Seal Tortie Point; Blue Tortie Point; Chocolate Tortie Point; Lilac Tortie Point; Seal Tabby Point; Blue Tabby Point; Chocolate Tabby Point; Lilac Tabby Point; Red Tabby Point; Cream Tabby Point; Seal Tortie Tabby Point; Blue Tortie Tabby Point; Chocolate Tortie Tabby Point; Lilac Tortie Tabby Point.

CFA: Seal Point; Blue Point; Chocolate Point; Lilac Point.

Breed Clubs:

Birman Cat Club. Address: 20 Hillside Drive, Little Haywood, Stafford, ST18 0NN, England. There is an annual publication, *The Birman Year.* Address: Gate Cottage, Church Hill, Sedlescombe, E. Sussex TN33 0QP, England.

National Birman Fanciers (NBF). Publishes a magazine, *NBF News.* Address: P.O. Box 1830, Stephenville, Texas 76401, USA. or 14007 Campaign St., Fredricksburg, VA 22407, USA.

Nine Silver Bells (Birmans). Address: 115 S. Springvalley Road, McMurray, PA 15317, USA.

Sacred Cat of Burma (Birman) Fanciers (SCBF). Address: 5542 Cleveland Road, Wooster, OH 44691, USA. (Through this club it is possible to obtain a copy of *The Birman Book* by Vivienne Smith.)

THERE ARE NOW MANY colour forms of the Birman Cat, but however much the colour of their points may vary, they all retain the diagnostic white paws.

2

Manx Cat

This very old breed, famous for being tailless, was originally found on the Isle of Man in the Irish Sea, between Northern England and Northern Ireland, and is now kept as a pedigree cat all over the world. Outside the Isle of Man, it appears to be more popular in the United States than in Europe.

Appearance: A sturdy, rounded, thick-coated short-haired cat with short front legs and long back legs. The tailless rump is higher than the shoulders. The head is large and broad. There are four recognized categories of Manx Cat:

1 'The Rumpy', completely tailless. This is the true Manx Cat, with a small hollow where its tail should be.
2 'The Rumpy Riser', with one, two or three vertebrae fused to the end of the spine, giving the animal a tiny knob where the tail should be.
3 'The Stumpy', with one, two or three normal tail vertebrae, giving the animal a short but movable tail-stump.
4 'The Longy', with an almost full-length tail.

In addition, there is a fifth type – the fake Manx Cat – created by ruthless dealers who have been known to amputate the tails of ordinary kittens to produce tailless adults that can be passed off as expensive pedigree Manx Cats. This is not a recent practice. It was recorded as long ago as 1903, when visitors to the island were offered tailless cats on the landing pier at Douglas, the capital of the Isle of Man. A commentator at the time remarks wryly that 'many more tailless cats and kittens than ever were born have been sold to tourists eager to carry home some souvenir of the island'.

The typical, traditional Manx Cat has a short, thick coat, but there is also a longhaired version, called the Cymric, which first appeared in Canada in the 1960s.

History: The Manx Cat from the Isle of Man is one of the oldest breeds of domestic cat. During its long history a rich assortment of fanciful legends has grown up around it, including the following:

1 The Manx Cat is the result of mating between domestic cats and rabbits. According to this myth, this cross accounts, not only for the reduced tail, but also for the fact that the Manx Cat

THE CONTROVERSIAL MANX CAT, much loved and hallowed by its long history, but now under fire
as a 'genetic abnormality'. Its tailless condition can indeed cause medical problems but it is
claimed that these can be avoided with proper breeding controls.

has a strange gait, caused by its unusually long back legs. (In some individuals the gait is so
strange that they are called 'hoppers', but this 'Manx Hop' may actually be an indication of
spinal deformity.)

2 The Manx Cat was the last animal to enter Noah's Ark. A pair of them insisted on one last
mousing trip as the flood waters were rising and they kept putting off the moment when they
would have to go aboard the Ark. Finally, when heavy rain began to fall, they rushed on board,
just as Noah was closing the door. As they squeezed through, the heavy door slammed shut on
their beautiful bushy tails and severed them, so that although the cats themselves were saved
from the flood, their tails were lost for ever.

3 The Manx Cat was a survivor from the Spanish Armada. According to this legend, several
tailless cats managed to avoid drowning when a galleon from the defeated Armada was
shipwrecked in 1588 on rocks off the coast of the Isle of Man, in the extreme south-west of the
island. There they managed to find shelter until low tide when they were able to clamber ashore
at a location now known as 'Spanish Head'. Finding themselves isolated from other cats on this
small island, they began to reproduce and established themselves as a distinctive, tailless cat.
(Unfortunately for this and the next story, there is no record of a ship from the Spanish Armada
ever coming near the Isle of Man.)

4 According to yet another legend, the ancestor of the Manx Cat was originally a (fully tailed) temple guardian in Tibet. He travelled from there to Spain, where he went aboard a Spanish galleon. This galleon was part of the Armada and was sunk near the Isle of Man. The cat swam ashore and settled on the island, where it produced a large number of kittens. Like the founding father of their breed, they all had long bushy tails. Because of these beautiful appendages, the kittens were repeatedly stolen and killed by Irish soldiers, who needed cats' tails as lucky mascots. (In a variant of this legend, the tails were taken by Viking invaders to adorn their helmets.) As a way of stopping this, the mother cats hit on the idea of biting off the tails of their kittens when they were born. The soldiers then lost interest, and the tailless Manx Cat breed came into existence.

5 In a variant of this last legend, the tails of the native cats of the Isle of Man were sliced off by Viking invaders, who wanted them as decorations for their helmets.

6 A mythological tale describes how Samson was taking a little light exercise by swimming the length of the Irish Sea. As he swam close to the Isle of Man, he was caught by a cat which nearly drowned him with its long tail. To defend himself, he severed the tail and from that day onwards, the cats of the Isle of Man had no tails.

7 A traditional Manx poem describes how Noah's dog bit off the tail of a cat as the Ark rested on Mt. Ararat, after the flood. The mutilated cat leaped through a window and started swimming. It went on swimming until eventually it arrived at the Isle of Man, where it came on to land and made its home.

8 The Manx Cat arrived at the Isle of Man on board trading ships coming from the Orient. (It has even been suggested that it was the Phoenicians who brought back tailless cats from Japan, over two thousand years ago.) This story is probably inspired by the fact that there has been a short-tailed domestic cat in Japan – the Japanese Bobtail Cat – since early times. Genetically, however, the two breeds are quite unrelated.

9 A variant of this last explanation has the breed arriving as a 'couple of kittens' brought home to the Isle of Man from the East Indies by a returning sailor.

10 A feudal lord increased his revenues by placing a tax on cats' tails. The population of the Isle of Man rebelled against this by cutting off the tails of all their cats. From then on, the cats remained tailless and no tax was paid.

Few breeds of domestic cat can have acquired such an amazing variety of speculative or nonsensical tales concerning their origins. The plain and far less colourful truth, however, is that the Manx gene almost certainly cropped up as a local, random mutation on the Isle of Man, centuries ago, and then became established there through prolonged in-breeding on the restricted island habitat.

Today Manx Cats have become so strongly associated with the Isle of Man that they have become a popular emblem there, appearing on local postage stamps and coins. At one point, the Tynwold (the Manx Parliament) became concerned that, although the Manx Cat was being bred all over the world, there was a risk that it might die out in its homeland. It was therefore decided to establish a government cattery to preserve a nucleus of breeding stock for all time. This was first done at Knockaloe Farm, where a group of 20 females and three males were installed. Then, in order to make the cats more available as a tourist attraction, a new cattery was built at Noble's Park in the capital, Douglas. With approximately 30 cats and kittens on display, this was opened to the public in July 1964.

Personality: Terms used to describe this breed include: active, hardy, lively, mischievous, playful, faithful, affectionate, speedy, patient, shy, docile, calm, quiet, doleful, undemanding and intelligent. It is said to be dog-like in some respects, will play a fetching game and will even accept the imposition of being taken for a walk on a leash. It is amenable to training and is good with children and other animals. One author describes it as a study in contradictions: 'quiet but active, shy but friendly, witty but reserved, clever but trusting'. Another called it a 'feline clinging vine' that will never leave you alone.

Critics of the breed see the loss of a tail as a deformity which robs the animals of one of their principal means of expression. Aldous Huxley commented: 'The Manx Cat is the equivalent of a dumb man.'

Breeding: The Manx Cat has never been particularly common, partly because the litters are rather small. There are usually only two to four kittens. An analysis of 237 litters gave an average figure of 3.4 kittens.

There is also the problem that the Manx gene is semi-lethal. If a Rumpy Manx Cat is mated with another Rumpy, the kittens die at an early stage of development. So there can never be a true-breeding Manx Cat. To create a completely tailless show cat, breeders usually mate a Rumpy with a partially tailed or fully tailed Manx.

A PURE WHITE FORM of the Manx Cat. Serious breeders claim that the deformities once associated with the Manx have now been reduced to the level of extreme rarities as a result of careful, selective breeding programmes.

The problem for Manx Cats is that the effect of the 'tailless gene' does not stop at the base of the tail. It modifies the whole of the spinal column, with the modification increasing from front to rear. The front parts show little more than a slight decrease in the length of the individual vertebrae, but towards the rear there is not only decrease in size, but also in number, and an increase in fusion. In the most extreme cases there is a condition similar to spina bifida, and interference with defecation because of a narrowing of the anal opening. Because of this the Manx Cat requires more careful and expert treatment on the part of breeders, than any other kind of domestic cat.

It has been said that, if the Manx Cat was a new breed, it would not be given pedigree status, and that it survives as a show cat only because of its long-established history. (A specialist breeders' club for Manx Cats was established as long ago as 1901.) This is unfair to modern breeders who have worked for years to improve the Manx Cat and to reduce the deformities without losing the essential, tailless condition. Some authors suggest that deformities are common but this is no longer the case. In two recent studies of spina bifida in Manx Cats, this condition was found in only 15 out of 806 and 2 out of 417 kittens. Other deformities, such as anal restrictions, deformed legs and a hopping gait, were also rare. It is claimed that, bred with care, the vast majority of Manx kittens are perfectly healthy today, thanks to intelligent selective breeding programmes, and that the breed is now safe for the future.

Colour Forms:

GCCF: All patterns and colours are accepted, except for Siamese markings. Those specifically listed are: White; Black; Chocolate; Lilac; Red Self; Blue; Cream; Silver Tabby (ten variants) (Classic and Mackerel); Red Tabby (Classic and Mackerel); Brown Tabby (nine variants) (Classic and Mackerel); Tortie; Chocolate Tortie; Lilac Tortie; Tortie and White; Blue Tortie and White; Chocolate Tortie and White; Lilac Tortie and White; Blue-Cream; Brown Spotted (ten variants); Silver Spotted (ten variants); Black and White Bi-colour (six variants); Black Smoke and White (ten variants); Brown Tabby and White (ten variants); Silver Tabby and White (ten variants); Black Smoke (ten variants); Black Tipped (ten variants).

CFA: All colours are permitted (except those involving chocolate, lavender or the Himalayan pattern). Specifically listed as accepted colours are: White, Black, Blue, Red, Cream, Chinchilla Silver; Shaded Silver; Black Smoke; Blue Smoke; Classic Tabby Pattern; Mackerel Tabby Pattern; Patched Tabby Pattern; Brown Patched Tabby; Blue Patched Tabby; Silver Patched Tabby; Silver Tabby; Red Tabby; Brown Tabby; Blue Tabby; Cream Tabby; Tortie; Calico; Dilute Calico; Blue-Cream; Bi-color.

Breed Clubs:

American Manx Club. Address: P.O. Box 15053, Colorado Springs, CO 80935-5053, USA.

International Manx and Cymric Society. 254 S. Douglas, Bradley, IL 60915, USA.

Note: There is also a breed publication: *Manx Lines.* Address: 19324 2nd Avenue, N.W. Seattle, WA 98177, USA.

3

Norwegian Forest Cat

The Viking cat. A large, long-haired Norwegian breed. In its homeland it has been known as the Skaukatt or Skogkatt, or more formally as the Norsk Skaukatt or Norsk Skogkatt. Its Norwegian nickname is the 'Wegi' or 'Wegie'. They are also often referred to as 'Skogs' or 'Norgies'. In 19th-century Norwegian folk-tales it is an enchanted cat and is referred to as the 'Fairy Cat'. In France it is called the *Chat de Bois Norvégian,* the *Chat des Forêts Norvégiennes,* or simply the *Norvégien;* in Germany it is the *Norwegische Waldkatze.*

Appearance: A large, powerfully built cat with long hair, a full ruff, tufted ears and a bushy tail. The front legs are slightly shorter than the hind legs. It is a giant among cats, similar in size to the American Maine Coon. The long outer coat is glossy and water-resistant, while the thick undercoat adds protection against the cold. The winter coat is even thicker than the summer one. Inevitably, this means a heavy moult once a year.

Legendary History: Norse folk-tales often speak of huge cats, perhaps inspired by the genuinely impressive bulk of the real-life Norwegian Forest Cat. One legendary cat was so heavy that even the god Thor could not lift it off the ground. The wagon of Freya, the blue-eyed, blonde-haired goddess of love and beauty, was drawn by two powerful cats. Any mortals who placed pans of milk in their cornfields for her cats to drink would have their crops protected by her. It was Freya who gave us Friday ('Freya's day') and this became a popular day for marrying. If the sun shone on her wedding day it was said of the bride 'she has fed the cat well', meaning that she had not offended the feline favourite of the goddess, who, in return, had bestowed upon the bride the good weather.

Cats were chosen to serve the goddess Freya because their fecundity reflected hers. The early Christians declared her a witch and banished her to the mountains. From their association with her, her cats were also seen as evil forces and were thereafter condemned to torture and death at the hands of the pious.

Factual History: The true story of how the Forest Cat came to be in the Norwegian countryside may never be known. There are six current theories:

1 Long ago, Viking ships brought Scottish Wild Cats to Norway, where they gradually changed into the Forest Cats we see today. (There are no indigenous wild cats in Scandinavia.)

2 Domestic cats from Europe reached Scandinavia on board trading ships. Once there, they

THE IMPRESSIVE Norwegian Forest Cat, with its magnificent, heavy coat, is one of the largest of all domestic breeds. An ancient breed, it has recently grown in popularity all over the world.

escaped and hybridized with the imported Scottish Wild Cats, in the process gaining a thicker coat and larger bone structure.

3 Angora Cats were carried by boat from the Middle East to the ports of the Mediterranean and from there to Scandinavia in the 16th century, where they crossed with the descendants of the imported wild cats, creating a bigger-boned, heavier-coated Angora.

4 Angora Cats, arriving by ship and escaping into the freezing Norwegian countryside, simply became bigger and bigger, with a thicker and thicker coat, as an adaptation to the climate, without the intervention of any imported wild cat stock.

5 Long-haired Russian Cats (modern Siberian Forest Cats) found their way to Norway on board ships plying the Baltic and North Sea routes.

6 Ordinary local domestic cats that became feral and lived rough slowly became bigger and more heavily furred.

ALTHOUGH THE NORWEGIAN FOREST CAT *(opposite),* now appears in many forms, it is always distinguishable by its large body size and luxuriant ruff.

Of these various theories, those involving Scottish Wild Cats seem to be the least likely. Any breed of domestic cat exposed to sub-arctic conditions will soon become larger and thicker-coated if it is to survive. A more elaborate explanation of the origin of this breed is hardly necessary.

We are certain of one thing, however, namely that, whichever way it may have arrived, the Norwegian Forest Cat lived in Norway for centuries as a farmyard cat, without any particular attention being paid to it. Then, in 1912, the first named Norwegian Forest Cat, a male called Gabriel Scott Solvfaks, was recorded by the Norwegian Cat Society. Nothing much more was heard about the breed for a while until, in the 1930s, cat enthusiasts began to take a greater interest. Planned breeding programmes followed, and the first Norwegian Forest Cat Club was formed in 1938, but further progress was interrupted by World War II.

Thanks to the tireless efforts of the Norwegian enthusiast Carl-Fredrik Nordane, the Forest Cat found favour again in the 1970s and before long was being seen at cat shows in many different countries, where its impressive size, elegant shape and magnificent coat made a great impact. It was given the international name of Norwegian Forest Cat in 1972, and it gained international championship status in 1977. In a few years it had been exported as a pedigree cat to the United States and most European countries, although it was late arriving in England, a breed club there not being formed until 1987. In 1995 it was estimated that there were approximately 1,000 of these cats in the British Isles.

Personality: Terms used to describe this breed include: rugged, sturdy, intelligent, agile, confident, calm, quiet, athletic, strong, quick, bold, mischievous, outgoing, affectionate, good-natured, playful, alert, responsive, inventive, independent, adventurous, adaptable, brave and loving. A skilful tree-climber, this is definitely not an indoor cat.

Colour Forms: In Norway, the most popular colour form is the Black and White. Outside Norway, the tabby is generally favoured. According to one source, all colours except chocolate, lilac and Siamese pointing are acceptable; according to another source, all colours except chinchilla and Siamese pointing are acceptable. Colour combinations that have been bred so far include: Black Smoke and White, Blue Tabby and White, Blue Tortie Smoke and White, Brown Tabby and White.

Breed Clubs:

Norwegian Forest Cat Club. Address: 9 Sundridge Road, Woking, Surrey, GU22 9AU, England.

National Norwegian Forest Cat Club. Address: 17 Ashwood Road, Trenton, NJ 08610-1328, USA.

Norsk Skogkattering, Danmark. Formed in 1975. A Danish breed club with 400 members worldwide. It issues a quarterly magazine in Danish – *Huldrekatten* – and an English newsletter. Address: Hermelinvaenget 8, DK-2880 Bagsvaerd, Denmark.

Norwegian Forest Cat Breeders Consortium. Address: 1859 Vintage Court, Corinth, TX 76205, USA.

Norwegian Forest Cat Fanciers' Association. Address: 2094 Sandpiper Court, Ponte Vedra Beach, FL 32082, USA, or 2507 Ocean Drive S., Jacksonville Beach, FL 32250, USA.

4

PERSIAN CAT

One of the oldest breeds of domestic cat, the exceptionally long-haired Persian became popular as soon as competitive cat showing began, at the end of the 19th century. Although its origins are obscure, the breed quickly became clearly defined and standardized.

As the glamorous 'luxury' breed of pedigree cat, it is still known throughout the world today by the name 'Persian', with one inexplicable exception. Among the officials of the British cat fancy, it is confusingly referred to simply as the 'Longhair'. This is done despite the fact that (1) outside feline officialdom, the entire British public (like the rest of the world) calls it the Persian, and (2) it creates considerable confusion with domestic cat classification systems, because of all the other, quite different, long-haired breeds that now exist. Some authors opt for a compromise. By calling it the 'Persian Longhair' they hope to keep British officialdom happy without mystifying the general reading public.

In France it is known as the *Persan;* in Germany as the *Perser, Perserkatzen* or *Persisch Langhaar;* and in Holland as the *Perzisch*.

Appearance: The Persian has a uniquely rounded shape, with a thick woolly coat, short neck and body, stocky legs, thick bones, bushy tail and massive, broad head with small, tufted ears set low on the head. The face has become much flatter in modern specimens, when compared with the profile seen a century ago. The thick fur has a dense, woolly undercoat.

History: As with most early breeds, there is considerable argument concerning the origin of the Persian. The truth is that detailed information is lacking, so that authors can speculate freely. No less than nine different views (some nonsensical, some plausible) have been expressed in the past; they are as follows:

1 It is descended from the long-coated wild cat called Pallas's Cat *(Felis manul).*
2 It is descended from the long-coated wild cat called the Sand Cat *(Felis margarita).*
3 It is descended from a cross between Pallas's Cat (or the Sand Cat) and local domestic cats in the Middle East.
4 It is descended from the European Wild Cat *(Felis sylvestris).*
5 It is descended from a cross between Pallas's Cat and the European Wild Cat.
6 It is descended from the Russian Longhair Cat, one of the original longhair breeds (see Siberian Forest Cat). It has been suggested that the 'Persian' is not really Persian at all, but that it is simply the thick-coated, cold-country cat from the north of Russia that was somehow

A BLUE AND WHITE Bi-colour Persian. One of the oldest of domestic breeds, the Persian Cat is by far the most spectacular and has retained its dominant position at cat shows throughout the 20th century.

accidentally associated with Persia. This could have happened if these cats were first seen in the West when they arrived on board ships from the Middle East.

7 It is descended from a cross between the Russian Longhair and local domestic cats in the Middle East.

8 It is descended from a cross between the Russian Longhair and the Turkish Angora. The appeal of this theory is that it explains the nature of the Persian coat, the thickness coming from the Russian cat and the long flowing silkiness from the Angora.

9 It is a long-haired mutant that appeared spontaneously in the Iranian region of the Middle East. This is the simplest theory, but it fails to explain why a long-haired mutant should have been successful in the intense heat of the Iranian region. The only suggestion offered so far to overcome this objection is that the mutation occurred in the most mountainous regions of Iran where lower temperatures do occur.

Of these nine suggestions, the first five, involving wild species, can almost certainly be discounted. The sixth overlooks specific reports of cats being brought to Europe from Persia. Of the other three, each is plausible enough. The most likely idea would seem to be that, one way or another, thick-coated cats from the frozen north were brought south where they managed to survive the amazing temperature contrasts of what is now Iranian territory.

The idea of an indigenous, long-haired breed arising inside Persia cannot, however, be discounted. The German author Hermann Dembreck has assembled a fairly detailed historical account of such an origin, but it is not entirely clear how much is based on precise records, and how much on his imagination. In summary, he claims the following:

When King Cambyses of Persia conquered Egypt in 525 BC, the invaders took large numbers of the sacred Egyptian cats home with them. There, the winters were much more harsh and, as the generations passed, these cats began to develop longer and longer coats. In 331 BC, Alexander the Great invaded Persia, and King Darius and his court fled to the mountains, taking with them their valuable cats. About 2,000 metres (7,000 feet) up, they built their strongholds and there, in the even colder air, generations of cats gradually grew even longer fur. Their main centre was north-west of the present-day city of Meshed, in the Chorassan district of Eastern Persia. These mountainous regions were heavily forested and in the forests roamed local wild cats, which mated with the domesticated castle cats and created a stockier, sturdier build. By AD 247, these Parthian lords had established a culture of their own and began to export some of their precious cats. By the eighth century, Islam was expanding and invaded Persian territory. They took some of the cats they found there and passed them on to other Islamic regions. By the 15th century they had reached Anatolia and were to be found in Angora, where they changed their shapes again, becoming slightly sleeker. Some of these Angoras Cats were then exported west to Europe, where they created a sensation, being the first long-haired cats ever seen there. A little later, the even fluffier cats from Persia itself were taken to the West.

Whichever theory one cares to follow, it is clear that, by the 17th century, a remarkable breed of thick-coated cat had somehow developed in what was then Persia. It was at that time that the Italian traveller, Pietro della Valle, first encountered it and was so impressed by its beauty that he brought breeding stock back to Europe with him. He set sail from Venice in 1614, travelling to Persia via Egypt, the Holy Land and Arabia. He spent five years in Persia before returning to Italy in 1626, via India, Mesopotamia and the Levant. (Some authors have reported that he brought Angora Cats back from Turkey, but he does not appear to have visited that country, so this is probably an error.) Of the cat he met in Persia, he recorded the following description: 'There is in Persia a cat of the figure and form of our ordinary ones, but infinitely more beautiful in the lustre and colour of its coat. It is of a blue-grey, and soft and shining as silk. The tail is of great length and covered with hair six inches long.'

It is not clear how well his breeding plans fared, but we do know that, by the 19th century the Persian had become a highly desirable breed, especially in France. Its only serious long-haired rival at that time was the Angora from Turkey.

The Persian's impact on the first cat shows in Britain was such that it quickly came to dominate the scene. Its long-haired Turkish rival was soon eclipsed. Already, by 1903, Frances Simpson was able to say: 'In classing all long-haired cats as Persian I may be wrong, but the distinctions . . . between Angoras and Persians are of so fine a nature that I must be pardoned if I ignore the class of cat commonly called Angora, which seems gradually to have disappeared from our midst.' She then goes on to devote no fewer than 127 pages to the various colour forms of Persians. Clearly, by the turn of the century, the Persian had won the day. It was soon being referred to as 'the aristocrat of the cat family'.

As the years passed, more and more colours and patterns were added to the Persian repertoire, until there were more than 60 different coat variants on show. At the same time, the Persian body-type was made more and more extreme, with even longer coats and flatter, broader faces. The degree to which these changes have been taken has varied from country to country, with the result that international judging of pedigree Persians at cat shows sometimes leads to strong disagreements and much heated debate.

Personality: Terms used to describe this breed include: docile, quiet, intelligent, aloof, gentle, easygoing, good-tempered, sweet-natured, affectionate and friendly. In this respect, it would seem that selective breeding during the last hundred years has greatly modified the breed. Writing in 1889, Harrison Weir paints a very different picture of the character of the Persians he encountered at the early cat shows: 'My attendant has been frequently wounded in our endeavour to examine the fur, dentition, etc., of . . . the Persian.' He goes on to say that 'I find this variety less reliable as regards temper than the short-haired cats . . . In some few instances I have found them to be of almost a savage disposition, biting and snapping more like a dog than a cat.' This forms a striking contrast with the temperament of the modern Persian, which is now generally thought of as the most placid of breeds.

Colour Forms: Uniquely and strangely, in Britain, the different colour forms of the Persian have been classed as different breeds since the early days of cat-showing. Separate breed colour clubs were established and the cats were treated as though there was much more than a mere colour-gene difference between them. Back in the days when there were only a few colour forms available, this did not matter, but today, when almost every colour and coat pattern imaginable has been created for the Persian, the situation requires re-examination.

GCCF: SELF: Black; White; Blue; Red Self; Cream; Chocolate; Lilac.

SMOKE: Black Smoke; Blue Smoke; Chocolate Smoke; Lilac Smoke; Red Smoke; Tortie Smoke; Cream Smoke; Blue-Cream Smoke; Chocolate Tortie Smoke; Lilac Tortie Smoke.

CHINCHILLA: Chinchilla; Golden Persian; Shaded Silver.

CAMEO: Red Shell Cameo; Red Shaded Cameo; Tortie Cameo; Cream Shell Cameo; Cream Shaded Cameo; Blue-Cream Cameo.

PEWTER: Pewter.

TABBY (classic pattern only): Silver Tabby; Brown Tabby; Blue Tabby; Chocolate Tabby; Lilac Tabby; Red Tabby.

TORTIE TABBY: Tortie Tabby; Blue Tortie Tabby; Chocolate Tortie Tabby; Lilac Tortie Tabby.

TORTIE: Tortie; Blue-Cream; Chocolate Tortie; Lilac-Cream.

TORTIE AND WHITE: Tortie and White; Blue Tortie and White; Chocolate Tortie and White; Lilac Tortie and White.

TORTIE TABBY AND WHITE: Tortie Tabby and White; Blue Tortie Tabby and White; Chocolate Tortie Tabby and White; Lilac Tortie Tabby and White.

BI-COLOUR SOLID: Black and White Bi-colour; Blue and White Bi-colour; Chocolate and White Bi-colour; Lilac and White Bi-colour; Red and White Bi-colour; Cream and White Bi-colour.

BI-COLOUR TABBY: Brown Tabby and White; Blue Tabby and White; Chocolate Tabby and White; Lilac Tabby and White; Red Tabby and White; Cream Tabby and White.

VAN BI-COLOUR: Black and White Van; Blue and White Van; Chocolate and White Van; Lilac and White Van; Red and White Van; Cream and White Van.

VAN TRICOLOUR: Tortie and White Van; Blue Tortie and White Van; Chocolate Tortie and White Van; Lilac Tortie and White Van.

THE DRAMATIC appearance of the Persian Cat has created many thousands of slaves to its undeniable beauty, owners who must daily devote themselves to hours of laborious grooming.

CFA: SOLID: White; Blue; Black; Red; Peke-face Red; Cream; Chocolate; Lilac.

SILVER AND GOLDEN: Chinchilla Silver; Shaded Silver; Chinchilla Golden; Shaded Golden.

SHADED AND SMOKE: Shell Cameo; Shaded Cameo (Red Chinchilla); (Red Shaded); Cream Shell Cameo (Cream Chinchilla); Cream Shaded Cameo (Cream Shaded); Shell Tortie; Shaded Tortie; Shell Blue-Cream (Blue-Cream Chinchilla); Shaded Blue-Cream; Black Smoke; Blue Smoke; Cream Smoke; Cameo Smoke (Red Smoke); Tortie Smoke; Blue-Cream Smoke.

TABBY: Classic Tabby Pattern; Mackerel Tabby Pattern; Silver Tabby; Silver Patched Tabby; Blue Silver Tabby; Blue Silver Patched Tabby; Red Tabby; Peke-face Red Tabby; Brown Tabby; Brown Patched Tabby; Blue Tabby; Blue Patched Tabby; Cream Tabby; Cameo Tabby; Cream Cameo Tabby.

PARTI-COLOR: Tortie; Blue-Cream; Chocolate Tortie; Lilac-Cream.

BI-COLOR: Calico; Van Calico; Dilute Calico; Van Dilute Calico; Chocolate Calico; Chocolate Van Calico; Lilac Calico; Lilac Van Calico; Bi-color; Van Bi-color; Smoke and White; Van Smoke and White; Tabby and White; Van Tabby and White.

NOTE: For Colourpoint versions, see Himalayan Cat.

Persian Variants Recent breeds for which the Persian has been used as the ancestral cat include the following (see separate entries for further details):

1 HIMALAYAN (Longhair Persian with Colourpoint coat pattern)
2 PEKE-FACED (Longhair Persian with flattened face)
3 EXOTIC (Shorthair Persian)

Breed Clubs:
Persian Bi-color and Calico Society. Address: 187 N. Madison Drive, S. Plainfield, NJ 07080, USA.
United Silver (Persian) Fanciers. Address: 663 N. Dayton Lakeview Road, New Carlisle, OH 45344, USA.
NOTE: In the United States there is a quarterly magazine which is devoted exclusively to the Persian Cat: *Persian Quarterly*. Address: 4401 Zephyr Street, Wheat Ridge, CO, USA. There is also a publication called *Persian News*. Address: 746 North Crescent Drive, Hollywood, Florida

IN THE EARLY DAYS of cat-showing, the few known colour forms of the Persians were each classed as a separate breed. Now that there is a huge number of colours available, that antique arrangement requires revision.

THE CHINCHILLA PERSIAN is arguably the most glamorous of all cats. It appeared in 1882, was first exhibited at a cat show in 1894, and had its first breed club in 1901. In the 1960s it became famous as the pampered pet of a James Bond villain.

33021, USA. And specifically for Silver Persians there is *Silver Lining*. Address: 491 Valencia Lane, Vacaville, CA 95688, USA.

5

RUSSIAN BLUE CAT

This early breed of short-haired cat has enjoyed many names: Blue, Maltese, Maltese Blue, Archangel Blue, Chartreuse Blue, Foreign Blue, Russo-American Blue, Spanish Blue, Blue Russian and Russian Shorthair. Another name for it was the American Blue Cat. According to Rush Shippen Huidekoper, writing in 1895, this name is 'probably due to the fact that the Maltese for some years has been a very favourite cat in America, and has probably been bred more carefully than any other breed of cat, so that its representatives formed a distinctive type of good quality'. Yet another early name referred to by Huidekoper in 1895 was the Russian Cat. Confusingly, this was also an early name for the Russian Longhair Cat, used by Harrison Weir in 1889. Although some authors still like to refer to the Russian Blue simply as the Russian Cat, this is best avoided because of its earlier ambiguity. The official title of Russian Blue was finally agreed in the 1940s. It has sometimes been referred to as 'The Connoisseur's Cat'. In France it is the *Bleu Russe;* in Holland the *Russisch Blauw;* in Germany the *Russisch Blau.*

Appearance: Originally a robust cat with a strong build and rather average proportions, but more recently modified by the introduction of Siamese genes, making it more elongated and angular. Its diagnostic feature is its lustrous, plush, dense, but short coat of grey fur. It has a characteristic wedge-shaped head.

History: Like other domestic cats with a long history, there are a variety of theories about the supposed origins of this breed:

1 The oldest tradition, and the one which gave the cat its geographical name, states that the breed originated in the cold northern regions of Russia. It adapted to this harsh climate by developing, not a long furry coat, but a short, thick, seal-like one. It is, in fact, a double coat, there being an outer coat of remarkably strong guard hairs and an inner coat of unusually water-resistant down hairs. The breed was hunted for its pelt in early times and may even have been kept, not so much as a pet or vermin-destroyer, but as a valuable source of clothing in the cold north. In this role, it is thought to have spread west through Scandinavia and became a favourite of the Vikings, eventually travelling with them to Britain and many other locations.

2 An alternative version sees these animals being taken as ships' cats from the port of Archangel (now known as Archangel'sk), on the White Sea, to Sweden and from there to Britain (hence their early alternative name of Archangel Blue).

THE RUSSIAN BLUE, one of the earlier breeds of show cat, which has been exhibited for well over a century. It is famous for its plush, dense coat of bluish-grey fur.

3 Another variation on this theme suggests instead that they came to Britain from Northern Norway. The earliest blue cats to reach England were certainly from that region, but they may not have been true Russian Blues. They were described at the time as 'Shorthaired Blue Tabbies' and were also known as 'Canon Girdlestone's breed'.

4 Another story envisages them being collected from Archangel by visiting British sailors who acquired them for sale in their home country. One version of this story depicts them being brought back at a very early date – during the reign of Elizabeth I, in the 16th century. Another version suggests the much later date of 1860.

Whichever origin is the true one, we do know that by the end of the 19th century, the Russian Blue had become a popular short-haired breed at the early cat shows. Writing in 1889, Harrison Weir commented that he thought it might be just another form of Blue British Shorthair, but he had 'to admit that those that came from Archangel were of a deeper, purer tint than the English cross-breeds . . . they had larger ears and eyes, and were larger and longer in the head and legs, also the coat of fur was excessively short, rather inclined to woolliness, but bright and glossy.'

Frances Simpson, writing in 1903, reported on the continuing clash between the British Blues and the Russian Blues. One owner complained that there should be separate classes: 'it is disappointing for a Russian owner, who seeing "Russian Blue" only given in the schedule, enters his cat accordingly and gets beaten by a short-haired blue failing in just the points that the Russian is correct in.' Simpson provided a detailed description of the two breeds and the Russian Blue was eventually given a separate class in 1912. Arguments about its origins, however, had it reduced to the official title of 'Foreign Blue'. Russian Blue breeders were not happy about this, but it was not until 1939 that the name Russian Blue was officially reinstated.

During World War II, the Russian Blue nearly disappeared in Europe. In Britain, only one breeder, Marie Rochford, managed to keep a pure line going, and it was from her stock that the post-war redevelopment of the breed began. Unfortunately, because of the small numbers of pure Russian Blues available, it was decided to introduce other lines, supposedly to improve the breed. Blue Point Siamese were favoured and the result was that the Russian Blue became increasingly lanky and angular and less and less like the heavy, tough cat it had been in its early days. By 1950 the official description of the breed had to be rewritten, making the cat little more than an all-blue Siamese.

In 1965/1966 British breeders decided to reverse this trend and to work back towards the original type of the Russian Blue. The extent to which this reversal has succeeded has varied in different parts of the world, creating some minor inconsistencies in the breed, worldwide, at the present time. (For example, the British version is today slightly heavier and has a rounder head than the American.) In Britain, a Russian Blue Association was founded in 1867.

The Russian Blue arrived early in the United States and Canada, appearing there around the turn of the century. Some give the date as between 1888 and 1890, but others place it a little later. The first one for which there is a specific record is a male called 'Blue Royal', which was imported by Clinton Locke of Chicago in 1907. As in Britain, there was at first some confusion between the Russian Blue and the local blue shorthair.

For some reason, after being shown at early cat shows in the United States, the breed disappeared from the American scene. When the 'orientalized' Russian Blues started to cross the Atlantic in the late 1940s, there was a new surge of interest in the breed and in 1950 a Russian Blue Club was formed by a group of American enthusiasts led by C.A. Comaire of Buda in Texas, who had imported post-war stock from both Britain and Denmark.

According to one author, this breed was 'a cherished pet both at the courts of the Russian Tsar and of Queen Victoria of England'.

Personality: Terms used to describe this breed include: affectionate, shy, pensive, intelligent, tranquil, timid, reserved, serene, placid, hardy, obliging, independent, unintrusive, quick-witted, acrobatic, elegant, resourceful, sensitive, temperamental, quiet, sensitive and loyal.

Colour Forms: The so-called blue colour is in reality a silvery-grey. In some countries there are three other, minor colour forms – White, Black and Red – but the creation of these variants seems rather perverse in a breed that is specifically named for its colour.

Breed Clubs:

Russian Blue Breeders Association. Address: 53 Percy Road, Shirley, Southampton, Hants, SO1 4LP, England.

Russian Blue Society. Address: 1602, Southbrook Drive, Wadena, MN 56482, USA.

6

SIBERIAN FOREST CAT

An ancient long-haired breed now believed to have been ancestral to all modern long-haired cats including both the Angora and the Persian. Sometimes referred to simply as the 'Siberian Cat' or the 'Siberia', it is most commonly found in Northern Russia, especially around St. Petersburg where its thick fur protects it from the harsh winters. In Germany it is known as the *Sibirische Katze*.

Appearance: A strongly built, long-bodied cat with a broad, round head and powerful legs. The long fur has a dense, heavy under-coat. There is a thick ruff and a bushy tail. In many respects it is similar to the Norwegian Forest Cat, to which it is no doubt closely related.

History: It would seem that this breed has been present in Russia for centuries. In the Victorian era, when it first appeared in the West, it was known as the Russian Longhair Cat. It was crossed with the other long-haired breeds popular at the time, such as the Angora and the Persian, and its separate identity was soon lost. By the early part of the 20th century it had been eclipsed by the softer-coated Persian and before long had vanished from the pedigree cat scene.

The breed presumably continued to thrive in its homeland but was taken for granted to such an extent by the local people that nobody bothered to develop it as a pedigree cat. (A recent survey revealed that 64 per cent of the cats in St. Petersburg carried the long-haired gene.) The result was that, in the world of cat shows, it became a forgotten breed. Even today it remains rare outside its homeland. However, this seems set to change. In 1987 a young male and female were collected from the region of St. Petersburg and taken to Berlin by enthusiasts, who invented the new name 'Siberian' and started a serious breeding programme. The male was called Tima and the female Mussa. The female was discovered in a city market. Within a few months they had produced their first litter. By 1990 a number of them had been registered in Germany and elsewhere in Europe, using the name of Siberian Cat, or Siberian Forest Cat.

Since then there has also been increased interest in Russia itself, as pedigree cat breeding has at last started to flourish there. There is now a birth registry for Siberian Forest Cats at the Kotofej Cat Club in St. Petersburg.

The breed was first imported into America in 1990 and the first litter was born there in October of that year. It was exhibited at the International Cat Show in New York in 1991.

As Russia was probably the original source of all domestic long-haired cats, before they were taken to Turkey and Persia and thence to the rest of the world, the re-appearance of these

THE SIBERIAN FOREST CAT is similar in appearance to the better-known Norwegian Forest Cat.
Coming from cold northern regions, both are large cats with heavy coats. The Siberian Forest
Cat is thought by some to be the original ancestor of all our long-haired breeds.

northern cats is to be welcomed. A close study of their genetics may help to unravel some of
the uncertainties concerning the origins of the other pedigree long-haired breeds.

Personality: The original Russian cats were said to be hardy, preferring to be outdoors even in
the coldest weather, less agile, and less affectionate towards their human companions, than other
breeds. The latest (Siberian) ones are reported to be charming, quiet, gentle, slightly shy, shrewd,
docile, lively, rugged, affectionate, devoted, relaxed and active. They are vocally quiet, like the
Persians.

Colour Forms: The typical colouring is tabby, usually with a white ruff and white paws, but now
that Russian breeders are taking an interest in it, many new colours are being developed.

Breed Club:

Comrade Cat Club (Siberian Cat). Address: RR 1, Box 2460, Bowdoinham, ME 04008, USA.

7

TURKISH VAN CAT

A native Turkish cat found in the region of Lake Van, in eastern Turkey near the border with Iran. Also known as the Van Cat, the Turkish Cat, the Swimming Cat, and the Turkish Swimming Cat. In Turkey it is called the *Van Kedi*.

Appearance: The Van Cat looks like a slightly larger version of the Angora, with the same long, silky fur. There is no undercoat, which gives the animal a sleek, elegant, long-bodied appearance. The coat is white except for the head and the plumed tail, which are auburn in colour. There are from five to eight faint ring-markings on the tail. (But see below for controversy concerning the auburn markings.) The eyes are unusual because they are often of different colours – one amber and one blue. This feature, combined with their glamorous coat and their unusual love of water, quickly made them favourites with the public.

Legendary History: The city of Van, in Eastern Turkey, is close to Mount Ararat, the legendary site of Noah's Ark. A local folk-tale tells of the day when, after the Ark came to rest on the mountain and the floods receded, the cats left its protection and made their way down the mountain slopes and into the ancient settlement of Van. As they left the Ark the cats were blessed by Allah and the patch of auburn hair at the front of their bodies is believed to be the place where he touched them.

Factual History: There is archaeological evidence to suggest that domestic cats have been present in Turkey for over 7,000 years. A recent excavation by the British Archaeological Institute in Ankara, at the Neolithic site of Hacilar, revealed small terracotta figurines thought to show women playing with cats.

Much later, during the Roman occupation of the Van region (then part of ancient Armenia) in the period AD 75 to 387, a large, pale, self-coloured cat with rings on its tail appears on battle-standards and armour. These relics, now housed in the Louvre, suggest an early presence for the Turkish Van Cat.

Whether this ancient evidence is accepted or not, we can be sure that these cats have been well known locally for centuries and were valued highly as pets. Despite this, they were not discovered by Western enthusiasts until the year 1955, when two British photographers, working for the Turkish Tourist Board, visited the Lake Van region. Laura Lushington and Sonia Halliday were given a male and female kitten which were named Van Attala and Van Güzelli Iskenderün respectively. Fascinated by these unusual cats, they took them back with them to Britain.

The cats became known to the public as 'Swimming Cats' because of a report about the behaviour of this first pair. Driving through Turkey in the intense summer heat, Laura Lushington stopped to cool off in a river and, without prompting, the two newly acquired kittens joined her in the water. Writing about the incident in 1962, she commented: 'To my astonishment, the Van kittens strolled into the water too and swam out of their depth – apparently thoroughly enjoying themselves. This, I suppose, is the reason they were dubbed "Swimming Cats" by the Press on my return to Britain.' (In his 1965 feline dictionary, Frank Manolson included the Van Cat under the title of 'Turkish Swimming Cat', commenting wryly, 'It's the answer for those people who dislike Labradors and are afraid of otters, but who simply must have a furry ornament to enhance the pool.' In reality, its interest in the water was primarily a response to the intense heat of the Turkish summers.)

After the inevitable long period of quarantine, the two animals arrived at Laura Lushington's Buckinghamshire home, where it soon became clear that they belonged to an exceptionally attractive breed which was new to the world of pedigree cats. In order to start a serious breeding programme with them, they collected five more examples on subsequent trips to eastern Turkey, again putting them through the lengthy British quarantine process.

Then began the even longer procedure of establishing them as an officially recognized new breed. This was not achieved for 14 years. Although their owners' photographs – especially those showing them swimming – had made them unusually familiar to the general public, they were not so popular with the conservative feline authorities. Delays were caused because of their owners' decision to use the name of 'Van' for both the cats and their registered cattery. (This was not permitted by the GCCF rules and the name of the breed had to be changed from Van Cat, or Turkish Van Cat, simply to 'Turkish Cat'. Outside the GCCF this name did not find favour because it was felt to be too vague and led to confusion with the related Turkish breed, the Turkish Angora. Also, the name 'Van' had already become so widely popular for the breed, that public opinion simply ignored officialdom and everywhere continued to refer to it as the 'Turkish Van Cat'. Eventually, when Laura Lushington retired from cat breeding, the GCCF was able to revert to the more suitable title of Turkish Van Cat.)

The owners also had to agree to allow other breeders to acquire specimens, to create a competitive situation for showing purposes. Furthermore, because the original Turkish owners had never kept records of the ancestry of their cats, there had to be four generations of true-breeding before they could be accepted as pedigree animals. When all this had been done, the breed was at last given recognition in 1969.

The Turkish Van Cat was late appearing in America, the first specimens not arriving there until 1982, and the first official registrations not occurring until 1985.

There, the history of this attractive breed might have rested, but an unforeseen problem arose. A curious discovery about the true colouring of the Van Cat was made by feline expert Roger Tabor during location filming for his 1991 television series *The Rise of the Cat*. He visited Lake Van and discussed the breed with local people, only to find that they considered a true Van Cat to be an all-white animal, without any darker markings on the head or tail. There were some specimens with the auburn markings that are so well known in the West, but those were

A TURKISH VAN CAT *(opposite)* at the water's edge of Lake Van, its traditional homeland in eastern Turkey. When it first arrived in the West, this breed became known as the 'Swimming Cat'.

A TURKISH VAN CAT with her kittens. These auburn and white markings, essential for showing this breed in the West, are viewed as inferior in Turkey, where all-white cats are preferred.

considered to be inferior to the all-white ones. For these local people, the key difference between their Van Cats and the typical Angoras from further west in Turkey was to be found in their eyes. The Angora has blue eyes, whereas for them, the Van Cat ideally has one blue and one amber eye.

This came as no surprise to Turkish Van Cat breeder Lois Miles who, in 1989, had been given the same information when she had contacted the Turkish Cultural Attaché in Van to ascertain the true status of the breed in its city of origin. She had become concerned that all the 300 Van Cats registered at that time were descendants of the small, foundation group imported in the 1950s. The original cats, now known as 'the magnificent seven', had been able to provide only a small gene pool for the further development of the breed, and none of the seven had actually come from the city of Van itself.

What Lois Miles now wanted was a genuine Turkish Van Cat *from* Van, and it was clear to her that, despite the difficulties it might cause with Western show-judges, to be correct it would have to be an all-white, odd-eyed cat. In 1992 she persuaded two friends, John and Pamela Hulme, who already owned four Turkish Vans, and who visited Istanbul each year, to make the long trek eastwards across Turkey to Lake Van, to find new blood. The Hulmes agreed, but when they reached Van they initially encountered difficulties in locating pure stock. Then they had the good fortune to meet a local professor, Yusef Vanli, and discovered that the Yüzüncü

Yil University in the lakeside city had recently established a Van Cat Research Centre. Careful surveys by this centre had revealed the surprising fact that in 1992 there were only 92 pure Turkish Van Cats surviving in the whole of Turkey. For this reason, the continued breeding of pure lines outside Turkey was clearly even more important, and the Hulmes managed to persuade the professor to introduce them to a family with four generations of the all-white, odd-eyed cats. They reserved one of the three small kittens that were present, but which was too young to travel and then, three months later, John returned with Lois Miles to collect it. It was a female, called Garip (meaning 'alone'), who was renamed Layla. She was flown to Heathrow and placed in quarantine, waiting for the day when she could inject new Van blood into the inbred Western population.

Like Roger Tabor, Lois Miles found that the local Turks preferred the all-white Van Cat. She feels it was purely accidental that the original pair brought back to England in 1955 happened to have auburn markings on the head and tail. These markings became enshrined as the diagnostic feature of the breed and, in the world of pedigree show cats, are now considered essential. To the Turks themselves it is something of a joke that what they consider to be an inferior version of their breed should have become the only form that is officially recognized in the West.

With the advent of Layla, this situation should soon begin to change, as modern Western ways finally fall into line with ancient Eastern traditions. Since her arrival in the West she has already produced 16 kittens from three litters, and one of her first female offspring has also bred. Among her progeny there have been several of the 'Turkish Ideal' – the all-white, odd-eyed cats – so the future for the breed looks interesting if complicated. Lois Miles has already been refused permission to exhibit her true, all-white Turkish Van Cats as such, and it remains to be seen how long it will take for the irony of this situation to be recognized by the Western cat-show officialdom.

Personality: Terms used to describe this breed include: adaptable, affectionate, independent, tranquil, sociable, soft-voiced, friendly, intelligent and modestly playful. The earliest Van Cats taken to cat shows were notorious for being difficult to hold, but later examples have become more amenable. The inhabitants of Van themselves describe the cat as 'proud and brave as a lion', making 'lovable, affectionate pets with a remarkably long lifespan'.

Colour Forms: The officially accepted Van pattern, of white with dark patches on the head and a dark tail, is always the same, but there are variations in the head and tail colour. The typical form is white and auburn, but the auburn may be replaced by certain other colours.

GCCF: Blue-eyed Auburn Turkish Van; Odd-eyed Auburn Turkish Van; Blue-eyed Cream Turkish Van; Odd-eyed Cream Turkish Van.

CFA: White body with head and tail coloured: Red (= Auburn); Cream; Black; Blue; Red Tabby; Cream Tabby; Brown Tabby; Blue Tabby; Tortie; Dilute Tortie; Brown Patched Tabby; Blue Patched Tabby.

Breed Clubs:

The Classic Turkish Van Cat Association. Publishes a twice-yearly magazine, *Vantasia*.
  Address: 2a Woronzow Road, St. Johns Wood, London, NW8 6QE, England.

Progressive Turkish Van Cat Association. Address: 4 Rockwood Close, Darton, Barnsley, South
  Yorkshire, S75 5LR, England.

The Turkish Van Cat Club. Formed in 1981. Address: The Cheratons, 129 Balgores Lane, Gidea
  Park, Romford, Essex, RM2 6JT, England.

8

JAPANESE BOBTAIL CAT

A stump-tailed Eastern cat, sometimes referred to as the *Mi-Ke* Cat (pronounced mee-kay), which means 'three colours'. Among their owners, these cats are affectionately known as 'Bobs' or JBTs. In Holland the breed is known as the *Japanse Stompstaartkat*.

Appearance: A short-haired cat with a lean, muscular body and slender legs. The hind legs are a little longer than the front legs, giving an upward tilt to the rump region. The unique tail is a stump 5–10 cm (2–4 inches) long, tightly curved on itself and with restricted movement. The hair covering of the tail is thick and fluffy, giving it a pompom-like quality. The delicate head is slightly pointed, with slanted eyes.

Despite its superficial resemblance to the Manx Cat, the two breeds are genetically quite distinct.

History: This is an ancient breed which, although now thought of as exclusively Japanese, originally appears to have been observed in many regions of the Far East, including Malaysia, Burma and Thailand. There are 19th-century references to a breed called the Malay Cat, which from its description sounds identical. Victorian zoologist St. George Mivart, discussing the various breeds of domestic cats known to him in 1881, comments: 'In Pegu [part of Lower Burma], Siam and Burmah, there is a race of cats – the Malay Cat – with tails only of half the ordinary length, and often contorted in a sort of knot, so that it cannot be straightened . . . Its contortion is due to deformity of the bones of the tail.' This information is repeated by Lydekker in 1896. Judging by the description of the tail, it seems likely that the Malay Cat was related to, or identical with, the Japanese Bobtail Cat.

There is some disagreement as to the precise date at which the Bobtail arrived in Japan. Some authorities claim that it was introduced from China about a thousand years ago, probably at the instigation of the cat-loving Japanese Emperor Ichijo. Others put the date even earlier, in the ninth, eighth, seventh or even sixth century, because of the existence of very early woodcuts and paintings of cats, especially those from the Gotokuji and Niko Temples.

For centuries the Bobtails were the exclusive pets of the nobility, who used to walk them on a collar and lead, and it was not until the beginning of the 17th century that they were allowed to spread to the general population. The reason for this change of heart was that it was officially decreed that all the noble cats had to be set free to act as badly needed pest-controllers. From this point onwards it became known as the *Kazoku Neko*, the Family Cat of Japan.

THE JAPANESE BOBTAIL CAT, with its characteristic pom-pom tail, is an ancient Oriental breed.
Although today it is strongly associated with Japan, it seems to have had a much wider range in
the past, from Burma and Thailand, through Malaysia.

The Bobtail has been pictured in Japanese works of art from many epochs. The most famous representation is in the woodcut 'Cat in Window' by the 19th-century artist Ando Hiroshige.

The favoured type is the *Mi-Ke* (meaning three-coloured, or, literally, 'three fur') which is white with bold patches of black and red. It was believed that to own such a cat would bring good luck, and it has become identified with the legendary 'Beckoning Cat'.

An additional factor that may help to account for the popularity of this short-tailed cat is the existence of a folk-myth in Japan which warns that long-tailed cats can change into human form and bewitch their owners.

The breed attracted the attention of the West when the American soldiers of the occupying army encountered it at the end of World War II. In 1968, an American called Judy Crawford, who had been living in Japan for 15 years and who had been breeding these cats during most of that time, sent a pair to the United States. The pair consisted of a tortoiseshell and white female called Madame Butterfly and a red and white male called Richard. They were sent to the well-known breeder Elizabeth Freret, who had already discovered the breed and become intrigued by it. (She also received a third one, a cinnamon tabby female, which she did not keep.) The pair soon produced kittens, which Mrs Freret took to an American cat show in 1969, where they aroused great interest. Judy Crawford herself was soon to return to America, accompanied by 38 of her Japanese Bobtails. There she continued to breed her cats and to create a circle of enthusiasts. In 1970 the International Japanese Bobtail Fanciers Association was formed and the breed was well on the way to acceptance as an exciting addition to the world of pedigree cat showing. In 1978 the CFA granted it full recognition.

Despite its growing popularity in America, the Japanese Bobtail did not arrive in Great Britain until the 1970s, when a single female Bobtail was brought to England from Japan by its owner.

A long-haired version also now exists (see Japanese Bobtail Longhair Cat).

Personality: Terms used to describe this breed include: friendly, loyal, intelligent, affectionate, playful, outgoing, lively and inquisitive. Vocally, they are said to have a 'melodious chant' unique to their breed, which they use when they are pleased.

Colour Forms: The following are the favoured ones, although many other combinations are accepted: Black, red and white (Mi-Ke); Black, red and cream (tortoiseshell); Black and white; Red and white; Tortoiseshell and white; White; Black; Red.

Breed Club:

Japanese Bobtail Breeders Society. Address: 1272 Hillwood Lane, Vineland, NJ 08360, USA.

Note: There are also two breed publications: *Bobs.* Address: 1069 Gridley Street, Bay Shore, NY 11706, USA; and *Pom!* Address: P.O. Box 338, Napanee, IN 46550-0338, USA.

THE JAPANESE BOBTAIL has a tail that is not merely shortened but also tightly twisted. Genetically, this is quite distinct from the tail-shortening of the Manx Cat.

9

CHARTREUX CAT

An old French breed, dating from the 1300s or even earlier. The name of 'Chartreux Cat' was first used for this breed in 1750. It is sometimes referred to as the 'Chartreuse Cat', the 'Carthusian Cat', the 'Monastery Cat', or the 'Blue Cat of France'. Sometimes known as the 'smiling cat'. In France it is called the *Chat des Chartreux;* in Germany it is the *Kartäuser;* in Holland it is the *Karthuizer;* and in Italy the *Certosino.*

Appearance: A strong, heavily built, broad-headed, short-haired, blue-coated, orange-eyed cat with rather finely boned legs. Affectionately described by one American breeder as 'a potato on toothpicks'.

History: A cat of obscure origin. As with several other ancient breeds, there are a number of conflicting stories as to how it began:

1 It originated as a cross between an Egyptian Cat and a Manul Cat. There is no scientific evidence whatever to support this fanciful idea.

2 It was originally imported into France, in the 17th century, from the Cape of Good Hope in South Africa by Monks of the Carthusian Order. La Grande Chartreuse, just north of Grenoble, in south-east France near the Italian border, was the principal monastery of the Carthusians, a Roman Catholic order established in the year 1084. Renowned for their yellow and green liqueurs, the Carthusian monks have also become famous for their own special breed of monastic cat. The oldest reference to link the monks with this breed is found in Bruslon's 1723 *Universal Dictionary,* in which he says it 'is called Chartreux because of the monks of this name who owned the breed first'. Thirty years later, a little doubt has crept in: 'Chartreux cats, perhaps named because it was the monks of this name that were the first to have this breed.' (Chevalier de Jancourt in the *Grand Encyclopédie* of 1753). Unfortunately there is no archival evidence that they ever possessed such a breed. Replying to a query about the Chartreux Cat in 1972, the Prior of the Grand Chartreuse had this to say: 'We have never had the Chartreuse order . . . at the Cape of Good Hope. As for the subject of a breed of cat which had been of use by the Grand Chartreuse, our archives stand silent. Nothing lets us assume that a breed of this type of cat had been utilized in any epoch of our long history.'

3 It originated in the Middle East and was given to the Carthusian Monks by the knights returning from the Crusades. The fact that blue-grey cats were recorded from Syria, Cyprus and

Malta, all places where the crusaders were active, has been offered in support of this theory. But again, there is no archival evidence that the monks ever received this type of cat.

4 It originated in the Middle East and arrived in Europe about 450 years ago, where it was exploited by the fur trade, its woolly pelts being highly prized for their fine, dense texture.

5 It began in Northern Europe and Siberia, where its thick, woolly coat protected it from the intense cold, and later developed into both the Russian Blue and the Chartreux. If this is true, then the famous Blue Cat of France may simply have been a non-pedigree European domestic, wandering the fields and alleyways until it was taken up as a special breed. An early encyclopedia published in London in the 1780s suggests that blue cats were, at that time, the dominant form of domestic feline in France. The author of the encyclopedia, George Howard, states categorically: 'In France the cats are all of a bluish-lead colour.'

If either of the last two stories is correct, it begs an obvious question. How did this cat become associated with the Chartreuse Monastery? A possible answer may lie in a reference to the word 'Chartreux', in Bruslon's 1723 *Universal Dictionary*. There, mention is made of a fine wool imported into France from Spain, which was called the 'Pile de Chartreux'. Bearing in mind the very fine, woolly coat of this breed of cat, it may well have been that the animal was named after the wool and that the monks of La Grande Chartreuse had nothing to do with it. Later, their connection may have been assumed, simply because they had the same name. In this way, legends can easily be born and then repeated time and again until they are part of a widely accepted tradition.

Whichever of these stories is true, we do know for certain that the breed is recorded, named and illustrated by Buffon in his 18th-century *Natural History*. And 19th-century British authors were also aware of the breed, although by then it seems to have become less common: 'Bluish-grey is not a common colour; this species are styled "Chartreux Cats", and are esteemed rarities.' (Charles Ross, 1868).

By the 1920s, French cat breeders had started to take a serious interest in the Chartreux. In 1928, two spinsters, the Leger sisters of the Guerveur Cattery, began a selective breeding programme on the small island known as the Belle-Ile-sur-Mère. Their foundation pair were a male called Coquito and a female called Marquire. They made good progress and, by 1931, were able to exhibit the breed in Paris. Sadly, however, their efforts were interrupted by the chaos of World War II.

After the war the breed was barely surviving and the decision was taken to reconstruct it using non-pedigree French cats that had blue-grey coats. This was done until the original shape and style of the Chartreux had been achieved. These reconstituted cats comprise the foundation stock of the modern Chartreux. (This also explains why some authorities now refuse to distinguish between the British Blue, the European Blue and the modern Chartreux.)

In 1970 ten of these new Chartreux were imported into the United States by the California breeder Helen Gamon. There, an enthusiastic group of breeders continued to develop them until they had gained championship status.

THE CHARTREUX CAT *(opposite)*, an early French breed with a long history and an obscure origin. It is sometimes referred to as the Monastery Cat, because of its close association with the Carthusian Order.

Personality: Terms used to describe this breed include: friendly, good-natured, accommodating, playful, self-assured, hardy, uncomplaining, quiet, devoted, gentle and placid. The cat is said to like children and dogs. It is characteristically lazy until a rodent appears, when it becomes a savage hunter.

Related Breeds: There are several breeds of blue-grey cat and the relationship between them has been hotly disputed for many years. They are: the Russian Blue; the British Blue; the Maltese; the Chartreuse Blue; the Blue European Shorthair; the Exotic Shorthair Blue.

Other blue breeds, not confused with the above, include: the Blue Burmese; the Korat; the Foreign Blue; the Blue Longhair.

Colour Form: Only one colour is recognized: Blue-Grey. (Genetically, this is a 'diluted black'.)

ALTHOUGH THE CHARTREUX CAT is sometimes known as the Blue Cat of France, its true colour
is a diluted black which is, in reality, a plain grey.

10

SIAMESE CAT

The best known of the ancient cats of Siam (now Thailand), it appears in *The Cat Book Poems* written some time between 1350 and 1767 (most probably in the 1500s) in the old Siamese capital of Ayudhya. It is depicted as a pale-coloured cat with black tail, ears, feet and lower face. Known as the *Vichien Mat,* it was only one of 17 varieties that appeared in the poems. It later acquired the name 'Siamese' (rather than a more specific title) because it was the first, and most strikingly unusual one to be seen in the West. Because of its traditional association with Siamese royalty, it has sometimes also been called 'The Palace Cat', 'The Royal Siamese', or 'The Royal Cat of Siam'. In France is it known as the *Siamois;* in Germany as the *Siamkatzen;* and in Holland as the *Siamees.*

Appearance: The blue-eyed Siamese has a highly characteristic shape, being slim, elongated and angular. The earliest examples of this breed to reach the West had two additional, unusual features: a crooked, kinked tail and inward-squinting eyes. Both these features were soon removed by selective breeding. The angularity of the breed, on the other hand, has been retained and greatly exaggerated during recent times, creating an extreme type of Siamese which some feel has moved too far from its original form.

The diagnostic feature of the Siamese Cat has always been its unique coat pattern. The body of the animal is light in colour, but its extremities are dark. This configuration, which is referred to as a 'colourpoint' pattern, or 'points' pattern, develops in an unusual way. To understand this, it is best to think of this cat as a dark-coated animal carrying a gene which inhibits the pigmentation of its fur if its body temperature rises above a certain level. So, where the cat's surface is coolest – on its extremities – the pigment is able to develop normally. But where its surface is hottest – around the main trunk of its body – the pigment is unable to develop and the coat remains pale.

Needless to say, when Siamese kittens are born, emerging from the heat of the womb they are hot all over and therefore pale all over. But then, as they grow older, their extremities gradually become cooler and darken. In elderly Siamese, the whole body becomes slightly cooler and all the fur then darkens a little.

It is easy enough to confirm that the fur of the Siamese is temperature-dependent. Any Siamese that has, say, a foot injury which needs bandaging for a long period of time will eventually show a pale foot where the bandages increased the heat of that extremity. Any Siamese that suffers a high-temperature fever will also eventually develop paler fur.

Legends: There are several popular fables connected with the special features of the Siamese:

1 The kinked tail and the squinting eyes of this breed, which so intrigued those who first encountered the early specimens, are said to be the result of escapades of an intoxicated monk. This particular monk, who served in a temple that housed a golden goblet once used by the Great Buddha, was in the habit of disappearing for days on end, leaving his pair of Siamese Cats to guard the sacred goblet. Eventually the male Siamese decided to seek a replacement for the monk and set out in search of another holy man. The female Siamese Cat stayed behind to guard the precious goblet on her own and she stared at it so hard and so long that she developed a permanent squint. As the days passed she became so exhausted that she wrapped her tail around the goblet and sank into a deep sleep. When the male cat finally returned with a new monk, they found the female, still protecting the goblet, but now surrounded by a litter of five kittens, all with crossed eyes and kinked tails.

2 The kinked tail was the result of a Buddhist monk tying a knot in his cat's tail to prevent him from forgetting something important.

3 The kinked tail was the result of a Royal Princess, preparing to bathe in a stream, threading her rings on her cat's tail and then tying a knot in its tip to stop them sliding off.

4 A variant of this last story omits the tying of the knot. In this version it is the cat itself that deliberately kinks its own tail to prevent the loss of its mistress's rings.

5 The blue eyes of the breed were gained as a result of the devoted courage of these cats when defending a sacred altar. When raiders had driven the priests from their temple, the intruders were confronted by menacing cats, sitting on the altar steps. Frightened of the teeth and claws of the loyal felines, they left the altar untouched. When the priests were able to return to the temple, they marvelled at the cats' loyalty and from that day forward, the fiery red of the animals' eyes was turned into a heavenly blue, reflecting the way in which they has served heaven in their stand against the barbarians.

History: There are five theories concerning the possible origin of this ancient breed:

1 The Siamese is descended from an Oriental wild cat species, thus giving it a different zoological origin from all other domestic cats and thereby explaining its striking differences in voice and personality. Although this has been put forward as a serious suggestion as recently as 1992, there is no scientific evidence to support it.

2 Egyptian traders took their domestic cats with them to the Far East, where they developed directly into the Siamese breed, without any European influence on the way. This direct route might be sufficient to explain the special features of the breed.

3 An extremely rare and greatly prized, pure white cat was given to the King of Siam as a special gift and from this animal the Siamese breed was developed by crossings with the dark-furred temple cats.

4 During the victory of the Siamese and Annamese people over the Cambodian Empire of the Khmers about 300 years ago, Annamese Cats were imported into Siam, where they crossed with specimens of the Sacred Cat of Burma to produce what we now call the Siamese Cat.

5 Centuries ago, a natural mutation occurred in the local cats of Siam in which an all-over dark brown coat became temperature-dependent in such a way that it resulted in a dark-pointed coat pattern.

To THE GENERAL PUBLIC there is only one Siamese colour pattern – the Seal Point, shown here.
To modern Siamese specialists, however, this is just one of many variants.

In the absence of any hard evidence, it is impossible to decide between these five alternative theories, and it is unlikely that we will ever know, with complete certainty, the true origin of this breed of cat.

It is often stated that the Siamese Cat was of such elevated status that it was confined solely to the Royal Palace of the King of Siam and that the theft of one was punishable by death. Such a strict degree of confinement is certainly an exaggeration. A modified view suggests that this type of cat was also present in many princely homes, in the mansions of the Siamese aristocracy, and in the precincts of the sacred temples. This view insists that, although it may not have been an exclusively royal cat, it was nevertheless a cat of high social standing.

According to one frequently repeated tale, the role of this breed was not merely to rid the palaces and mansions of rodents, but to provide a repository for the souls of the human occupants when their earthly lives ended. When a member of the royal family died, one of their favourite cats would be entombed with them. This was not as cruel as it may sound because there were a number of holes in the roof of each tomb, through which an athletic feline could make its escape. When it did so, it was considered that the dead person's soul was now successfully reincarnated in the cat.

In this sacred role the animal was said to have played a vital part in the religious lives of the people and, for this reason, it was supposed to be highly unusual for a foreign visitor to be allowed to take away any Siamese Cat. Only if it was felt necessary to pay some great tribute to honour a foreigner, would one of these cats be offered as a special gift. It follows that, if this was true, the number of these cats leaving the country was extremely small.

There are early records of occasional ones being exhibited as curiosities at European zoos. And we know that a few must somehow have been obtained as pets because of their presence at the very first of the British cat shows, held in 1871. Unfortunately there are no detailed records of these cats. How they came to be there remains a mystery.

Part of the problem with these very first references to Siamese Cats is that, at that time, individual animals were often named by their country of origin. In other words, a 'Siamese Cat' would simply mean one that came from Siam, without saying anything about its appearance. The earliest confirmation we have of the exhibition at a cat show of a true Siamese, with typical coat pattern, dates from 1879, when an article in the London *Daily Telegraph* refers to a 'couple of juveniles of Siamese extraction, with black muzzles, ears, feet and tail setting off a close yellowish drab coat . . . the exhibitor of these curiosities being a Mrs Cunliffe-Lee'.

The next specific reference to the breed appears in St. George Mivart's classic work on feline anatomy, *The Cat*, published in 1881. There he mentions that: 'The Royal Siamese Cat is of one uniform fawn colour, which may be of a very dark tinge. There is a tendency of a darker colour about the muzzle . . . It also had remarkable blue eyes [and] a small head.'

A little later, in 1889, we have the following comment from Harrison Weir: 'it will be seen how very difficult it is to obtain the pure breed, even in Siam, and on reference to the Crystal Palace catalogues from the year 1871 to 1887, I find that there were *fifteen* females and only *four* males, and some of these were not entire; and I have always understood that the latter were not allowed to be exported, and were only got by those so fortunate as a most extraordinary favour, as the King of Siam is most jealous of keeping the breed entirely in Siam as royal cats.'

The first fully documented export of a Royal Siamese bears out Weir's words, for it was a special gift to the White House in Washington: a present for Lucy Webb Hayes, the wife of the American President, from David Stickles, the American Consul in Bangkok. A female called Siam, she started her long sea journey in 1878 by being sent from Bangkok to Hong Kong. From there she was shipped to San Francisco after which she had to travel by land across America. Arriving at the White House early in 1879, she did not survive long. She fell ill in September of the same year and died in October, despite being offered the finest cuisine the White House kitchens could provide. In her short spell at the presidential home she did, however, become immensely popular and created great interest in this exotic new breed.

The earliest properly documented case of Siamese Cats being exported to Britain dates from the year 1884, when Mr Edward Blencowe Gould, an Acting Vice-Consul (not the Consul General as usually stated) at Bangkok, acquired a pair. It is claimed that he obtained them directly from King Chulalongkorn (who ruled from 1868 to 1910 and who was the son of the King of Siam so well known in the West as the central figure in the musical *The King and I*). Apparently, when the Vice-Consul paid his farewell call on the King, he was offered any gift he liked from the Royal Palace, to take away with him. He chose a pair of the magnificent royal cats. The king was dismayed, but reluctantly honoured his obligation.

Some authors take a sceptical view of this incident, viewing it as pure invention designed to add glamour to the new breed. Brian Vesey-Fitzgerald flatly rejects it with the words: 'We can dismiss the "direct gift from the King" story straightaway.' Milo Denlinger is particularly scathing: 'There is no record that Mr Gould, himself, claimed that these two cats were a present, reluctantly made to him, by the King of Siam, but much romantic drivel has been printed about his difficulty in obtaining them. It seems more likely that they were merely purchased at some bazaar in Bangkok, like any other commodity.'

A partial confirmation of this unromantic view is to be found in a letter written by Gould's sister, Mrs Lilian Velvey, for whom the cats were a gift. Many years later, in 1930, she wrote: 'It is curious to note now that my original queen, Mia, a very beautiful cat, only cost my brother three ticals or about 7/6d.' However, although this seems to destroy at least half the legend, it should be remembered that no mention is made in this letter concerning the male cat, who was called Pho. So it is still possible, though unlikely, that Gould did acquire the male from the King and then purchased the female from a less noble source to make up a breeding pair.

However he obtained them, we do know that the Vice-Consul gave these two cats to his brother, Owen Gould, who brought them to England as a gift for their sister. These are the oldest 'official' Siamese and are recorded as 1a and 2a in the Siamese Cat Register. They produced a litter, and the kittens, who were given the exotic names of Duen Ngai, Kalahom and Karomata, were exhibited by Mrs Velvey at the 1885 Cat Show at Crystal Palace. They enjoyed great success there, winning both the 'best shorthaired cat' prize and the 'best cat in show', out of 480 entries. This created a huge demand for Siamese Cats and, in the final decade of the 19th century, the royal embargo (if it ever existed) was weakened and many more were imported and shown. Mrs Velvey herself was involved in the importation of many of these Siamese between 1885 and 1890, a fact that is perhaps not entirely unrelated to the report that her brother, the Consul, had by then built his own cattery in Bangkok.

Despite Mrs Velvey's triumph in 1885 (or perhaps because of it), when more Siamese Cats began to appear at cat shows in Britain, they met with a mixed reception. One critic, who had seen the breed at one of the first exhibitions, had called it 'an unnatural nightmare kind of cat'. Another, writing in a magazine in 1889 commented that 'all our informants agree in confessing that almost any other cat is pleasanter and safer to live with'. However, Harrison Weir, who organized the early shows, declared (also in 1889) that: 'Among the beautiful varieties of the domestic cat brought into notice by the cat shows, none deserve more attention than "The Royal Cat of Siam".'

In January 1901, the Siamese Cat Club was formed to promote and protect the breed. Without delay, its members contacted the Siamese Legation in London to find out a little more about their favourite feline. The Legation's reply, dated 17th September 1901, held a few surprises for them: 'the fawn-coloured animal with the dark points and blue eyes is rare in all parts of the country. In Bangkok because there are more leisured people who can devote time to hobbies of the sort, these cats are bred a good deal . . . The King of Siam does not keep any special breed, nor are there any specially preserved in his palace . . . There is no Royal Cat of Siam . . . Nor does any religious sanctity attach to any cat of Siam . . . These ideas have probably arisen from the fact that the Siamese generally are fond of animals, cats included.'

If these statements are true, and not merely the unverified comments of a snobbishly dismissive Legation bureaucrat, then they contradict all the earlier stories concerning the exotic background of this breed. A similar and equally unromantic view was offered 30 years later by a Dr Hugh Smith: 'I was well acquainted with cats in Siam . . . There are no "palace" cats . . . There are no "royal" cats . . . Any person can have a Siamese Cat, and as a matter of fact there are many people outside the palaces and many foreigners who keep such cats as household pets . . . There are no "temple" cats . . . '

However, whether true or not, these negative comments had little impact on the cat world and were soon forgotten. The romantic legends of the Siamese Cat, both regal and sacred, stubbornly survived and are still being told retold to this day.

For those who find the unromantic dismissals depressing, there is a glimmer of hope in remarks made by a Mr A.N.M. Garry who, in 1930, visited Siam and remarked that: 'Having been a contemporary of the then King [of Siam] at Eton, I got a special permit to see the Bangkok Palace . . . and I saw one or two of these "Royal" cats . . . ' So perhaps there was something feline in the Royal Palace, after all. And a Major Walton of the Rice Purchasing Commission, who became a personal friend of the Prince Regent of Siam in the 1940s, tends to confirm this because, before leaving Siam, he was presented with a pair of Siamese as a special gift from the Prince Regent. This again suggests that the breed had some sort of royal connections. But more solid, historical evidence is needed before we can be sure of this.

Returning to the earlier days of the cat fancy, at the very end of the 19th century a few of the famous European Siamese Cats found their way across the Atlantic. Under the aegis of Mrs Clinton Locke of Chicago, the 'Mother of the American Cat Fancy', they were soon appearing in cat shows there, also with great success. In 1899 she founded the Beresford Cat Club, and in the club's first stud book published in 1900, the first two American Siamese Cats recorded were a champion male called Siam and a female called Sally. Their full names were Lockhaven Siam and Lockhaven Sally Ward, which indicates that they were owned by Mrs Locke herself.

Among these early Siamese there was a high mortality. Despite this, rich Americans were paying as much as $1,000 at the turn of the century to import a British-bred Siamese Cat. Translated into today's monetary value, this would make an early Siamese one of the most expensive felines of all time. Presumably this also gave them a certain glamour and they soon became favourites in American high society. By 1909 the Siamese Cat Society of America had been formed and the breed was firmly established as an important new type of show cat.

From that point onwards, on both sides of the Atlantic, the Siamese went from strength to strength. Throughout the 20th century its popularity has continued to spread worldwide as it has progressed to becoming one of the most celebrated of all pedigree breeds.

Personality: Terms used to describe this breed include: unpredictable, demanding, noisy, thieving, mischievous, determined, lively, active, agile, demonstrative, domineering, graceful, loyal, affectionate, devoted, intelligent and resourceful.

Perhaps the most unusual feature of the Siamese, that sets it apart from other breeds, is its voice. No other cat is quite so noisy. As one owner commented plaintively: 'He is so vocal with his incessant yowling and mewing that he drives a person forced to listen to him almost to distraction. He talks all the time he is awake . . . with his raucous and always persistent voice. There are frequent alterations in the tone, pitch, timbre and volume of that voice.' For some this may be an irritant, but for many Siamese owners it is one of the qualities that helps to give this unusual breed its unique charm.

Several authors have referred to the Siamese as 'more like a dog than like a cat'. Although this is an exaggeration, it is fair to say that, of all the various cat breeds, the Siamese is the one nearest to the dog in personality.

A MODERN GRAND CHAMPION Seal Point Siamese (*opposite*), in all its graceful, elongated splendour. Throughout the 20th century the breed has become increasingly angular and slender.

Colour Forms: When it first arrived in the West, the Siamese Cat displayed only one colour pattern: *Seal Point.* This was to be the only colour form recognized for half a century – from 1871 until the 1930s. Even today, when there are many different variants, it has remained in the public mind as 'the' Siamese colour.

The history of the development of the other Siamese colours is complex. In the early days, when a variant occurred, it was usually written off as 'poor seal'. From time to time, however, a particular breeder would become attached to one of these alternative colour forms and start a serious breeding programme. Then, after a while, the variant would be given official recognition and become registered as a distinct breed. For example, the *Blue Point,* first noticed as early as 1894, was not recognized as a breed by the GCCF until 1936. (In America it was recognized a little earlier, in 1932.) Another early variant, the *Chocolate Point* was not given the official blessing until 1950. The *Lilac Point* had to wait until 1960. (To avoid confusion, it should be mentioned that the Lilac Point had already been accepted in America in 1954 under the title of Frost Point.)

The *Tabby Point, which was* mentioned as early as 1902, was finally recognized in 1966, along with the *Cream Point, Red Point* and *Tortie Point.* However, these four breeds (and other, later ones) are not considered true Siamese in the United States. There, they are called Colourpoint Shorthair Cats.

In recent years many other colour combinations have been added until, today, there is a huge variety from which to choose, including the following:

GCCF: Seal Point; Chocolate Point; Blue Point; Lilac Point; Cinnamon Point; Caramel Point; Fawn Point; Seal Tabby Point; Blue Tabby Point; Chocolate Tabby Point; Lilac Tabby Point; Red Tabby Point; Cream Tabby Point; Cinnamon Tabby Point; Caramel Tabby Point; Fawn Tabby Point; Seal Tortie Tabby Point; Blue Tortie Tabby Point; Chocolate Tortie Tabby Point; Lilac Tortie Tabby Point; Cinnamon Tortie Tabby Point; Caramel Tortie Tabby Point; Fawn Tortie Tabby Point; Red Point; Seal Tortie Point; Blue Tortie Point; Chocolate Tortie Point; Lilac Tortie Point; Cinnamon Tortie Point; Caramel Tortie Point; Fawn Tortie Point; Cream Point.

CFA: Seal Point; Chocolate Point; Blue Point; Lilac Point.

Siamese Variants: The Siamese has been used as the ancestral cat for a number of recent breeds, each modifying the original form in one way or another. These modern descendants of the Siamese include the following:

1 BALINESE (Longhair Siamese with points)

2 JAVANESE (Longhair Siamese with new-colour points)

3 ORIENTAL LONGHAIR (Longhair Siamese without points)

4 ORIENTAL SHORTHAIR (Shorthair Siamese without points)

5 COLOURPOINT SHORTHAIR (Shorthair Siamese with new-colour points)

6 HAVANA (Shorthair Siamese with solid brown coat)

7 FOREIGN WHITE (Shorthair Siamese with all-white coat)

8 SEYCHELLOIS (Shorthair Siamese with splashed white coat)

In addition there are three breeds that have an important Siamese element in their make-up, but which also have a strong 'rival' element present:

9 OCICAT (Shorthair Siamese/Abyssinian)

10 SNOWSHOE (Shorthair Siamese/American Shorthair Bi-colour)

11 TONKINESE (Shorthair Siamese/Burmese)

Some of these names, especially the Javanese, are used slightly differently in different countries.)

Note: Because modern show Siamese have developed such an extreme body-type, there has recently been a movement to return to the old-style Siamese with a less angular body and more rounded head. These types of Siamese have been given a number of different names, including the following: Applecat; Apple-head Siamese; Classic Siamese; Old-fashioned Siamese; Opal Cat; Thai Cat; Traditional Siamese.

Breed Clubs:

National Siamese Cat Club. Address: 5865 Hillandale Drive, Nashport, OH 43830, USA.

Siamese Cat Association,. Publishes a *Journal.* Address: Wrenshall Farmhouse, Walsham Le Willows, Bury St Edmunds, Suffolk, IP31 3AS, England.

Siamese Cat Club. One of the oldest of all breed clubs, founded in 1901. It issues a twice-yearly *Newsletter.* Address: Fistral, 10 Noak Hill Close, Billericay, Essex, CM12 9UZ, England.

Siamese Cat Society of America. Publishes a *Siamese News Quarterly.* Address: 304 S.W. 13th Street, Fort Lauderdale, FL 33315, USA.

Siamese Cat Society of the British Empire. Woodlands Farm, Bridford, Exeter, Devon, EX6 7EW, England.

11

KORAT CAT

An ancient domestic breed from Thailand. Known there as the Si-Sawat, its existence is recorded in *The Cat Book Poems* written in the Ayudhya Period, some time between 1350 and 1767, and now lodged in the Bangkok National Library. In the 1970s, a Thai cat expert, Pichai-Ramadi Vasnasong, described this cat as one of the eight types of 'Siamese Cats' (using the term in an unusually broad sense) known to exist in Thailand: '1. The Koraj. This is better known as the Si Sawat (purple grey, the colour of the Sawat nut).' This Thai spelling, Koraj, has been changed to Korat by European breeders because the Thai pronunciation of 'j' is equivalent to our soft 't'.

Appearance: A trim, medium-sized, muscular, short-haired cat with tall ears and a heart-shaped head. The luminous green eyes are unusually large and prominent. The silver-blue coat is glossy and fine, lying close to the body – essentially a hot-country coat. The hairs have a delicate, silver tipping, eloquently known in the East as 'sea-foam'.

History: The word 'Sawat' also carries a meaning of 'good fortune' or 'prosperity', and in its native Thailand, where to own one is thought to bring good fortune, the Korat has been a highly prized cat for centuries. The symbolism of their colours has led to their being used in rain-making ceremonies. At the end of the dry season they are taken in procession and water is poured over them to bring the rains. They have sometimes been called the 'Cloud-coloured Cat' and, because their eyes are the colour of young rice, they have been thought to help in producing a good crop. Traditionally, a pair of Korats was given to a bride on her wedding day to bring her prosperity in the years ahead. Because of the sheen on their coats, they were said to symbolize a gift of silver.

It is said to have acquired its present name from King Chulalongkorn at the turn of the century, when he asked where such beautiful cats came from. He was told that they were found in Korat *(Cao Nguyen Khorat)*, one of the eastern provinces of the country. It was this same king, also known as Rama V, who commissioned a monk (with the catchy name of Somdej Phra Buddhacharn Buddhasarmahathera) to paint a copy of the ancient *Cat Book Poems*, with its revealing illustrations of the different types of local cats. This *Smud Khoi* (papyrus book) is on

LIKE THE OTHER so-called 'blue' cats, such as the Chartreux and the Russian Blue,
the Korat *(opposite)* in reality, displays a pure grey coat.

THE KORAT CAT, an ancient Thai breed known locally as the Si-Sawat because it has the unusual, purple-grey colour of the Sawat nut. In modern times it was developed in the West in the 1960s by the American breeder Jean Johnson.

view in the Minor Arts Room at the National Museum in Bangkok and carries a lyrical description of the Korat breed: 'The hairs are smooth, with roots like clouds and tips like silver./ The eyes shine like dewdrops on a lotus leaf.'

This book also says of the Korat: 'The cat "Ma-led" has a body colour like "Doklao".' The word 'Ma-led' is used to describe the silvery-grey seed of a wild Thai fruit called the 'Look Sawat'. 'Doklao' refers to the silvery-tipped flower of a local herb. The name 'Si-Sawat' means 'Colour of the Sawat Seed'. This insistence of the specific hue of the Korat makes it clear that, for this particular breed, any individual animal deviating from the traditional coat colour would cease to be a true Korat.

Because this breed was valued so highly, it was never sold. As a result, exported examples were extremely rare. Only occasionally was one presented as a special gift to honour some dignitary or aristocrat.

The first record of a Korat Cat being seen in the West dates from 1896, when one was exhibited in London at the Holland House Show. According to the well-known cat judge, C.A. House, writing some years later, it was entered by a Mr Spearman, a young Englishman just back from Siam. It is not clear how he obtained it, although it is clear that he had brought it personally from its country of origin. Sadly, despite his protestations that it was a distinct and separate breed, the judge of the day, the famous cat artist Louis Wain, disqualified it because, in his ignorance, he foolishly considered it to be a poor specimen of a blue Siamese.

After this, the breed then disappeared without trace for many years. It was not heard of again until 1959, when a pair, called Nara and Darra, was presented to the American Ambassador to Thailand. They were sent to Mrs Jean Johnson in the United States, who had become fascinated by the breed when she had visited what was then Siam in 1947. She had been searching for a typical Siamese Cat, but was shown the Korats and told that these, and not the local colourpointed varieties, were the most important local felines. Twelve years later she now had a pair of these 'special cats' and was able to use them to start a breeding programme. In the early 1960s more Korats were obtained and brought safely back to the United States. In 1965 a Korat Cat Fanciers' Association was formed in America and published a quarterly newsletter called *Mai Pen Rai*. It insisted that, to be accepted as a true Korat, a cat must have a pedigree stretching back to an origin in Thailand. Others clubs were also formed, including the Si-Sawat Society, the *Sa-Waat-Dee* and the Korat Fanciers of the East. The Korat was eventually recognized as a pedigree breed there in 1966.

Korat breeding stock did not reach Britain until the 1970s – to be precise, at 10.30 am on the morning of 11th March 1972: a five-weeks pregnant female called Saeng Duan and an unrelated male kitten called Sam. The female gave birth to six kittens in quarantine on Easter Sunday – the first Korats ever born in Britain. Twelve years later the breed was given full recognition and granted championship status.

Personality: Terms used to describe this breed include: intelligent, inquisitive, gentle, active, soft-voiced, cautious, shy, powerful, faithful, shy, reserved, calm, friendly, intuitive, swift, agile and playful.

Korat Cat males are said to make good fathers if left with their kittens. They are unusually territorial and will hiss and growl at unknown intruders. According to legend, the males were sometimes taken into battle on the shoulders of the warriors and would launch themselves ferociously at the enemy.

Colour Forms: All Korats are a slate blue/grey colour.

Breed Clubs:

The Korat Cat Association. Publishes a regular newsletter. Address: 25 Stapleford Road, Whissendine, Oakham, Leics., LE15 7EY, England.

Korat Cat Fanciers' Association. Formed in 1965. Address: 1601 North Federal Highway, Lake Worth, FL 33460-6695, USA. The KCFA publishes a quarterly newsletter, *Mai Pen Rai*. Address: 2790 Newberry Avenue, Green Bay, WI 54302, USA.

Si-Sawat Circle. Address: 23 Kingsway Avenue, West Point, Manchester, M19 2DH, England.

Si-Sawat (Korat) Society. Publishes a *Newsletter*. Address: 251 Connell Ct., Reynoldsburg, OH 43068, USA.

12

BURMESE CAT

A short-haired breed named after the country of origin of the founder cat. In reality, its ancestors may have been found over a wider range of the Far East, including Thailand (where it is known locally as 'The Copper'). Because of recent breeding variations, some owners refer to their cats as 'Traditional Burmese'. In Germany the breed is known as the *Burma*; in Holland as the *Burmee*. Among English-speaking breeders it is usually nicknamed 'The Burm'. (The name 'Zibeline Cat', meaning 'like the sable' – that is, very dark brown – was suggested as an alternative to 'Burmese', but was never widely accepted. Dechambre, writing in 1957, proposed that the modern, pedigree Burmese Cats should be called 'Zibelines or Sables, because of their coat, and to distinguish them from the true Burmese'.) A lesser-known, alternative name is the Copper Cat. Thai cat expert Pichai-Ramadi Vasnasong comments that of the eight types of 'Siamese cats' (using the term in a broad sense), number eight is 'the Copper – which is better known to foreigners as the Burmese'.

Appearance: A muscular, athletic, compact, short-haired cat with a glossy, rich, dark brown coat. The underparts are slightly lighter in colour than the rest of the body, but the change from light areas to dark is gradual. The rounded, domed head, with ears set wide apart, has a short face with golden-yellow eyes.

History: It is claimed that this breed is mentioned as the Su-pa-lak, or Thong Daeng, in one of the poems of the ancient Thai Cat Book, written during the Ayudhya Period, which stretched from 1350 to 1767. It is recorded there as a courageous, protective cat and described in the following words: 'Of magnificent appearance with shape the best/ Coloured like copper, this cat is beautiful:/ The light of her eyes is as a shining ray.'

According to local folklore, these beautiful brown, golden-eyed cats – presumably the ancestors of what we now know as the Burmese Cat – were kept as sacred animals in the temples, monasteries and palaces of Burma. Pampered by the rich and holy, these revered felines were provided with personal servants in the form of student-priests. These servants acted as guardians to ensure the safety of their charges and were severely punished if they failed in their duties. The purity of the breed was maintained by the strict control over the movements of the cats that prevented them from mating with the highly varied felines that roamed the rest of the country. Occasionally, a single cat was presented as a special gift to a visiting dignitary, but apart from that they seldom left their Burmese strongholds.

The story goes that a certain Major Finch, stationed in the East during World War II, who made good use of his spare time there by visiting Buddhist temples, saw many beautiful examples of these sacred brown cats. He called them 'Rajah Cats', but it is clear from his description that what he was calling Rajah Cats and what we today know as Burmese Cats were one and the same. He claimed that they were the true 'Royal Cats' and were held in high esteem in the Royal courts long before the pale-bodied Siamese Cats put in an appearance. In fact, in his opinion, the Rajah Cat was the parent form of the Siamese Cat, which in ancient times was viewed merely as a poorly coloured, semi-albino version of this sacred, rich brown cat.

Whether this is all true, or merely a romantic legend, by the 1930s a key event occurred in the history of the breed. It was then that the 'founding female' of the modern Burmese Cat arrived in the United States and was used as the starting point for a carefully developed breeding programme. Even at this more recent date, however, there is some confusion as to precisely how she came to be on American soil. There are four contradictory versions:

1 She was brought from Rangoon to the United States in 1933, where she was sold as a 'Brown Siamese'.
2 She was brought from India to the United States in the early 1930s.
3 A sailor brought her to New Orleans in 1934, where he sold her to a local pet shop, saying he had obtained her in Burma and that she was a 'Burmese Cat'. She was eventually purchased by a retired ship's doctor (ex-US Navy) by the name of Joseph C. Thompson.
4 She was purchased from a native carnival in Rangoon by the famous wild-animal dealer Frank ('Bring 'Em Back Alive') Buck, who sold her, in Burma, to Dr Joseph Thompson, who then took her back with him to his home in San Francisco in 1930.

We may never be certain which of these four 'arrival' stories is the true one, but we do know for sure that, one way or another, a remarkable brown female cat did come into Dr Thompson's possession in the early 1930s. It is instructive to read Dr Thompson's own words, from an article he wrote with three of his colleagues in 1943 (the year of his death) on *The Genetics of the Burmese Cat*: 'The First "Burmese" cat was a female imported into the United States from Burma by the senior author [Dr Thompson himself] in the year 1930.' This statement firmly fixes the date, but is ambiguous concerning the mode of acquisition of the cat. 'Importing a cat from Burma' leaves open the question of whether Dr Thompson himself brought the animal in, or whether it was brought into the country for him. The original source of the animal therefore remains something of a mystery.

Once Dr Thompson had acquired the cat, however, the picture becomes much clearer. A brown female cat, she was named Wong Mau. At the time of her arrival, Dr Thompson was working as a psychiatrist in San Francisco and was employing a rather unusual type of treatment. His enlightened form of therapy consisted of giving each of his rich patients a pregnant Siamese Cat to look after. The problems these patients faced – and the rewards they gained – from raising a litter of kittens were so successful in taking them out of themselves, that they soon forgot their neuroses, started to look outward instead of inward, and rapidly regained their mental balance.

Thompson had been fascinated by the Far East for many years, at one time becoming a monk in a Tibetan monastery, and became especially attached to this new arrival from Burma. Wong Mau was allowed to sit at his side during his consultations, and soon became the most important cat in the doctor's feline collection. At first, she was looked upon as simply a brown Siamese, but careful breeding experiments revealed that she was in fact a cross between a Siamese and a dark-coated breed that was new to the West. Enlisting the aid of some geneticist friends, Dr Thompson was able to segregate this brown breed, which was given the name of Burmese Cat. By crossing Wong Mau with a Siamese male (the first mating took place in 1932 with a Siamese stud called Tai Mau) and then back-crossing the male offspring with her, it was possible to create three types of kittens: those that had Siamese markings, those that were brown but with darker points (like Wong Mau herself) and those with all-over brown colouring. This last type became the foundation stock for the Burmese Cat breed.

These first true Burmese Cats were used in further breeding programmes in a deliberate attempt to establish a new pedigree cat. In the early 1940s, three more individuals were imported into America from Burma, to strengthen the stock. These were a male and two females. They left Rangoon in 1941 on the S.S. *Chart* and had to endure a wartime sea voyage lasting five months, during which they had to survive attacks by bombers. At last, they arrived in New York in 1942 and became the property of Guy Fisher. Only one of the three, a female called Tangyi of Forbidden City, appears on any of the pedigree lists of the period, but she was able to provide a valuable addition of new blood to the breeding programmes. Unfortunately, once again we do not appear to have any information about Tangyi's original source in Burma. The arrival of these three additional cats from Rangoon does, however, suggest that the brown Burmese Cat was a true breed in its original homeland, and that Wong Mau was not an isolated oddity, as has been suggested by some critics.

After some initial setbacks, the success of the breeding programme was recognized in the United States when the CFA officially accepted the Burmese breed. In the late 1940s three Burmese Cats (a male and two females) were imported from America into Britain by breeders Sydney and Lillian France of Derby, and in 1952 the breed was also recognized there by the GCCF. In 1955, the Burmese Cat Club was formed in Britain and now has 1,500 members.

Finally, although it is generally accepted today that Wong Mau was the founding cat of the modern breed it has been pointed out that, back in the 19th century, dark brown 'Siamese' cats were being exhibited at cat shows in Britain, and that these were probably of the same type. Writing in 1889, Harrison Weir explains that there are two types of 'Royal Cat of Siam', one pale-bodied and one dark: 'light rich dun is the preferable colour, but a light fawn, light silver-grey or light orange is permissible; deeper and richer browns, almost chocolate, are admissible . . . the last merely a variety of much beauty and excellence; but the dun and light tints take precedence.' He also refers to an exhibitor who 'possesses a chocolate variety of this Royal Siamese cat . . . Although this peculiar colour is very beautiful and scarce, I am of the opinion that the light grey or fawn colour with black and well-marked muzzle, ears, and legs is the typical variety . . . I take that to be the correct form and colour, and the darker colour to be an accidental deviation.'

The owner of the 'Chocolate Siamese' is then quoted as saying, 'The dun invariably beats the chocolate at shows.' This situation obviously led to a favouring of the pale-bodied Siamese with dark extremities, and the rapid disappearance of the overall dark-bodied form. As far as can be

THE BURMESE CAT *(opposite),* believed to be an ancient breed from South-east Asia where it was once revered as a sacred animal. Modern Burmese are descended from an individual imported into the United States in 1930.

A DILUTE COLOUR FORM of the Burmese Cat. From the 1950s onwards, new colour varieties were developed and the traditional Brown colour of this breed was joined by several delicate, paler hues such as Blue and Lilac (or Platinum).

told, the chocolate specimens were never specially bred from or developed and soon vanished without trace. However, their brief appearance at these early shows indicates that a Burmese-type of cat has been around for a very long time and supports the view that Wong Mau had an ancient Eastern lineage.

Personality: Terms that have been used to describe this breed include the following: affectionate, alert, active, agile, sociable, inquisitive, athletic, ingenious, intelligent, curious, zestful, adaptable, lively, energetic, smart, playful, devoted, vocal, highly strung, rumbustious, boisterous, bold, bossy, stubborn and demanding. In general, its character is felt to be close to that of the Siamese.

Colour Forms: The traditional colour for this breed is Brown. Other colours were added later: Blue in 1955; Cream in 1971; Chocolate, Lilac and Red in 1972; Brown Tortie, Chocolate Tortie, Lilac Tortie, Blue Tortie in 1973.

In the United States the colour forms of the Burmese are more restricted than in Europe. The CFA recognizes only four colour forms: the original Sable (brown) and its dilutions, known as Champagne, Blue and Platinum. Because some American breeders have imported pedigree Burmese with other colours from Europe, a separate class has been established by the CFA for 'European Burmese'.

GCCF: Brown; Blue; Chocolate; Lilac; Red; Cream; Brown Tortie; Blue Tortie; Chocolate Tortie; Lilac Tortie.

CFA: Sable (= Brown); Champagne (= Chocolate); Blue; Platinum (= Lilac).

The CFA also lists 'European Burmese' colours, as follows: Brown; Blue; Chocolate; Lilac; Red; Cream; Seal Tortie; Blue Tortie; Chocolate Tortie; Lilac Tortie.

Breed Clubs:

Burmese Breeders Society. Address: 11 Hawksworth Avenue, Guiseley, Leeds, LS20 8EJ, England.

Burmese Cat Club (with a membership of 1,250). Issues a quarterly magazine, *The Burmese Cat Club News*. Address: Southview, Landmere Lane, Edwalton, Nottingham, NG12 4DG, England.

Burmese Cat Society. Address: 11 Hawksworth Avenue, Guiseley, Leeds, LS20 8EJ, England.

Burmese Limited. Address: 168 Delavan Avenue, Newark, NJ 04104, USA.

Burmese Please. Address: 2184 Oneida Crescent, Mississauga, Ontario, Canada.

National Alliance of Burmese Breeders. Address: 11057 Saffold Way, Reston, VA 22090, USA.

National Burmese Cat Club. Address: Normandy Heights Road, Morristown, NJ 07960, USA.

Top Burmese Academe. Address: Route 1, Box 344A, Florence, SC 29051, USA.

United Burmese Cat Fanciers. Address: 2395 N.E. 185th Street, North Miami Beach, FL 33180, USA. (Originally there were two pioneer Burmese clubs in the United States, The Burmese Cat Society and Burmese Breeders of America, but they amalgamated in 1960 to form the United Burmese Cat Fanciers.)

13

ANGORA CAT

An ancient Turkish breed of long-haired cat. (Angora means Ankara. The capital city of Turkey changed its spelling in 1930, but the animals named for it, such as the Angora Cat and the Angora Goat, have retained their original forms. Ankara Cat was an alternative name; it was most commonly used in the middle of the 19th century, but occurs occasionally in later writings.) According to Turkish legend, their great national hero, Kemel Ataturk, will one day be reincarnated as a pure white Angora Cat.

Appearance: Traditionally a blue-eyed, white-coated cat with long, soft fur. The hairs are especially long on the neck, underside and tail, but less so on the rest of the body. This, and the absence of a woolly undercoat, gives the Angora a slender, bushy-tailed look that clearly distinguishes it from the heavier-coated Persian with its more rounded silhouette. The Angora kittens are slow to develop the typical adult coat, it not being fully displayed until the age of two years. Perhaps because of their hot-country homeland, the summer moult is extreme and leaves them looking almost like a short-haired breed.

History: There are three rival ideas concerning the origin of the Angora Cat. The first theory suggests that it was originally developed from the wild Pallas's Cat *(Felis manul)* by the ancient Chinese and the Tartars, and only later taken to Turkey. There is no scientific evidence to support this.

A more acceptable theory envisages an old-established Russian domestic cat developing an unusually long-haired coat as a protection against the intense winter cold. This breed, taken south to Asia Minor on board trading ships, eventually arrived in Turkey and Iran, giving rise in these two warmer regions to the Angora and Persian Cats respectively. This theory would explain the apparent anomaly of long-haired cats being named after hot countries.

An alternative theory suggests that the Angora was taken from the cold mountains of eastern Persia by Islamic invaders in the 15th century. Once in Turkey, its coat changed slightly, becoming less thick and fluffy than that of its Persian ancestors. (For details see Persian Cat.)

Whichever is true, in Turkey there were soon several colour forms of Angora Cat, each with its own title. There was, for example, a red tabby called the *sarmen* and a silver tabby called the *teku*. There was also an odd-eyed white cat with one blue eye and one amber eye, called the *Angora kedi*. In some circles, the white form became the favoured one and purists usually insist on this as the 'only true Angora colour'.

THE ANGORA CAT, one of the most ancient of all domestic breeds, having been known since at least the 15th century in Turkey. It was the first glamorous long-haired cat to reach Western Europe, arriving in the 16th century.

The Angora Cat is recorded as a distinct breed in Turkey as early as the 1400s, and was the first long-haired cat to be brought to Western Europe. The earliest specimens arrived in the 16th century as special gifts from the Turkish Sultans to noble families in England and France. In addition, at about the same time, it is reported that the French naturalist Nicholas Claude Fabri de Pereise brought some of these cats back to France from Turkey as novelties. It was only later, in the 17th century and especially towards the end of the 18th century, that this lithely elegant breed was joined by the even longer-coated Persian Cat.

By the 19th century, the more luxurious Persian had come to dominate the scene and the true Angora was becoming something of a rarity. Eventually, by the turn of the century, the traditional Angora Cat had been completely eclipsed by the glamorous Persian and pure Angora specimens eventually vanished from the West.

However, in the 1960s some British breeders set about recreating the delicately beautiful Angora and achieved this goal by the careful selection of Angora types from long-haired Oriental cats. The soft-coated, bushy-tailed look was soon regained, but the typical Angora head was less easily perfected. The angular, pointed face of the typical Oriental cat persisted, setting these new, 'pseudo-Angoras' apart from the true originals. The new Angoras also retained the more vocal personality of their Oriental ancestors.

Happily, although the original breed had long ago vanished from the show rings, it was not entirely extinct. A few pure lines remained in the Ankara region of Turkey and, thanks to the intervention of the Ankara Zoo, the true Angora was eventually rescued from oblivion. The zoo collected together a number of the surviving Turkish specimens and began a serious breeding programme with them, keeping only white cats with blue, amber or odd eyes. Some of the progeny of this programme were exported and two unrelated pairs reached North America in the 1960s to form a new breeding nucleus there. These cats and their descendants are now referred to as Turkish Angoras, to distinguish them from the reconstituted British Angoras.

The re-introduction of the true Turkish Angoras in the 1960s was due to the efforts of Walter and Leisa Grant. In 1962 they visited Ankara and, with the blessing of the Governor of the city, purchased a pair of cats from the zoo there. The male was an odd-eyed white called Yildiz and the female an amber-eyed white called Yildizcik. They were joined by a second pair, also white, but this time with the male amber-eyed and the female odd-eyed, called Yaman and Marvis, in 1966. Together, these four animals became the foundation stock for the re-introduction of the ancient breed, and in 1970 the Turkish Angora was finally accepted back into the show ring as a distinct category by the CFA in America. At about the same time, American breeders formed the Original Turkish Angora Society to consolidate the revival of this distinguished cat. In the 1970s additional cats were imported from Ankara Zoo, this time to Britain and Sweden, and the breed has since become re-established in many parts of Europe.

Personality: Terms that have been used to describe this breed include: polite, courteous, responsive, fastidious, gentle, kind, sweet, affectionate, alert, loyal and intelligent; sometimes shy and aloof, sometimes outgoing and gregarious. Graceful in movement, but unusually immobile – the ideal indoor house cat.

One of the earliest descriptions of this breed, by Sir William Jardine in 1834, reads as follows: '[Angora Cats] are frequently kept in this country as drawing-room pets, and are said to be more mild and gentle in their tempers than the common cat . . . We have not heard much in praise of their utility.' Charles Ross, writing in 1868, provides another early evaluation of the character of this breed: 'The Cat of Angora is a very beautiful variety, with silvery hair of fine silken texture . . . they are all delicate creatures, and of gentle dispositions. Mr Wood, while staying in Paris, made the acquaintance of an Angora, which ate two plates of almond biscuits at a sitting. This breed of Cats has singular tastes; I knew one that took very kindly to gin and water, and was rather partial to curry. He also ate peas, greens and broad beans (in moderation).'

Colour Forms: The traditional Angora is the blue-eyed white. Many other colours are now acceptable. Because there are two 'Angoras', it is important to consider their colour forms separately. The GCCF lists the British Angora simply as the 'Angora', and ignores the Turkish Angora. The CFA ignores the British Angora and lists only the Turkish Angora.

GCCF: (British) Angora: White; Black; Chocolate; Lilac; Red Self; Cinnamon; Caramel; Fawn; Blue; Cream; Silver Tabby; Red Tabby; Brown Tabby; Tortie; Chocolate Tortie; Lilac Tortie; Cinnamon Tortie; Caramel Tortie; Fawn Tortie; Blue Tortie; Brown Spotted; Black Smoke; Colourpointed; Black Shaded; Brown Ticked Tabby.

CFA: (Turkish) Angora: White; Black; Blue; Cream; Red; Black Smoke; Blue Smoke; Classic Tabby Pattern; Mackerel Tabby Pattern; Patched Tabby Pattern; Silver Tabby; Red Tabby; Brown Tabby; Blue Tabby; Cream Tabby; Tortie; Calico; Dilute Calico; Blue-Cream; Bi-color.

Breed Club:

The Angora Breed Club. Address: 26 Essex Road, Enfield, Middlesex, EN2 6UA, England.

PURISTS INSIST on a pure white coat for the Angora Cat, but even from early times there were several distinct colour forms in Turkey, including a red tabby known locally as the sarmen.

14

MAINE COON CAT

One of the first truly American breeds, the Maine Coon Cat is a big, tough, outdoor, cold-country cat, similar to the Norwegian Forest Cat and the Siberian Forest Cat from the Old World. Early names for it included the Maine Coon Cat, used by Frances Simpson in 1903, and the American Coon Cat. It has also been called the Maine Cat, the Maine Trick Cat, the American Longhair, the American Forest Cat, the American Shag and the American Snughead. It has been described as a 'gentle giant with the face of a lynx'. This is a powerful working cat with physical beauty as a bonus.

Appearance: One of the largest of all domestic breeds. Long-bodied but with a relatively small head. Well-muscled and strong-boned. The protective coat is long, heavy and silky, with a large ruff and bib and, above all, a magnificently luxuriant tail.

History: As with all early breeds, there are a number of alternative explanations concerning the origin of the Maine Coon Cat:

1 It is a cross between a house-cat (or a wild cat) and a raccoon. Although this is zoologically impossible, the legend could at least have given the breed its distinctive name. The idea first arose because the original Maine Coons were tabbies with ringed tails and were fond of climbing trees. This made them look raccoon-like and sparked imaginative speculations concerning their unlikely parentage.

2 It is a cross between a house-cat and an American Bobcat or Canadian Lynx. This is another preposterous theory which was seriously considered by some authors. Although it is true that a variety of feline hybrids have occurred in the past, there is nothing about the anatomy or behaviour of the Maine Coon that suggests any non-domestic genetic elements.

3 It is descended from six Angora cats that belonged to the Queen of France, Marie Antoinette. A Captain Samuel Clough of Wiscasset, Maine, is said to have brought the cats to Maine on board his ship, *The Sally,* along with other precious belongings of the beleaguered Queen. It is claimed that she was planning an escape from the dangers of the French Revolution and had sent all her most treasured possessions on ahead of her, including furniture, cloth, wallpaper, china, silver, ornaments and her six beloved long-haired cats. She herself never followed because she was beheaded before she could leave. Her cats broke free, or were turned loose in Maine, and began to fend for themselves in the New England countryside. Her other

A BROWN MACKEREL Tabby and White example of the impressively built Maine Coon Cat from
North America. A splendidly tough, sturdy, long-haired, cold-country cat that is rapidly gaining
in popularity.

belongings were disposed of, and it is claimed that some of the furniture is still to be seen in
Wiscasset. Without more detailed, documented evidence, all one can say in favour of this story
is that a cross between Angoras and local tabby cats would probably result in something
approaching a Maine Coon in appearance.

4 It is descended from Norwegian Forest Cats, or Skogkatts, that were sent to America by Marie
Antoinette during the French Revolution, when she hoped to escape to the New World. The
reason the French Queen might have owned Norwegian Skogkatts is that one of her most
devoted admirers at the French court was the Swedish diplomat Count Axel von Fersten, who
would have had access to Scandinavian felines and might have offered her some as an exotic
gift. Sadly, there is no hard evidence to support this.

5 It is descended from Angora Cats sent to America by Marie Antoinette during the American
War of Independence. She is said to have made a gift of some to the Marquis de Lafayette on
one of his voyages.

6 It is descended from Persians and Angoras brought to New England by an English sea captain
by the name of Coon. In his trading vessel, he is reputed to have been a regular visitor to the
ports up and down the coast and was always accompanied by his feline 'army'. Whenever he
went ashore, some of his cats managed to follow suit and fraternize with the local cats. In this

A SILVER TORTIE SMOKE AND WHITE MAINE COON CAT. This breed has the unique distinction of
being the only one to boast its own glossy colour magazine: *Maine Coon International*.

way, they founded the long-haired cat population of North America – a population that was
named after him. (In some versions of this story, Captain Coon is identified as Chinese.)

7 It is descended from Norwegian Skogkatts brought to North America as ships' cats at a very
early date by the Vikings. To believe this, you have to accept the controversial view that Vikings
were regularly visiting North America in the 500 years before Columbus 'discovered' the New
World. (It is claimed that Columbus was only able to make his voyage successfully because he
had set eyes on some of the early Viking maps of North America.) In support of this theory it
has been pointed out that the Norwegian Forest Cat and the Maine Coon Cat are remarkably
similar in appearance. One expert cat judge, seeing both breeds together at a show in Berlin,

remarked that in her opinion they belonged to the same breed. (It could, however, be argued that it is only similar climatic conditions which have made them look the same – both breeds being well protected from the cold.)

8 It is a descendant of Russian Steppe Cats (Russian Long-haired Cats) that were brought to Maine by sailors on trading ships.

9 It is a descendant of a French breed from the mountains of the Pyrenees known as the 'French Domestic', which looks very similar to the Maine Coon. It is thought that early French explorers first brought these long-haired cats to the New World to trade with the local Indian tribes as valuable rodent-destroyers. (The North American Indian tribes had no domestic cats available to them before the arrival of Europeans.)

10 It is a cross between local house cats that were running wild in the New England forests and Angora Cats that had been imported as exotic novelties by New England sailors and had escaped. The custom in the early days of sea travel was for sailors to bring back unusual 'curios' from faraway places for sale in their home ports. Angora Cats could have been acquired on voyages to Turkey any time from the 17th century onwards.

11 It is a result of British sailors bringing Angoras over as ships' cats in the 1850s. When these cats escaped and mated with the local cats, the outcome was the Maine Coon. The weakness of this idea is that ships' cats would almost certainly have been the tough, local British shorthairs, rather than the then highly valued long-haired imports from Turkey.

12 It is the descendant of local house-cats that became semi-wild and, as a result of living in the cold forests, gradually developed a heavier body and a thicker coat as a natural protection against the cold.

Of all these various explanations the last one is the simplest, but there may well have been occasional injections of long-haired cats from abroad, by one or other of the routes mentioned.

Whichever origin is the true one, we do know that Maine Coons have the remarkable distinction of being the very first cats ever to be exhibited in competitive cat shows. The first official cat show in the world is usually dated at 1871, in London. The first in North America is usually given as 1895, in New York. But Maine Coon shows had been taking place regularly before either of these. From the early 1860s, New England farmers had been holding an annual cat show at the Skowhegan Fair. Maine Coons were brought there from all over the region to compete for the title of 'Maine State Champion Coon Cat'.

When the bigger shows began at the end of the century, the Maine Coons had a considerable advantage, having already been exposed to over 30 years of competitive showing. As a result they were extremely popular and highly successful in those first days of major, national pedigree competition. But it was not to last. As cat shows became more and more popular, the exotic Persians and Siamese began to appear and gradually took over the show scene, as they had done in Europe. The Maine Coons were eclipsed and gradually vanished.

The problem was familiarity. As one Maine Coon enthusiast put it, early in the 20th century: 'The Maine people having had them so long, it is difficult to arouse any great enthusiasm about them.' The farmers may have taken pride in them, but these new cat exhibitions were city affairs. The recently arrived breeds from overseas were rare novelties and therefore much more appealing to the sophisticated urbanites who were flocking to the big shows.

Interest in the New England breed did, however, return in the 1950s and a Maine Coon Cat Club was formed in 1953. In 1968 the Maine Coon Breeders and Fanciers Association was established and in 1976 this was joined by the International Society for the Preservation of the Maine Coon. From this point onwards, the breed began a full revival and in the 1980s its fame started to spread abroad. It arrived in Britain in 1983/84 (although the first Maine Coon in Europe was a pregnant female sent to Austria in 1953/54). (See also Rexed Maine Coon.)

Personality: Terms used to describe the breed include: hardy, rugged, dignified, reserved, amiable, gentle, elegant, loving, faithful, self-confident, responsive, durable, affectionate, playful, intelligent, resourceful, shy, good-tempered, soft-voiced, active and healthy.

Colour Forms: Traditionally, this is a tabby cat, but today almost any colour is allowed, including all solids, tabbies, shadeds and smokes, Bi-colours and Parti-colours. The British Maine Coon Cat Club lists no fewer than 64 colour forms. Specifically excluded are: Chocolate, Lilac and Siamese Points; blue or odd eyes in cats of a colour other than white; and Bi-colour or Parti-colour cats with more than one-third of the fur white.

Breed Clubs:

British Maine Coon Cat Club was founded in 1985. In 1995 it published a guide to the breed: *Introducing the Maine Coon.* Address: 12 St Joseph's Road, Handsworth, Sheffield, South Yorkshire, S13 8AU, England.

Internationaler Maine Coon Cat Club (IMCCC). Address: Ziegelleiweg 18, 51149 Köln, Germany.

Maine Coon Fanciers of Great Britain. Address: Woodsview Cottage, Fowley Lane, High Hurstwood, East Sussex, TN22 4BG, England

Maine Coon Breeders and Fanciers Association. Address: 4405 Karrol S.W., Alburquerque, NM 87121, USA; or 2669 Skeel Street, Brighton, CO 80601, USA.

Maine Coon Club. 59 Ninth Street, Wyoming, PA 18644, USA.

United Maine Coon Cat Association. 7 Mason Drive, Milford, MA 01757, USA.

NOTE: In 1994, the Maine Coon had the unique distinction of being the only breed to have its own glossy colour magazine: *Maine Coon International* has been published quarterly since then by MCI Group, P.O. Box 59, Uckfield, East Sussex, TN22 4ZY, England.

15

ABYSSINIAN CAT

At the turn of the century sometimes called the 'Ticked' or 'British Tick' (both referring to its ticked coat), 'Cunny', 'Rabbit Cat', 'Hare Cat' or 'Bunny Cat'. According to Frances Simpson, writing in 1903, 'The colour of an Abyssinian should be a sort of reddish-fawn, each individual hair being "ticked" like that of a wild rabbit – hence the popular name of "bunny cat".' It is often referred to today as the 'Aby'. In France it is known as the *Abyssin;* in Germany as the *Abessinier;* and in Holland the *Abessijn.*

Appearance: Medium-sized, muscular, slender-bodied, short-haired cat with characteristically ticked coat. Each of the orange-brown hairs is marked with two or three dark bands; the darkest of the bands is the one nearest the tip of the hair. Head slightly wedge-shaped, with large ears and almond-shaped eyes. Soft, dense fur. Long, tapering tail. There is a long-haired variant of this breed, recently developed from it, called the Somali.

History: We probably owe the existence of the modern Abyssinian breed to a bizarre historical incident. In the 1860s, the Emperor of Abyssinia (now Ethiopia) wrote a letter to Queen Victoria in which, among other things, he asked for her hand in marriage. Not surprisingly, the letter was ignored. Her failure to respond so incensed the Emperor that he proceeded to arrest a number of Europeans, including the British Consul.

Overreacting in a spectacular fashion, the British government sent a force of 32,000 to ensure their release. This so panicked the Emperor that, as the troops approached, he blew his brains out with a pistol that had, ironically, been an earlier gift from Queen Victoria.

The British troops, having no need to fight, offered gifts to a local chief and set off for home. Along the way, some of the soldiers appear to have acquired pet kittens from the now friendly locals, and brought these back with them to Britain.

Gordon Stables, writing in 1874, reports that the first Abyssinian Cat to be identified as an individual was called 'Zula' (not 'Zulu' as some books say) and was brought to England by the wife of Captain Barrett-Lennard in 1868. This date coincides with the end of the Abyssinian confrontation and it seems likely that she obtained the animal from one of the returning soldiers. This idea is reinforced by the fact that Zula is the name of the northern Abyssinian port at which the British military force established its first base, in 1867.

Early writers on this breed, noting the proximity of Abyssinia to Egypt, suggested that it might be the direct descendant of the sacred cat of the ancient Egyptians. Although the Abyssinian Cat

THE ABYSSINIAN CAT, a breed famous for its ticked coat. Known affectionately as the 'Aby', it may owe its existence as a pedigree show-cat to a bizarre incident involving Queen Victoria and a pistol.

does, indeed, have the correct body proportions when compared with the many small bronze statuettes of the cat goddess Bastet, there is no hard evidence to support this theory.

A less romantic version of the Abyssinian's origin sees it as a cat 'more at home on the Thames than the Nile' – created by careful selective breeding in England at the end of the 19th century. This view holds that individual cats with ticked coats were brought together repeatedly to fix the 'ticked' quality and create the breed out of existing British Shorthairs.

The truth probably lies in a combination of these theories. It seems quite likely that a few unusual cats with ticked coats, distantly related to those of nearby Egypt, were brought back to England after the brief 'war' with Abyssinia. These cats were probably then mated with carefully chosen British Shorthairs in order to develop the new breed of 'ticked' cats.

According to several authors, the Abyssinian was first listed as a distinct breed in 1882, but its status was strongly contested by certain authorities of the day. The first Standard of Points for the breed was published in 1889, by Harrison Weir, and the first Abyssinians to be registered in the National Cat Club Stud Book had their names entered there in 1896. In 1907 the first specimens were sent to the United States.

In the inter-war period, in 1929, the Abyssinian Cat Club was formed in England by Major E.S. Woodiwiss. After a dormant period during World War II, it was reactivated in 1947. Barely a dozen pure-bred Abyssinians had survived the austerity and destruction of the war years, but serious breeding was soon started again and the Club went from strength to strength until it was eventually able to celebrate 60 years of existence with a special Jubilee Show in 1989.

Personality: Terms that have been used to describe this breed include: intelligent, affectionate, gentle, graceful, sinuous, energetic, companionable, friendly, fearless, quiet, active, playful, alert, fast, sun-worshipping. Lithe and pantherine in its movements. Requires considerable freedom and dislikes close confinement.

A critic of the breed has commented that it is difficult to handle, undisciplined, introverted, shy and cautious, but against this, an eminent cat judge has declared: 'The quiet unassuming Abyssinian combines all the good points and none of the failings of his more widely advertised relations.'

Colour Forms: The original colour form of this species was described as 'ruddy'. It stood alone as the sole acceptable colour until, in 1963, it was joined by a 'sorrel' or 'red'. Blue was not added as a championship colour until 1984. Today a number of further colours have been added, and the recognized lists read as follows:

GCCF: Usual (=Ruddy/ Ruddy Brown/ Burnt Sienna); Sorrel (= Red/ Cinnamon/ Russet); Chocolate; Blue; Lilac (Chocolate Dilute); Fawn (Sorrel Dilute); Red (Sex-linked Red); Cream (Sex-linked Cream); Tortie; Sorrel Tortie; Chocolate Tortie; Blue Tortie; Lilac Tortie; Fawn Tortie; Silver; Sorrel Silver; Chocolate Silver; Blue Silver; Lilac Silver; Fawn Silver; Red Silver; Cream Silver; Tortie Silver; Sorrel Tortie Silver; Chocolate Tortie Silver; Blue Tortie Silver; Lilac Tortie Silver; Fawn Tortie Silver.

CFA: Ruddy (= Usual/ Ruddy Brown/ Burnt Sienna); Red (= Sorrel/ Cinnamon/ Russet); Blue; Fawn.

Breed Clubs:

Abyssinian Cat Association. Address: Danum, Fields Road, Chedworth, Glos., GL54 4NQ, England.

Abyssinian Cat Club. Publishes a twice-yearly journal, *Papyrus.* Address: Alwyne, 15 Cramhurst Lane, Whitley, Surrey, GU8 5RA, England.

Abyssinian Cat Club of America. Address: 4060 Croaker Lane, Woodbridge, VA 22193, USA.

16

BRITISH SHORTHAIR CAT

The modern pedigree British Shorthair has been developed from the ancient British working cats whose ancestors arrived with the Romans somewhere between the first and fourth century AD.

Appearance: A sturdy, muscular cat with a massive, broad head, rather short neck and legs and thick tail. The coat, although short, is dense and plush. The pedigree version of this cat is an altogether stockier, heavier animal than the typical domestic pet shorthair.

History: It is difficult to be certain of the precise date that domestic cats arrived in Britain. During the Roman period there were many wild cats in the country, and it is not always easy to tell from skeletal remains whether a particular animal was wild or domesticated. There are some feline footprints impressed into tiles in the foundation of a third century temple in Roman Chelmsford. It has been argued that these are unlikely to have been made by wild cats, but we cannot be certain.

One of the earliest known examples of an undeniably domestic British cat was discovered during excavations at Lullingstone in Kent. There, in the basement of a rich man's house dating from the second half of the fourth century, was a skeleton of a cat that had perished in a fire. Its bones and teeth showed that it was a domesticated specimen and not a trapped wild cat.

During the 1,600 years that followed, the domestic cat survived as a pest-controller, despite repeated, systematic persecution and torture by pious Christians, who believed that the feline body housed the spirit of the devil. Eventually, in the Victorian era, cats were at last treated as appealing household pets.

With the advent of competitive cat shows, starting in 1871, the best examples of the British working cats were selected and developed as pedigree animals. A large number of colour forms was soon available. These short-haired animals dominated the earliest cats shows because the long-haired breeds were so new and were outnumbered by about ten to one. By 1896, however, the longhairs has become the favoured breeds and were given the place of honour at all shows.

By the turn of the century it was reported that the short-haired cats were 'in a very small minority'. So popular were the new longhairs that there was at one point a danger that the old,

THE RED TABBY COLOUR FORM of the stocky, muscular, broad-headed
British Shorthair Cat *(opposite)*, the modern pedigree version of the ancient British working cat.

original shorthairs might have been completely eclipsed. However, dedicated supporters came to their rescue and in 1901 the Short-haired Cat Society was formed to promote them. Since then they have always had a significant part to play in competitive cat showing.

In Continental Europe there used to be no difference between the British Shorthair and what was referred to as the 'European Shorthair'. The British breed clubs had been the first to develop shorthairs as pedigree cats, so they had precedence over the Continentals, and many of the first pedigree 'European Shorthairs' were imported British Shorthairs. But then the Continentals began to develop and improve their own shorthair cats and, in 1982, a distinction was made between the two breeds. After that, inevitably, they began to diverge. Today, the main differences are that the British Shorthair has a cobbier, sturdier body and a heavier, wider head.

The bluish-grey version of the British Shorthair is known as the British Blue Cat. Because it has always been the most popular colour for the breed, some authorities have in the past raised it to the level of a separate breed. Writing in 1955, Rose Tenent comments: 'The British Blue has been called the "aristocrat" of short-hairs.' She continues: 'In the United States the British Blue is known as the Maltese cat, and recently has enjoyed much popularity there as a household pet. On the Continent, too, this cat is becoming increasingly popular, and there its name is the Chartreuse.' This is confusing, since the name 'Maltese' has also in the past been given to the Russian Blue Cat. Furthermore, there is disagreement about the relationship between the British Blue and the French cat called the 'Chartreux' or 'Chartreuse'. Some authorities consider them to be so similar as to be the same breed. Others see them as distinct breeds and classify them separately. The British Blue is said to have the plushest coat of any shorthair. In recent times the preferred colour of this breed has shown slight changes, the dark slate-blue of the early days becoming much paler.

Personality: Terms used to describe this breed include: hardy, good-natured, calm, affable, loyal, intelligent, reserved, prosaic, stolid, loving, untemperamental, tranquil, dignified, independent and affectionate.

Colour Forms: The traditional and most popular colour for the British Shorthair is Blue. Black is also one of the earliest colours. Today, however, almost every colour is accepted and the list has grown longer and longer, year by year. To simplify the list, the colours are grouped into convenient categories.

GCCF: SELF COLOURS: White; Black; Chocolate; Lilac; Red Self; Blue; Cream.

TABBY (both Classic and Mackerel): Red Tabby; Brown Tabby; Blue Tabby; Chocolate Tabby; Lilac Tabby; Cream Tabby.

SILVER TABBY: Silver Tabby; Blue Silver Tabby; Chocolate Silver Tabby; Lilac Silver Tabby; Red Silver Tabby; Cream Silver Tabby.

TABBY AND WHITE: Brown Tabby and White; Blue Tabby and White; Chocolate Tabby and White; Lilac Tabby and White; Red Tabby and White; Cream Tabby and White.

SILVER TABBY AND WHITE: Silver Tabby and White; Blue Silver Tabby and White; Chocolate Silver Tabby and White; Lilac Silver Tabby and White; Red Silver Tabby and White; Cream Silver Tabby and White.

SPOTTED: Brown Spotted; Blue Spotted; Chocolate Spotted; Lilac Spotted; Red Spotted; Cream Spotted;

SILVER SPOTTED: Silver Spotted; Blue Silver Spotted; Chocolate Silver Spotted; Lilac Silver Spotted; Red Silver Spotted; Cream Silver Spotted;

TORTIE TABBY: Tortie Tabby; Tortie Silver Tabby; Tortie Spotted; Tortie Silver Spotted.

THE BRITISH BLUE, the most popular colour form of the British Shorthair Cat, is sometimes referred to as the 'aristocrat of shorthairs'. In appearance it is similar to the French Charteux.

TORTIE: Tortie; Blue-Cream; Chocolate Tortie; Lilac Tortie.

TORTIE AND WHITE: Tortie and White; Blue Tortie and White; Chocolate Tortie and White; Lilac Tortie and White.

BI-COLOUR: Black and White Bi-colour; Blue and White Bi-colour; Chocolate and White Bi-colour; Lilac and White Bi-colour; Red and White Bi-colour; Cream and White Bi-colour.

SMOKE: Black Smoke; Blue Smoke; Chocolate Smoke; Lilac Smoke; Red Smoke; Cream Smoke; Tortie Smoke; Blue Tortie Smoke; Chocolate Tortie Smoke; Lilac Tortie Smoke.

SMOKE AND WHITE: Black Smoke and White; Blue Smoke and White; Chocolate Smoke and White; Lilac Smoke and White; Red Smoke and White; Cream Smoke and White.

TIPPED: Black Tipped; Blue Tipped; Chocolate Tipped; Lilac Tipped; Red Tipped; Cream Tipped; Black Tortie Tipped; Blue Tortie Tipped; Chocolate Tortie Tipped; Lilac Tortie Tipped; Golden Tipped.

SELF POINTED: Seal Colourpointed; Blue Colourpointed; Chocolate Colourpointed; Lilac Colourpointed; Red Colourpointed; Cream Colourpointed;

TORTIE POINTED: Seal Tortie Colourpointed; Blue-Cream Colourpointed; Chocolate Tortie Colourpointed; Lilac Tortie Colourpointed;

TABBY POINTED: Seal Tabby Colourpointed; Blue Tabby Colourpointed; Chocolate Tabby Colour Pointed; Lilac Tabby Colourpointed; Red Tabby Colourpointed; Cream Tabby Colourpointed;

TORTIE TABBY POINTED: Seal Tortie Tabby Colourpointed; Blue-Cream Tabby Colourpointed; Chocolate Tortie Tabby Colourpointed; Lilac Tortie Tabby Colourpointed.

CFA: White; Black; Blue; Cream; Black Smoke; Blue Smoke; Classic Tabby Pattern; Mackerel Tabby Pattern; Spotted Tabby; Silver Tabby; Red Tabby; Brown Tabby; Blue Tabby; Cream Tabby; Tortie; Calico; Dilute Calico; Blue-Cream; Bi-color.

Breed Clubs:

British Shorthair and Tipped Club. Address: Rowan, Shas Lane, Uppermill, Oldham, Lancs OL3 6HP, England.

Short Haired Cat Society. Address: Highridge, Parsonage Hill, Somerton, Somerset TA11 7PF, England.

NOTE: In America there is a breed publication, *The British Shorthair Newsletter.* Address: 17275 Hammock Lane, Fort Pierce, FL 34988, USA.

17

MEXICAN HAIRLESS CAT

An apparently extinct breed known from the turn of the century.

Appearance: Similar to the modern Sphynx Cat, with a long body and tail, a wedge-shaped head and large ears. They did, however, differ from the Sphynx Cat in two ways: in the winter they managed to grow a little hair on their backs and tails, though this was shed in the summer; also, they had long whiskers.

History: In 1902 an American couple, Mr and Mrs F.J. Shinick, living in Albuquerque, New Mexico, were presented with a pair of hairless cats by local Pueblo Indians. They were told by Jesuit priests that these cats were the last survivors of an ancient Aztec breed of cat.

The male was called Dick and the female Nellie. Mrs Shinick reported that 'Nellie has a very small head, large amber eyes, and long whiskers and eyebrows . . . Dick was a very powerful cat and could whip any dog alone. His courage, no doubt, was the cause of his death . . . one night he got out and several dogs killed him.' This happened before the male had become sexually mature, so that the pair were never able to breed. Mrs Shinick searched all over New Mexico for a hairless mate for Nellie, but without success. Sadly, she was forced to conclude, 'I fear the breed is extinct.'

For some reason, it did not occur to her to mate Nellie with a normally haired male and then back-cross to her in an attempt to continue the line. Nor is it clear what she did with Nellie, although a report in the following year, 1903, suggests that she may have sold the female to an English cat-lover. In that year Charles Lane, in his book *Rabbits Cats and Cavies,* shows an illustration of a Mexican Hairless Cat called Jesuit, with the caption: 'Believed to be the only specimen ever exhibited in England. Owner, Hon. Mrs McLaren Morrison.' He says he hopes this 'may prove they are not quite extinct'. It seems likely that 'Jesuit' was in reality a renamed Nellie, brought to England at great expense to cause a sensation at major cat shows. This view is strengthened by the comments in a letter, dated 1902, sent by the Shinicks to an English cat exhibitor: 'I have priced Nellie at $300. She is too valuable a pet for me to keep in a small town. Many wealthy ladies would value her at her weight in gold if they knew what a very rare pet she is. I think in your position she would be a very good investment to exhibit at cat shows and other select events, as she doubtless is the only hairless cat now known.'

If Nellie did cross the Atlantic and become Jesuit, she may well have introduced a wider public to the Mexican Hairless breed, but there are no records that she was ever used for

THE EXTRAORDINARY Mexican Hairless Cats, photographed at the turn of the century. Known as Dick and Nellie, they failed to launch a naked feline dynasty because brave Dick was killed by a pack of dogs.

breeding, and it would appear that, after her day, the Mexican Hairless Cat finally vanished without trace.

Some authors referred to this breed as the 'New Mexican Hairless' because earlier hairless examples of domestic cats from Latin America had been described by naturalists as far back as 1830. As in several other instances, in different parts of the world (including France, Czechoslovakia, Austria, Morocco and Australia), these naked mutant cats appeared and then soon vanished. Only the modern Sphynx Cat (see separate entry) has been treated seriously as a potential pedigree breed.

18

HIMALAYAN CAT

This is the American name for a Persian Cat with Siamese colourpoint markings. Its popular nickname is the 'Himmy' or 'Himmie'. It is sometimes referred to as a 'Colourpoint Persian'. In Britain it is officially called a 'Colourpoint Longhair'.

In the 1920s references occur to a breed called the 'Malayan Persian'. This appears to have been an early, alternative name for the Himalayan which was soon abandoned. In 1947, the name 'Masked Silver' was given to certain Persians which carried Siamese markings – presumably yet another (now obsolete) name for the Himalayan.

Appearance: Almost exactly as for the Persian Cat, with snub nose, flat face, broad head, short body and thick, heavy, very long-haired coat. The only difference is that this breed shows the colourpoint coat pattern of the Siamese.

History: In the 1920s and 1930s, breeders in several countries were striving to produce a cat with a typical Persian body, but with Siamese markings. The idea was to borrow only the coat pattern from the Siamese and nothing else. In 1924, in America, attempts to produce a Colourpoint Persian cat by crossing Siamese with White Persians resulted in animals that were christened 'Malayan Persians'. For some reason this line disappeared. In 1924, Dr T. Tjebbes was making Persian/Siamese crosses in Sweden. In 1930, Dr Clyde Keeler and Virginia Cobb started a serious breeding programme in the United States with the same aim. After six years, the first true Himalayan kitten was born. It was appropriately named 'Debutante'. In September 1936 Miss Cobb was able to write an article for *The Journal of Heredity* describing the successful progress of their programme.

After World War II, the development of the Himalayan was taken up in earnest by Marguerita Goforth of San Diego. As the years passed, great improvements were achieved and the breed was finally given official recognition in the United States in 1957.

In Britain, similar breeding experiments were being carried out by Brian Stirling-Webb at Richmond in Surrey. Although his cats were condemned to the unimaginative title of 'Colourpoint Longhairs', their quality was so impressive that they gained official recognition as early as 1955 – two years before the American Himalayans.

Even today, some cat organizations still do not like to give this breed its own separate name. The fact that they carry a genetic contribution – admittedly a relatively small one – from Siamese Cats seems to be sufficient to justify the separate title, but in the end it is simply a matter of taste.

THE HIMALAYAN CAT, a breed that displays the attractive combination of a Persian Cat body with Siamese Cat markings. In Britain it is known officially by the more cumbersome name of Colourpoint Longhair.

Personality: Terms used to describe this breed include: docile, gentle, intelligent, outgoing, devoted, affectionate and demanding. The voice is slightly louder than that of the full Persian, but much quieter than the Siamese. Because of their mixed ancestry it is inevitable that they will show some characters derived from both their Persian and their Siamese backgrounds. Not surprisingly, they are closer to the Persian than the Siamese. One author commented that Himalayans 'are a rest cure to an owner who has endured the domineering ways and boisterous and violent affections of the Siamese'. On the other hand, Himalayans are said to be more enterprising than full Persians, perhaps borrowing a small slice of the Siamese vigour.

Colour Forms: To simplify the list, the colours are grouped into convenient categories.

GCCF: SOLID POINT COLOURS: Seal Point; Blue Point; Chocolate Point; Lilac Point; Red Point; Cream Point.

TORTIE POINT COLOURS: Seal Tortie Point; Blue-Cream Point; Chocolate Tortie Point; Lilac-Cream Point.

NON-TORTIE TABBY POINT COLOURS: Seal Tabby Point; Blue Tabby Point; Chocolate Tabby Point; Lilac Tabby Point; Red Tabby Point; Cream Tabby Point.

TORTIE TABBY POINT COLOURS: Seal Tortie Tabby Point; Blue-Cream Tabby Point; Chocolate Tortie Tabby Point; Lilac-Cream Tabby Point.

CFA: **HIMALAYAN (POINT) PATTERN:** Chocolate Point, Seal Point; Lilac Point; Blue Point; Flame (Red) Point; Cream Point; Tortie Point; Blue-Cream Point; Chocolate Tortie Point; Lilac-Cream Point.

HIMALAYAN LYNX (POINT) PATTERN: Seal Lynx Point; Blue Lynx Point; Flame (Red) Lynx Point; Cream Lynx Point; Tortie Lynx Point; Blue-Cream Lynx Point; Chocolate Lynx Point; Lilac Lynx Point; Chocolate Tortie Lynx Point; Lilac-Cream Lynx Point.

Breed Clubs:

Colourpoint Cat Club. Publishes a twice-yearly magazine. Address: 1 Chestnut Avenue, Ravenshead, Notts., England; Tel: 01623-793980.

Colourpoint Society of Great Britain. Address: 77 Nursery Hill, Shamley Green, Guildford, Surrey, GU5 OUL, England.

NOTE: There are also two breed publications: *Cat Tracks.* Address: 167 West Genesee Street, Chittenango, NY 13037, USA; and *The Western Edition.* Address: 1575 Hurlburt lane, Sebastopol, CA 95472, USA.

19

KARAKUL CAT

It is reported that in the 1930s curly-coated mutations occasionally occurred among short-haired cats in the United States. These individuals were referred to as Karakul Cats, but no attempt appears to have been made either to study them or to use them to establish a new breed. The so-called Karakul Cats were obviously isolated precursors of the Rex breeds that were developed after World War II.

PEKE-FACED CAT

A flat-faced breed developed in America, with head proportions similar to those of the Pekinese Dog. The depressed nose gives the breed an appealing facial configuration, but critics believe this is achieved at the expense of causing breathing difficulties.

THE CONTROVERSIAL Peke-faced Cat. The face of the Persian cat has grown flatter and flatter over the years, and the Peke-face is the ultimate expression of this trend. Although appealing, it can easily suffer from breathing problems.

Appearance: The Peke-faced Cat is essentially a Persian Cat with a face that is even flatter than usual. According to the standard for the breed, the nose should be 'short, depressed and indented between the eyes'. Unlike the Persian, which appears in many colour forms, the Peke-faced cat is only known in red and red tabby colours.

History: This variant of the ordinary Persian appeared spontaneously in litters of ordinary Reds. The earliest records of Peke-faced individuals date from the 1930s. They became highly valued by American and Canadian breeders and often won prizes at cat shows, being seen, in effect, as 'Super-Persians'. In Europe they have remained unpopular because of the physical abnormalities that are associated with them.

Abnormalities: Because of its excessively flattened face, this breed is likely to suffer from blocked tear-ducts which cause runny eyes, a poor bite when its mouth is closed, and respiratory difficulties due to the reduced size of its nasal cavities. The respiratory problems increase with age. Breeders are attempting to reduce these faults, but may not be able to do so without abandoning the extreme flattening of the face – the very feature which makes these cats so anthropomorphically appealing.

Personality: Terms used to describe this breed include: calm, affectionate, polite, friendly and sociable. Claimed to be 'the ideal indoor cat'.

21

PRUSSIAN REX CAT

Discovered in East Prussia in the early 1930s but not developed. Little is known about the Prussian Rex except that, like other Rex Cats, it carried the wavy-hair gene. According to one report, it was the offspring of a Russian Blue/Angora cross, was owned by a Frau Schneider and was called Munk. It is the earliest recorded example of a Rex Cat, but does not appear to have been used in a systematic breeding programme, and soon vanished. (See also German Rex Cat.)

BALINESE CAT

The long-haired version of the Siamese Cat. In the United States some colour forms (see below) are called Javanese Cats. When the breed first appeared it was given the name 'Long-haired Siamese' but this was unpopular with Siamese breeders and a new name was sought. 'Balinese' was selected for two reasons. First, Bali is close to Siam (Thailand) and secondly the elegant movements of the cats were thought to be reminiscent of Balinese dancers. In Australia it is also known as the Oriental Longhair. In France it is the *Balinais;* in Germany the *Balinesen*.

Appearance: Described as 'slim and dainty', it has been called 'the fashion model of the cat world'. The elongated, angular body of this breed, its colourpointed coat pattern and its vivid blue eyes are identical to those of the Siamese, the only difference being that the Balinese has a soft, silky, medium-long coat with a plumed tail.

History: The Balinese began as an accident. Siamese kittens started to appear with much longer fur than usual. At first they were looked upon as unfortunate oddities and were discarded from breeding programmes, until a Californian breeder decided to turn a negative into a positive and develop them as a distinct new breed. Marion Dorset is said to have first taken an interest in them as early as the 1940s and by the mid-1950s she had developed a planned breeding programme with them. In the early 1960s she was joined in this venture by a New York breeder, Helen Smith, and it was she who suggested changing the name to Balinese. Other breeders were soon attracted and in 1968 they formed a club called 'The Balinese Breeders and Fans International'. They also launched a magazine, *Speaking Balinese*. By the end of the decade the new breed had achieved championship status with all the American cat societies. In the 1970s it had spread to Europe and had also gained championship status there by the 1980s.

There are two theories as to how the long coat came to appear in pure-bred Siamese stock. One sees it as a spontaneous mutation, while the other regards it as the delayed result of the occasional introduction of Angoras into Siamese lines, in England back in the 1920s.

NOTE: The Balinese should not be confused with the Himalayan. Both could loosely be described as 'Long-haired Siamese', but they are very different. The Himalayan is essentially a modified Persian, with Siamese colourpoints, whereas the Balinese is a modified Siamese, with a long coat.

Personality: The following terms have been used to describe this breed: extrovert and lively, intelligent, eager, enthusiastic, active, athletic, acrobatic, expressive, regal, graceful, loyal, friendly, warm, curious and affectionate. Like their Siamese ancestors, they are vocally noisy.

A LILAC POINT BALINESE CAT. When this elegant breed first appeared, it was referred to simply as the 'Long-haired Siamese', but there were strong objections to this from Siamese breeders and it was eventually renamed.

Colour Forms: In the US, Seal, Chocolate, Blue and Lilac Point are the only colours permitted. Other colours, such as Red, Tortie and Lynx (Tabby) Point, are referred to as Javanese (see entry). In the UK this separation is not made, all the colours being included in the breed.

GCCF: Seal Point; Blue Point; Chocolate Point; Lilac Point; Red Point; Seal Tortie Point; Cream Point; Blue Tortie Point; Chocolate Tortie Point; Lilac Tortie Point; Seal Tabby Point; Blue Tabby Point; Chocolate Tabby Point; Lilac Tabby Point; Red Tabby Point; Seal Tortie Tabby Point; Cream Tabby Point; Blue Tortie Tabby Point; Chocolate Tortie Tabby Point; Lilac Tortie Tabby Point.

CFA: Seal Point; Chocolate Point; Blue Point; Lilac Point.

Breed Clubs:

American Balinese Association. Address: 29 Harvest Lane, West Hartford, CT 06117, USA.

Balinese and Siamese Cat Club. Address: Holly Tree Cottage, Clacton Road, Horsley Cross, Manningtree, Essex, CO11 2NR, England.

Balinese and Siamese Cat Society. Address: Lapislazuli, 10 Osborne Road, Westcliff-on-Sea, Essex, SS0 7DW, England.

Balinese Cat Society. Issues a magazine. Address: 5, Lamaleach Drive, Freckleton, Preston, Lancs., PR4 1AJ, England.

23

OHIO REX CAT

One of the American Rex Cats (the others being the Oregon Rex, the California Rex, the Selkirk Rex and the Missouri Rex), it first appeared in Ohio in 1953.

History: The first Ohio Rex Cat, a male kitten named 'Toni', was an unexpected mutation in an otherwise normal litter born to normal-coated domestic cats owned by Miss Mary Hedderman of Plainsville, Ohio. Toni died young, but was followed by three more Rex kittens from the same parents. No long-term breeding programme was pursued with these, however, and the Ohio Rex strain died out.

According to one authority, this breed was first discovered in 1944, but was ignored owing to wartime preoccupations.

24

AUSTRALIAN CAT

The Australian Cat is said to 'have arisen as a mutation from the Siamese breed'. In 1946 it was already said to be 'very rare'. Its body was shaped like that of the Siamese, but its coat varied in colour. The ears were large, the nose long, the whiskers short – sometimes completely absent.' Little more appears to be known about it.

GERMAN REX CAT

Discovered in 1946 (some authors say 1947 or 1948, but the early date seems most likely) in East Germany. Taken up by serious breeders in 1951, following the discovery of the Cornish Rex Cat in England in 1950.

Appearance: Its coat is very similar to that of the Cornish Rex: it has no guard hairs and the awn hairs and undercoat are both unusually short. However, it differs from the Cornish Rex coat in having awn hairs that are a little thicker than those of the undercoat, and this gives it a fuller, woollier look.

History: The first German Rex was a black female feral cat seen wandering in the gardens of the Hufeland Hospital in the ruins of East Berlin, shortly after the end of World War II. She was rescued by a Dr R. Scheuer-Karpin, who named her 'Lammchen'(= Lambkin). She was found to be carrying the same wavy-hair gene as the Cornish Rex Cats. This was designated GEN 1. Rex. No. 33, as distinct from the wavy-hair gene of the Devon Rex Cat, which was designated GEN 2. Rex. No. 33a.

Lammchen had many litters and, when she was ten years old, in 1957, she was mated with one of her sons. This mating produced a litter of Rex kittens. During the next few years more German Rex litters were born and eventually, in 1960, two female German Rex Cats, called Marigold and Jet, were taken to the United States for breeding purposes. In 1961 a black male called 'Christopher Columbus' followed them and these three cats, in conjunction with the already imported Cornish Rex Cats, formed the basis of the Rex breed in America.

For many years (until 1979), the American CFA only recognized one form of Rex Cat – the one forged from crosses between the German and the Cornish – and ignored the other main breed, the Devon Rex.

Since, genetically, the German and Cornish breeds share the same Rex gene and are therefore, in one sense, virtually the same animal, it was only a matter of time before one eclipsed the other. The German breed was still being shown in Germany in the 1980s, and in 1982 some European breeders came to regard it as a separate breed, not because of its Rex gene, but because it had a body form that differed from that of the Cornish Rex and was closer to the European Shorthair. Despite this, however, fewer and fewer of them appeared in shows and eventually the line seems to have almost disappeared, while the Cornish has gone from strength to strength.

THE GERMAN REX CAT, first discovered wandering in the ruins of East Berlin in the 1940s. Genetically it appears to be very similar to the Cornish Rex, although it has a slightly different body form.

There is a report of an even earlier example of a German Rex Cat being found, back in the 1930s in East Prussia, but details are scanty. (See Prussian Rex Cat.)

COLOURPOINT SHORTHAIR CAT

This is essentially a Siamese Cat with newly developed colouring to the points. In some cat societies it is referred to simply as 'New Colour Siamese'. In others, it is grouped separately under its own name.

Appearance: The body has the slender, angular shape of the typical Siamese, with the same close coat, and the same wedge-shaped head with huge ears and blue eyes.

History: For many years, breeders have been experimenting with new colours for the extremities of their Siamese Cats. Extreme traditionalists insist on the original Seal Point (a pale fawn coat with seal-brown extremities) and nothing else. Less extreme traditionalists accept both the seal-point and the Chocolate Point. Others also allow the two dilutants, Blue and Lilac. Any further colours are frowned upon and placed outside the strict 'Siamese' category, hence the introduction of the name 'Colourpoint Shorthair' for these other variants.

For non-traditionalists, they are all Siamese, regardless of the colour of their points, because they have the same body shape and personality and are truly Siamese in all but colour. The argument against this is that, in order to introduce these new colours, it was necessary to cross the Siamese foundation stock with other breeds, and this, therefore, makes them 'non-Siamese' to the purist.

The first seriously planned attempts to create new Siamese colours began in England in the 1940s, just after the end of World War II. In 1947 and 1948, red tabby cats and Abyssinians were mated with traditional Siamese Cats. When the offspring of these matings were back-crossed to Siamese Cats, the results were, as predicted, Red, Cream and Tortie Points. Some individuals were solid or full-coloured and these, too, were developed as a new breed: the Oriental Shorthair.

In the 1960s there was another special breeding programme that was designed to add further colours to the points, this time concentrating on 'tabby points'. (Tabby is called Lynx in America.)

Perhaps surprisingly, it is certain American cat societies that have adopted the more traditional stance and refused to allowed these new colour types to be called 'Siamese', while the British officials lump them all together in one class. Although breeding logic seems to be on the side of the Americans, an awkward fact has come to light that tends to support the British approach. Studying the feline population of Thailand recently, feline scholar Roger Tabor unexpectedly 'found tabby and tortie point Siamese among Thai temple cats'. Clearly, with true, home-bred Siamese, 'purity' is a matter of degree.

Personality: Terms used to describe this breed include: unpredictable, audacious, demanding, inquisitive, active, vocal, jealous, extroverted and arrogant, but also very loving and exceptionally intelligent. Their character was summed up by one owner with the phrase 'they are always on stage'.

Colour Forms: All Colourpoint Shorthairs have the typical Siamese points pattern, but *not* in the four traditional Siamese colours (Seal, Chocolate, Blue and Lilac). All other colours are permitted, and those already listed by the Cat Fanciers' Association in America are:

CFA: Red Point; Cream Point; Seal-Lynx Point; Chocolate Lynx Point; Blue-Lynx Point; Lilac-Lynx Point; Red-Lynx Point; Cream-Lynx Point; Seal-Tortie Point; Chocolate-Tortie Point; Blue-Cream Point; Lilac-Cream Point; Seal-Tortie-Lynx Point; Chocolate-Tortie-Lynx Point; Blue-Cream-Lynx Point; Lilac-Cream-Lynx Point.

Breed Club:

Colourpoint, Rex-coated and AOV Club. Address: 17 Rackenford, Shoeburyness, Essex, SS3 8BE, England.

THE COLOURPOINT SHORTHAIR CAT, an American breed not to be confused with the Colourpoint British Shorthair, is a Siamese Cat with newly developed colouring to the points. This one is a Seal-Lynx Point.

KASHMIR CAT

A solid-coloured version of the Himalayan Cat developed in North America. It has no connection with Kashmir. The name is based on the fact that this breed is close to the Himalayan breed and that Kashmir is close to the Himalayas.

Appearance: A Persian Cat with solid chocolate or lilac fur.

History: In the 1930s, breeding programmes were started to obtain a Persian cat with Siamese markings. This colourpointed Persian, called the Himalayan, was given championship status in the 1950s (1955 in Britain and 1957 in the United States). During the course of creating the Chocolate Point and Lilac Point versions of this breed, occasional specimens appeared with solid colours. Some breeders decided that these all-over Chocolate and all-over Lilac individuals should be given separate breed status under the name Kashmir. There was considerable opposition to this on the grounds that this was just another minor colour variation and did not justify a separate title. One author described the Kashmir as 'a taxonomist's daydream and a superfluous breed division'. Another says it is 'unnecessary splitting . . . simply in order to create another breed'. As a result, it remains controversial, welcomed by some but ignored by many. The Canadian Cat Association is one of the few major organizations to accept it as a separate category. For most others, the cats are merely Chocolate Persians or Lilac Persians.

Technically, the justification for calling these cats by a separate name is this: when the Himalayan Cats were being developed from traditional Persians, they acquired their Siamese colourpoints from an introduction of Siamese genes into the breeding programme. When a few self-coloured individuals arose by accident in this programme, they may have lacked the colourpoints, but still carried a Siamese genetic element in their make-up. They are therefore not pure Persians, even though they may look like them. In other words, this is a cat that is given a separate breed name, not for what you see when you look at it, but for what is hidden in its genetic make-up. For some authorities this is simply not enough.

Personality: Terms used to describe this breed include: gentle, intelligent, outgoing, calm, self-confident, devoted, demanding and affectionate.

ORIENTAL SHORTHAIR CAT

This is, quite simply, a Siamese Cat without the typical Siamese coat markings. It has been called the 'greyhound of cats'.

Appearance: As for Siamese, but with non-pointed coat colours.

History: When Siamese Cats were first introduced to the West they had a variety of colour patterns. Very early on (in the 1920s), it was decided to concentrate on one particular kind of colouring. The official, pedigree Siamese Cat was to display a Seal Point coat – that is, a pale coat with dark brown extremities – and intense blue eyes. Other forms were rejected and soon vanished. Over the years, the colour of the Siamese points was varied, but the basic pattern – of pale ground colour with darker extremities – was always retained. As time passed, this pattern became synonymous with the breed, and any cat without points could no longer even be called a Siamese.

When, in the 1950s, certain breeders decided to resurrect the original non-pointed type of colouring in their Siamese, they had to find a new name for their cats. The first type they sought was the all-brown cat which was eventually given its own name – the Havana. Other solid (or 'self') colours that were developed were referred to as 'Foreigns'. The more complicated colours, involving patterns such as tabby, spotted or tortoiseshell, were the ones called 'Oriental Shorthairs'. In America, this distinction between Foreigns and Oriental Shorthairs was not made; there, they were all called Oriental Shorthairs. In Britain, the GCCF followed suit in the early 1990s. They switched the names of specific colour forms from Foreign Shorthair to Oriental Shorthair in all breeds except the Foreign White.

The Foreign White is essentially a pure white Siamese. A dramatically elegant breed, it was created by crossing Siamese with white short-haired cats. Although it is a white cat with blue eyes, a combination that is usually associated with deafness, the Foreign White does not suffer from this disability. In the United States the Foreign White is classified as just another colour form of the Oriental Shorthair, but in Britain the GCCF still treats it as a separate breed. When the GCCF decided to abandon the use of the word 'Foreign', the breeders of the Foreign White objected, insisting that they wanted to keep their time-honoured name. This request was granted and so

THE ORIENTAL SHORTHAIR CAT *(opposite)* – a Siamese Cat without the typical Siamese markings. This breed is now available in a bewilderingly large range of colour forms.

YET ANOTHER COLOUR FORM of the Oriental Shorthair Cat, the Oriental Spotted Tabby. This one is given separate consideration here because the original intention was to develop it into a completely new breed. This plan was later abandoned.

the Foreign White became the only one of the many Oriental Shorthair colours to retain its old name.

Another colour variant, the Oriental Spotted Tabby Cat was an attempt by British breeders to re-create the ancient-Egyptian ancestor of the domestic cat. It was originally intended to become a distinct breed and was called the 'Egyptian Mau', but this title was later dropped in order to avoid confusion with the new American breed of the same name. (See Egyptian Mau for further details.)

The method used to create Oriental Shorthairs has been to introduce various other short-haired breeds into Siamese stock. This had to be done in such a way that only the colouring of these other breeds was added, and the Siamese type, with its slender, elongated build, was retained.

Personality: As for Siamese. It is said that these cats have an unusual personality, in that they are prepared to walk on a collar and leash with their owners and find physical restraint less disturbing than other cat breeds. This makes them especially suited to travelling and showing.

Colour Forms: All colours are acceptable except the typical Siamese-pointed coat pattern. The list of colours already developed has grown and grown. To simplify it, the colours are grouped into convenient categories.

GCCF: ORIENTAL SELF: Havana (= Brown); Lilac; Foreign White (the only colour form still using its older title of 'Foreign'); Black; Blue; Red; Cream; Cinnamon; Caramel; Fawn.

ORIENTAL TORTIE: Black; Blue; Chocolate; Lilac; Cinnamon; Caramel; Fawn.

ORIENTAL SMOKE: Black; Blue; Chocolate; Lilac; Red; Tortie; Cream; Blue Tortie; Chocolate Tortie; Lilac Tortie; Cinnamon; Cinnamon Tortie; Caramel; Caramel Tortie; Fawn; Fawn Tortie.

ORIENTAL SHADED: Black; Blue; Chocolate; Lilac; Red; Tortie; Cream; Blue Tortie; Chocolate Tortie; Lilac Tortie; Cinnamon; Cinnamon Tortie; Caramel; Caramel Tortie; Fawn; Fawn Tortie; Black Silver; Blue Silver; Chocolate Silver; Lilac Silver; Red Silver; Tortie Silver; Cream Silver; Blue Tortie Silver; Chocolate Tortie Silver; Lilac Tortie Silver; Cinnamon Silver; Cinnamon Tortie Silver; Caramel Silver; Caramel Tortie Silver; Fawn Silver; Fawn Tortie Silver.

SPOTTED TABBY: Brown; Blue, Chocolate; Lilac; Red; Tortie; Cream; Blue Tortie; Chocolate Tortie; Lilac Tortie; Cinnamon; Cinnamon Tortie; Caramel; Caramel Tortie; Fawn; Fawn Tortie; Black Silver; Blue Silver; Chocolate Silver; Lilac Silver; Red Silver; Tortie Silver; Cream Silver; Blue Tortie Silver; Chocolate Tortie Silver; Lilac Tortie Silver; Cinnamon Silver; Cinnamon Tortie Silver; Caramel Silver; Caramel Tortie Silver; Fawn Silver; Fawn Tortie Silver.

CLASSIC TABBY: (as for Spotted Tabby)

MACKEREL TABBY: (as for Spotted Tabby)

TICKED TABBY: (as for Spotted Tabby)

CFA: SOLID: Blue; Chestnut; Cinnamon; Cream; Ebony; Fawn; Lavender; Red; White.

SHADED: Blue Silver; Chestnut Silver; Cinnamon Silver; Cream Silver; Ebony Silver; Fawn Silver; Lavender Silver; Parti-color Silver; Red Silver.

SMOKE: Blue Smoke; Cameo Smoke; Chestnut Smoke; Cinnamon Smoke; Dilute Cameo Smoke; Ebony Smoke; Fawn Smoke; Lavender Smoke; Parti-color Smoke.

TABBY: Classic Tabby Pattern; Mackerel Tabby Pattern; Spotted Tabby Pattern; Ticked Tabby Pattern; Patched Tabby Pattern; Blue Silver Tabby; Blue Tabby; Cameo Tabby; Dilute Cameo Tabby; Cinnamon Silver Tabby; Cinnamon Tabby; Chestnut Silver Tabby; Chestnut Tabby; Cream Tabby; Ebony Tabby; Fawn Tabby; Fawn Silver Tabby; Lavender Silver Tabby; Lavender Tabby; Red Tabby; Ebony Silver; Tabby.

PARTI-COLOR: Blue-Cream; Cinnamon Tortie; Chestnut Tortie; Fawn-Cream; Lavender-Cream; Ebony Tortie.

Breed Clubs:

Foreign White Cat Society. Address: 17 George Street, Bletchley, Bucks., MK2 2NR, England.

Oriental Cat Association. Publishes a *Yearbook* and a series of pamphlets on various colour forms. Address: 3 Ownstead Gardens, Sanderstead, South Croydon, Surrey, CR2 OHH, England.

Oriental Shorthair Breed Council. Publishes a *Newsletter.* Address: P.O. Box 250066, West Bloomfield, MI 48325-0066, USA.

NOTE: There is also a breed publication, *Tailes of the Orient.* Address: 7828 Citadel Drive, Severn, MD 21144, USA.

29

TONKINESE CAT

The Tonkinese is a short-haired American hybrid created by crossing Siamese and Burmese. In its early days it was referred to as the Golden Siamese, and this name was used in print as recently as 1961. Its present name has sometimes been incorrectly spelled Tonkanese. It was christened the Tonkinese after the Gulf of Tonkin which, like the cat itself, is close to Burmese and Siamese (Thai) territories, but does not belong to either of them. Among owners they have the nickname of 'Tonks'. In France it is called the *Tonkinois;* in Germany the *Tonkinesen;* and in Holland the *Tonkanees.*

Appearance: Intermediate between Siamese and Burmese, with dark Siamese points, but a body colour that has a richer hue than that of the typical Siamese. The body shape is also intermediate, lacking the exaggerated elongation of the Siamese.

History: In the 1950s the American feline expert Milan Greer began a breeding programme to create what he called the Golden Siamese. He did this initially by crossing a male Burmese with a female Chocolate-point Siamese. At his specialist cat centre called *Fabulous Felines* he continued to develop the breed through five generations.

When Milan Greer was satisfied that the breed was secure, he passed the baton on to other breeders. Edith Lux was one of these and it was she who decided to change the name from Golden Siamese to Tonkinese.

Summing up the breed, Milan Greer commented: 'It has the better traits of both the Siamese and the Burmese. It is a perfect combination of brains and beauty . . . After developing this breed I discovered that I had created a prodigy in fur.'

Later, in the 1960s, Canadian breeders, especially Margaret Conroy, took a special interest in the breed and helped to gain recognition for it. In 1965 she was the first to register a Tonkinese with a cat club – the Canadian Cat Association. So great was her contribution that some authors incorrectly refer to the Tonkinese as a Canadian breed.

Most of the American societies soon accepted the breed. Before long there was a Tonkinese Breed Club of USA, Canada and Australia to promote this appealing cat, based in the United States at Gillette, New Jersey. By the 1990s it was accepted by all of the North American cat societies. In 1991 it was recognized by the GCCF in Britain.

As regards the breeding of this cat, if a Burmese is crossed with a Siamese all the kittens are Tonkinese. If a Tonkinese is mated to another Tonkinese, then half the kittens are Tonkinese,

THE TONKINESE, first developed as a breed in the United States during the 1950s, was initially referred to as the Golden Siamese. It was created from crosses between Siamese and Burmese.

a quarter are Burmese and a quarter are Siamese. It was for this reason that some feline authorities refused to accept it as a true breed.

Historically, it is interesting that the first Burmese Cat to arrive in America – a female called Wong Mau, who arrived in the United States in the early 1930s – was not, in fact, a pure-bred animal, being part Siamese. This means that the Burmese Cat who founded the modern Burmese breed was, in reality, what we would today call a Tonkinese, the very first one ever seen in North America. (For details see Burmese Cat.)

Personality: Terms used to describe this breed include: inquisitive, exceptionally intelligent, condescending, witty, wilful, clever, loyal, loving, mischievous, clownish, active, sociable, gregarious, outgoing, lively and affectionate.

Supporters of the breed claim that it has the good qualities of both parent breeds, but none of their bad qualities.

Colour Forms: It appears in a variety of colours. In America these colours have been given exotic names (see next page).

GCCF: Brown; Blue; Chocolate; Lilac; Red; Cream; Brown Tortie; Blue Tortie; Chocolate Tortie; Lilac Tortie; Brown Tabby; Blue Tabby; Chocolate Tabby; Lilac Tabby; Red Tabby; Cream Tabby; Brown Tortie Tabby; Blue Tortie Tabby; Chocolate Tortie Tabby; Lilac Tortie Tabby.

CFA: Natural Mink (warm brown with dark brown points); Champagne Mink (beige or buff-cream with medium brown points); Blue Mink (soft, blue-grey with darker, slate-blue points); Platinum Mink (pale silvery-grey with darker grey points). An additional colour is sometimes recognized: Honey Mink (ruddy brown with darker brown points).

Breed Clubs:

Tonkinese Breed Association. Address: 2462 Primrose Avenue, Vista, CA 92083, USA.

Tonkinese Breed Association UK. Address: 2 Rose Walk, Seaford, East Sussex, BN25 3DH, England.

Tonkinese Breed Club. This club issues a magazine, *Tonkinfo.* Address: Lansdale, 12 Robin Hood Lane, Winnersh, Wokingham, Berks, RG41 5LX, England.

Tonkinese Cat Club. This club issues a *Tonkinews* journal. Address: 2 Rose Walk, Seaford, East Sussex, BN25 3DH, England.

NOTE: There is also a breed publication called *Aqua Eye.* Address: P.O. Box 115, Sunland, CA 01041, USA.

ONE OF THE MANY new colour forms of the Tonkinese Cat. This particular combination of pale, blue-grey body with slate blue points is known in North America as the Blue Mink and in Europe simply as the Blue.

30

CORNISH REX CAT

Appeared in 1950 in the county of Cornwall, England. Originally called the 'English Rex', until a second form of Rex Cat was discovered in nearby Devon. Sometimes referred to in the popular press as the 'Poodle Cat' or 'Coodle'. (This is not to be confused with the new type of Rex Cat from Germany also known as the Poodle Cat – see Non-recognized Breeds.)

Appearance. A short-coated, wavy-furred cat with curly whiskers and eyebrows. Slim-bodied, with long, slender legs, the hind legs being taller than the front ones. The head is wedge-shaped and the ears large and pointed. The tail is long, fine and tapering.

In a typical feline coat there are three main kinds of hairs: guard hairs, awn hairs and down hairs; the guard hairs and awn hairs are together called the 'top-coat', and the down hairs are referred to as the 'undercoat'. It is generally stated that in the Cornish Rex Cat there are no guard hairs and that the coat is almost entirely made up of down hairs. This is not strictly true. Microscopic analysis of Rex hairs reveals that the awn hairs are present but greatly reduced, so that they are almost like down hairs. In fact, all the hairs, even the down hairs, are reduced in length by the Cornish Rex gene, giving the Rex Cat a coat that is about half the thickness of that on a typical cat. The fur is also much finer, each hair being about 60 per cent the typical thickness. This delicate coat falls into ripples or waves that give the animal its unique appearance.

Unusual Features: Because the thin coat lacks guard hairs, this breed suffers from exposure to extreme cold or heat. A feral Rex Cat would therefore be at a disadvantage in many climates. As with most thinly protected or naked species, the Rex Cat has a slightly higher body temperature than normal – one degree higher than typical breeds of domestic cat. Its metabolism is also higher, giving it a much bigger appetite. If its coat is brushed too vigorously, bald patches may appear. Generally speaking, this is a delicate cat that requires more careful attention than a typical breed. As a breed, it has one special advantage – namely, that it is less likely to cause allergic responses in people who are sensitive to normal cat hair.

This breed typically has a strange body posture, with the back arched and the underside 'tucked up'. Associated with this posture is a remarkable leaping ability, even from a stationary starting position.

History: The first Cornish Rex Cat was born in an old farmhouse on Bodmin Moor in Cornwall on 21st July 1950. A red tabby male in a litter of five kittens, born to an ordinary farm cat called

'Serena', was observed to have an unusual, curly coat. The owner, a Mrs Nina Ennismore, kept this kitten and, on the advice of a geneticist, mated it back to its mother, a tortoiseshell.

The new litter contained two curly-coated kittens and one plain-coated one. A second back-cross produced further curly-coated kittens, and the new breed was established.

Mrs Ennismore had, in the past, bred Rex Rabbits and decided to name this new feline mutation after the rabbit breed. The comparison is not particularly accurate. The first Rex Rabbit appeared as a mutation in France in 1919. It was given the name of Castorrex, meaning 'King of the Beavers', but this was eventually abbreviated simply to 'Rex'. The special quality of its coat was that it was 'heavily plushed and velvety' and lacking in guard hairs. If the dense, even coat showed any signs of being wavy or curly it was considered faulty. This is where the comparison with Rex Cats falls down, since for them a closely curled coat is an essential characteristic. A more correct term would have been 'Astrex' – the name given to another breed of rabbit, introduced in 1932, in which the fur is tightly waved. Despite this, the name Rex has survived and become generally accepted.

The first male Cornish Rex Cat, the founding father of the breed, was named 'Kallibunker'. He sired two litters, and then his son 'Poldhu' continued to act as a stud and produced several more litters by being mated to his female relatives.

Rather surprisingly, Kallibunker was put to sleep by his owner as part of an economy drive to reduce her growing cat population which, by 1956, had grown to 40 individuals. Mrs Ennismore, disillusioned at the lack of appreciation for her new breed, and short of funds to support her large feline family, had most of them destroyed, including both Serena and Kallibunker, a sad end for these historic felines. She did however, keep enough of the Rex cats to enable the breed to continue.

One of 'Poldhu's' daughters, called 'Lamorna Cove' was exported to America. She was already pregnant, having been back-crossed to her father, 'Poldhu', before leaving Cornwall. Arriving at San Diego in 1957, she produced a litter of four Rex kittens and established the breed in the United States.

Because the very first Cornish Rex Cats reputedly lacked stamina, careful outbreeding with a variety of non-Rex queens was undertaken to strengthen the breed. This was done using one of Kallibunker's sons, 'Champagne Charlie', and Burmese, Siamese, Russian Blue and British Shorthairs. This out-breeding reduced the number of Rex kittens in litters to one in four, but considerably improved the stock. It also added the possibility of a wider variety of colour forms.

The Cornish Rex Cat was eventually given official recognition, by the CFA in America in 1964, and by the GCCF in Britain in 1967.

The question has been asked as to why such a slender, elongated breed should be found living on a farm in southern England. Because of the climate, with its long, cold, wet winters, British feral cats tend to be of the stockier, heavy-bodied type. The Cornish Rex looks much more suited to a hot, dry climate, and it has been suggested that Kallibunker's ancestors may have arrived in Cornwall from North Africa or the Middle East, brought there in ancient times by Phoenician traders visiting the famous local tin mines. There is no proof of this, but it would certainly explain the rangy, skinny body of this remarkable breed.

THE CORNISH REX CAT *(opposite)*, first discovered in England in 1950. This Red Smoke example clearly shows the typical wavy coat and the elongated body of this unusual breed.

THE LILAC COLOUR FORM of the Cornish Rex Cat. All coat colours and patterns are acceptable in this breed.

Personality: Terms that have been used to describe this breed include: individualistic, playful, extrovert, intelligent, inquisitive, affectionate, spirited, sweet-tempered, gentle and friendly. It has been called 'the greyhound of the cat fancy'.

Related Breeds: The Cornish Rex is closely related to the German Rex. They share the same gene for curly-coat. The Devon Rex, despite its close geographical proximity to the Cornish Rex, has a different curly-coat gene.

Colour Forms:

GCCF: All coat colours, patterns and combinations of colours and patterns are acceptable in this breed.

CFA: Also accepts all colour and patterns, but specifies the following: White; Black; Blue; Red; Cream; Chinchilla Silver; Shaded Silver; Black Smoke; Blue Smoke; Classic Tabby Pattern; Mackerel Tabby Pattern; Patched Tabby Pattern; Brown Patched Tabby; Blue Patched Tabby; Silver Patched Tabby; Silver Tabby; Red Tabby; Brown Tabby; Blue Tabby; Cream Tabby; Tortoiseshell; Calico; Van Calico; Dilute Calico; Blue-Cream; Van Blue-Cream and White; Bi-color; Van Bi-color.

Breed Clubs:

Cornish Rex Society. Address: 720 Fisherville Road, Fisherville, KY 40023, USA.

Rex Breeders United. Address: 446 Itasca Ct. N.W., Rochester, MN 55901, USA.

ITALIAN REX CAT

First discovered in Italy in 1950, this wavy-haired cat was clearly carrying the Rex gene, but was not used for a serious breeding programme and seems to have vanished in one generation.

32

HAVANA (BROWN) CAT

Sometimes referred to simply as the Havana. Despite its title, this breed did not originate in Cuba. It is in reality an all-brown cat created in England in 1952. There are two theories as to how it acquired its name. One suggests that it was inspired by the colour of Havana Cigars, and the other that it was borrowed from the Rabbit Fancy, where there is a Havana breed with the same coat colour. However, even if the second theory is correct, it does not invalidate the first, because the Havana Rabbit itself was named after the 'Havana Brown' colour of Cuban cigars.

After a few years (in the late 1950s) it was decided to rename the breed. This was done, against the breeders' wishes, because it was feared that the name 'Havana' might give the false impression that this home-grown British breed had originated in the West Indies. Its new name was to be more mundane: the Chestnut Brown. It was exhibited in England under the full title of Chestnut Brown Foreign Shorthair until about 1970, but then, owing to popular demand, the original name resurfaced and has been used ever since.

There were a number of precursors for the breed which failed to survive: the Swiss Mountain Cat (an all-brown Siamese first shown in 1894 but soon forgotten) and the Brown Cat (shown in 1930).

Two discarded names for the breed were the Berkshire Brown and the Reading Brown. They were suggested because of the geographical location of the 1952 foundation stock, Reading in Berkshire, but were soon rejected in favour of Havana. Another rejected name used in the early days of the breed was Oriental Chocolate Cat.

Appearance: In Britain, because of repeated back-crossings to Siamese, this cat is now essentially an all-brown Siamese. In the United States, Canada and Japan, however, crossings with Siamese were outlawed and there, as a result, the breed has a slightly different, less Oriental build, closer to its original 1950s shape, with a rounder face and a shorter nose.

History: The Havana was the unexpected result of a mating between a Seal Point Siamese male called Tombee and a black short-haired female (which was half Seal Point Siamese and half

THE ELEGANT HAVANA BROWN CAT *(opposite).* Because it was developed in England rather than Cuba, a committee decided to alter its name to Chestnut Brown Foreign Shorthair, a title that only a committee could love. By popular demand this was later abandoned and Havana reinstated.

Black Persian) called Susannah. One of the kittens resulting from this cross was a Self-Brown male which was named 'Elmtower Bronze Idol'. This was the first Havana Cat, born on 24th October 1952. He was soon joined by a female, 'Elmtower Brown Study', resulting from a further mating between the Siamese stud and the black cat.

This foundation stock was created by Mrs Munro-Smith of Reading in Berkshire, although she had, in fact, been trying to obtain something quite different – namely, a Colourpoint Persian. The Havana Brown was merely a lucky accident, but she was quick to realize its value.

The Havana was first exhibited in Britain in 1953 and was given championship status in 1958.

In 1956 a pair of kittens, a male called Laurentide Brown Pilgrim and a female called Roofspringer Mahogany, were exported to a Californian breeder in the United States and became the foundation stock for the breed in North America. The Havana was given official recognition there as early as 1959.

Personality: Terms used to describe this breed include: intelligent, active, affectionate, lively, considerate, playful, mischievous, lordly, home-loving and outgoing. Because of the stronger Siamese element in the British Havana, it is more vocal than its American counterpart.

Colour Form: A rich, warm, chestnut brown. No variant colours are allowed.

Breed Clubs:

Havana and Oriental Lilac Cat Club. Address: Talisker Cottage, Tadwick, Near Bath, BA1 8AH, England.

Havana Brown Fanciers. Address: 2250 24th Street, Apt. 129, San Francisco, CA 94107, USA.

Havana (Brown) Preservation Society. Address: 40 Clinton Street, Brooklyn Heights, NY 11201, USA.

Havana, Foreign and Oriental Cat Association. Address: 26 Lethe Grove, Colchester, Essex, CO2 8RG, England.

International Havana Brown Society. Publishes a magazine, *Havana Happenings.* Address: 185 Bridgeside Circle, Danville, CA 94506-4452, USA.

33

EGYPTIAN MAU

A cat with spots or very short stripes that looks like the domesticated felines depicted in the art of ancient Egypt. There are two forms, one artificially created and the other a natural breed taken from the streets of modern Egypt.

Appearance: The artificial form of this breed has the build and personality of a Siamese, but with a tabby coat. The natural form of this breed has a rounder head and a less exaggerated, more muscular body.

History: The Egyptian Mau has two distinct origins that must be considered separately, as they relate to the two forms of Egyptian Mau:

1 In the 1960s a British breeder, Angela Sayer, decided to initiate a programme that would re-create the cat of the ancient Pharaohs. The appearance of the domesticated Egyptian cat was well known from wall paintings dating from the second millennium BC. It was shown as a long-legged, slender-bodied, big-eared animal with a coat covered in markings that were intermediate between stripes and spots. Each mark was a dash, or very short stripe, and these were sometimes shown, not only on the body but also on the legs, the tail and even the ears. In some cases, these short stripes were reduced to spots and in other cases they were elongated to create full striping, but these two extremes were the exceptions. The common form was always the 'dash' or abbreviated stripe.

To sum up, this ancient Egyptian cat looks to us today rather like a mackerel-tabby Siamese, and it was this type that Angela Sayer was seeking to reconstitute. The idea arose when, during a programme designed to produce a Tabby-pointed Siamese, certain individuals appeared with all-over short stripes. They were rejected from the programme, but Mrs Sayer decided to take one of them, a female called Panchusan Zerina, and use her as the foundation queen for her new project. Using back-crosses with Siamese and Havanas, she aimed to complete her Egyptian programme by the early 1970s.

At an earlier date, a second, quite separate attempt had been made to re-create the Egyptian cat, and this was eventually to overshadow the Sayer project. The name 'Egyptian Mau' was kept for the cat developed from this other line, and Sayer's cat became known by the less romantic title of 'Oriental Spotted Tabby'. (In some countries it is called the 'Oriental Shorthair Tabby' or the 'Spotted Oriental'.)

2 In 1953, a Russian expatriate, Princess Natalie Troubetskoy, who was living in Rome, became fascinated by a pair of spotted cats belonging to the Egyptian Ambassador to Italy. These cats, a silver female and a smoke male, were being kept not for breeding, but as mascots. The female was, in fact, spayed, so breeding was out of the question. With the help of the Ambassador, she did, however, manage to acquire a similar one from Cairo, a silver female kitten called Baba. When Baba was successfully mated with the Ambassador's male cat, Geppo, two bronze-coloured male kittens were obtained, called Jude and Joseph. Jude died, but Joseph, nicknamed Jo-Jo, was mated back to its mother to produce a female kitten called Lisa. Baba, Jo-Jo and Lisa were the first ever Egyptian Maus to be exhibited. This happened in Rome at the International Cat Show in 1955. Late in December 1956 the Princess left Italy to live in the United States and took her three cats with her. These were to form the basis of the breed in America. In 1957, Lisa was the first Mau to be shown there (at the Empire Cat Show) and quickly attracted the attention of other breeders. By 1968 the breed had gained Championship status with the CFF. Other cat organizations were soon to follow. By 1978, this line of Egyptian Maus finally arrived in Britain.

In the United States a special organization has been formed to promote this breed, called the Egyptian Mau Breeders and Fanciers Association.

Regarding the name of the cat, it should be mentioned that Princess Troubetskoy stated that she preferred the title 'Egyptian Cat' for this breed because the word Mau simply means 'cat' in Egyptian and should be translated as such. She was ignored, probably because the name had become so widely accepted, but it is worth pointing out that to call this breed by the full name of the Egyptian Mau Cat is an error, because this is, in effect, to call it the Egyptian Cat Cat.

Comparing the cats from these two lines – the British and the Italian – it is clear that there are slight differences. The British line is a colour variant of the Oriental Shorthair – effectively a Siamese with fine spotted-tabby markings, whereas the Italian line is closer to a spotted Abyssinian. Strangely, it is the artificial British breed that looks more like the ancient Egyptian cat in early wall paintings. The Italian breed, which is descended from Cairo alley cats, which were presumably themselves directly descended from the cats of the Pharaohs, is ironically slightly less convincing, being almost too elegant and too perfectly spotted.

Several authors make reference to a possible additional source for Egyptian Maus. They report that the first ones to reach America were a pair called Gepa and Ludol, and that they arrived there in 1953. If correct, this would put them three years ahead of the arrival of the Troubetskoy cats, but it seems more likely to be an error, with 'Gepa' being a garbled version of the original male 'Geppo'. Writing in 1995, American breeder Len Davidson mentions that further examples of Maus were later imported into the United States and were used to enlarge the gene pool of the breed. He comments: 'Traditionally, obtaining more Maus from Egypt has been nearly impossible. It was not until the early 1980s, when Cathie Rowan exported 13 beautiful cats, that additional Egyptian Maus were brought to the United States . . . Because no other allowable out-crosses exist, these efforts helped save the breed. In 1991 I brought four more Maus into the United States.'

Personality: Terms used to describe this breed include: good-tempered, calm, hardy, shy, agile, healthy, robust, reserved, quiet, good-tempered, loyal, affectionate, active, intelligent and with good memories. It is claimed that they can be walked on a collar and lead. Originally they were said to be unpredictable, aloof, excitable, fiery and wild, but after generations of selective breeding their temperament has clearly improved.

THE EGYPTIAN MAU, a spotted breed which has been selected to look like the domesticated feline of the Ancient Pharaohs. The word 'Mau' is Egyptian for 'Cat'.

Colour Forms:

GCCF: (Accepts the British version under the title Oriental Spotted Tabby. See under Oriental Shorthair for colour details.)

CFA: Silver (with charcoal markings); Bronze (with dark brown markings); Smoke (with jet black markings).

Breed Club:

National Egyptian Mau Club. Address: 52 Gregory Road, Framingham, MA 01701, USA.

JAPANESE BOBTAIL LONGHAIR CAT

In 1954 the Japanese began to develop a long-haired version of the Japanese Bobtail as a distinct breed. Previously, long-haired specimens had been frequently seen as street cats in the northern provinces, but had been ignored as undesirable oddities by the pedigree cat world. Then it was decided to isolate and pure-breed them and they soon gained a considerable following.

In America, they were accepted as a separate breed by TICA in 1991 and at the same time the standards for the ordinary, short-haired Bobtail were slightly revised.

THE JAPANESE BOBTAIL LONGHAIR CAT is an offshoot of the ancient breed and has only been taken seriously in the second half of the 20th century.

BOMBAY CAT

This American breed was called the Bombay because its intensely black coat is reminiscent of that of an Indian Black Leopard. It has been described as a 'Black Burmese', a 'mini-panther' or 'the patent-leather kid with new-penny eyes'.

Appearance: A compact, muscular black cat with a sheen to its very short, satin-like coat. It has large, golden eyes and wide-set ears on its rounded head.

History: The breed was deliberately created in Kentucky in 1958 by Nikki Horner, who crossed

THE BOMBAY CAT, a domestic breed developed in America in the late 1950s, is essentially a jet black Burmese. The aim of its creator was to produce a sleek, mini-panther.

sable Burmese with black American Shorthairs. Her aim was create 'a copper-eyed mini-panther with patent-leather fur' by combining the black colour of the Shorthair with the coat sheen of the Burmese. The Bombay achieved championship status in the United States in 1976, but is still fairly rare outside America. Some breeding had occurred in Britain, using British-type Burmese and black British Shorthair Cats. Because of slight differences between the American and British parental stock, the resultant Bombays are also slightly different from one another.

Personality: Terms used to describe this breed include: assertive, confident, gentle, vocal but soft-voiced, intelligent, sensitive, active, inquisitive, playful, patient and unusually friendly.

Colour Forms: Black is the only colour permitted in this breed.

Breed Clubs:

The Bombay Connection. Address: 200 Raintree Trail, Lafayette, LA 70507, USA.

International Bombay Society. Address: 5782 Dalton Drive, Farmington, NY 14425, USA.

36

CALIFORNIA REX CAT

First discovered in California in 1959, the California Rex is better known as the Marcel Cat.

Appearance: This cat has the wavy-haired coat of the typical Rex Cat, but with longer fur, giving it the look of 'marcel-waving', hence its alternative name.

History: Mrs F. Blancheri discovered two wavy-haired cats in a San Bernadino animal shelter, a female called 'Mystery Lady of Rodell', who was an odd-eyed tortoiseshell, and her son, who was a red tabby. They were acquired by Bob and Dell Smith who, on seeing that their curly coats were longer and silkier than those of typical Rex Cats, decided to give them a distinctive name – 'The Marcel Cat'. When the Smiths mated Mystery Lady with her son, the result was an even longer-coated offspring, a red tabby female. These were found to be genetically compatible with the Cornish Rex. They were later used in crossing experiments with shorthaired Rex Cats, but there seems to have been a general lack of interest in the breed in its own right.

OREGON REX CAT

First appeared in 1959 in the USA. It is one of five recorded American Rex Cat strains, the others being the Ohio Rex, California Rex, Selkirk Rex and Missouri Rex.

History: In 1959 Mrs M. Stringham of Warrenton, Oregon, a well known cat-breeder, found a wavy-haired black-and-white female kitten among an otherwise normal-haired litter, from a normal-haired tortoiseshell queen. This solitary Rex kitten was named 'Kinky Marcella' and became the founding female of a new strain of Rex Cats.

Crosses between this breed and the better known Cornish Rex and Devon Rex have produced only straight-haired kittens, revealing that the Oregon Rex gene is distinct from both. It has therefore been assigned a separate gene symbol: 'ro'.

According to one authority, this breed was first discovered in 1944, but died out because of wartime preoccupations.

AMERICAN BOBTAIL CAT

A short-tailed cat, similar to a Stumpy Manx. It should not be confused with the wild species, the American Bobcat *(Lynx rufus)*.

Appearance: The American Bobtail is a stocky, long-haired cat with an abbreviated tail. The double coat appears in two lengths: long and medium. The head is broad and rounded with wide ears and large eyes. The tail may be straight or slightly curled and is always well-haired. (This description is for Type 2 below.)

History: There appear to be several distinct origins for this breed. To put it another way, there seem to be at least three different breeds using this same name. They are as follows:

1 Writing in 1940, American zoologist Ida Mellen comments: 'The American domestic Bobtail Cat of the New England and Middle Atlantic States (called the Rabbit Cat) traces its ancestry to the Manx Cat, but the distribution of tailless cats is wide, covering the Crimea and other Parts of Russia, Japan, China, the Bismarck Archipelago, the Malayan Archipelago, Burma and Siam . . .' Nothing more seems to be known about this version of the American Bobtail.

2 A completely different source is given for the cat that is now widely recognized in pedigree circles as the true American Bobtail. The 'founding father' of this breed was a homeless male tabby kitten seen near an Indian Reservation in Arizona in the 1960s. A holidaying couple, John and Brenda Sanders, adopted him, christened him Yodie and took him home with them to Iowa. There, he eventually mated with their Siamese Cat, Mishi, producing a litter, some of which were short-tailed. One of these kittens grew up to mate with a 'cream point and white cat'. The kittens in this new litter were all short-tailed and they attracted the attention of Mindy Schultz, a friend of the Sanders family, who, in the 1970s, designated them as a new breed which she called the American Bobtail.

At first, these Bobtails had short coats, but when crossed with Himalayans, they produced thick-coated kittens. These kittens were to become the foundation stock of the breed.

Certain other crossing experiments resulted in completely tailless kittens, suggesting that the American Bobtail gene is similar to the Manx gene, which also gives rise to tails of varying length, from the Rumpy (no-tail) to the Stumpy (short-tail) to the long-tail.

3 One author has recently claimed that there is another distinct form of American Bobtail in existence. This one is supposed to be the result of crosses between domestic cats and wild

THE AMERICAN BOBTAIL CAT, a domestic breed with an abbreviated tail. It is generally accepted that it was first discovered near an Indian reservation in Arizona in the 1960s, but there are rival theories concerning its origin.

Bobcats that occurred in the late 1970s. Writing in 1992, Amy Shojai comments that 'Rose Estes has been breeding Bobtails for fourteen years . . . According to Rose, wild Bobcats interbreed most often with Siamese because the scent of the Siamese in season closely resembles the smell of the female Bobcat.'

Bearing in mind that the wild Bobcat belongs to a different genus *(Lynx)* from the domestic cat *(Felis)*, and is nearly twice as big, the idea that the two species would interbreed seems far-fetched, to say the least. However, before rejecting it out of hand, it is worth noting that Stanley Young, in his detailed study of the wild Bobtail published in 1958, had this to say about hybridization:

'There is evidence of a successful mating between a male Bobcat and a domestic cat at Sandy Creek, Texas during 1949. The offspring were observed by several persons in the area.' He also mentions a similar incident that occurred in 1954 in South Dakota. There, a black female domestic cat mated with a wild male Bobcat and in early June produced seven kittens. Three of the litter 'had bobtails, large feet, tufted ears, and were light grey in color with a speckling of black dots on the stomach, legs and sides. The ears were larger and hard and stiff. The tufts on them . . . were up to approximately a quarter of an inch [6mm] in length. This litter of kittens lived until 27th June 1954, when they were killed by a domestic tomcat.' It is impossible to tell whether these hybrid kittens would have been fertile or sterile when they became mature, but this report certainly makes the Rose Estes American Bobtails that were reported by Amy Shojai seem a little less unlikely.

It would seem from this that both the abbreviated tail and the name to go with it have cropped up more than once in the United States during the 20th century. Lisa Black, writing about the Bobtail in 1994, confirms this, commenting: 'Many other reports exist of this type of cat being produced.' For the time being, however, we must accept Type 2 above as the 'official' American Bobtail for show purposes.

Personality: Terms used to describe this breed (Type 2) include: friendly, patient, calm, watchful, intelligent, mischievous and good-natured. Inevitably, because of their lack of a balancing tail, they are not particularly fond of climbing. Vocally, they are described as having 'a scratchy little rambling voice which makes some people ask, "When will they learn how to meow?"'. They are said to be more doglike than other cat breeds.

Colour Forms: All colours are acceptable in this breed.

39

BRITISH ANGORA CAT

In the 1960s some British breeders decided to re-create the elegant Angora Cat. It had been immensely popular in Victorian times, but was soon to be eclipsed by the even more exotic Persian. By the early part of the 20th century the original Angora had virtually vanished in the West. A nostalgic desire for its return prompted certain breeders to reconstitute it by careful

THE BRITISH ANGORA CAT is the product of a 1960s breeding programme that set out to
reconstitute the traditional Angora Cat. Careful selection re-created the elegant Angora coat, but
the body-shape is more angular and elongated than the original.

selective breeding from suitable long-haired Oriental cats. The soft coat and the bushy tail were
successfully obtained, but the bone structure proved more difficult. The angular head typical of
the Oriental remained as a reminder that this new British Angora was a copy of the true Angora
and not the original.

Since then, the original breed has been rediscovered in its Turkish homeland and once again
brought to the West for development as a pedigree cat. This has led to some confusion, because
there are now two Angoras, with very different origins. Misunderstandings are avoided by
calling the new imports 'Turkish Angoras' and the re-created ones 'British Angoras'. (For further
details see Angora Cat.)

40

CYMRIC CAT

The long-haired version of the Manx Cat. The name (pronounced kim-rick) is taken from the Celtic word for Wales (Cymru) and was given to the breed because Wales is close to the Isle of Man, just as the Cymric Cat is close to the Manx Cat. Some cat societies do not use the breed's Welsh name, however, preferring to call it simply the Longhair Manx.

THE CYMRIC CAT *(above and opposite)*, the long-haired version of the short-haired, tailless Manx Cat. It was first developed in Canada in the 1960s, although long-haired examples of the Manx had appeared occasionally before.

Appearance: Exactly like the Manx Cat in every way except for the coat, which is long and thick. The woolly undercoat is even thicker than the outer coat. The texture of the fur has been compared with that of the Norwegian Forest Cat.

History: Long-haired kittens had been born to Manx Cat mothers on the Isle of Man on many occasions, but had always been discarded as unwanted variants. Then, in the mid-1960s, similar kittens born in Canada were treated with greater respect. They were carefully kept and developed as a separate breed. The driving force behind this project was Canadian cat breeder Althea Frahm, who first exhibited the cats as 'Manx Mutants', before they were given their own breed name. In 1976 a special group was formed to promote the breed, called the 'United Cymric Association'.

The earliest records that can be found for the showing of this breed are those from the American Cat Association (ACA), dating from late 1963.

Critics of the Cymric have suggested that it resulted from crosses between Manx Cats and Persians or Maine Coons, but there is no evidence to support this. Indeed, had these longhairs been involved in the cat's ancestry they would undoubtedly have altered its Manx conformation.

Personality: Similar to the Manx Cat. Confident, playful, intelligent, docile, friendly, alert, observant and relaxed. A good indoor cat.

Colour Forms: All colours are acceptable, though some authorities reject colour-point patterns.

41

JAVANESE CAT

A long-haired version of the Siamese Cat, closely related to the Balinese Cat. The definition of the Javanese is confusing, to say the least. The name has different meanings in different regions:

1 In the United States, long-haired Siamese Cats are called Balinese if they show one of the four basic Siamese colourpoint patterns (Seal, Chocolate, Blue, or Lilac) and Javanese if they show any other colour pattern. (Some American cat societies do not make this distinction, however, calling them all Balinese.)
2 In New Zealand, long-haired Siamese Cats are called Balinese if they show any colourpoint pattern, and Javanese if they have spotted or self-coloured coats.
3 In Britain, long-haired Oriental cats, which were originally bred to re-create the Angora, are now known as Javanese.

Appearance: The elegant, angular, elongated body, the wedge-shaped head, the large ears and the blue eyes are all typically Siamese. The Javanese only differs from the Siamese in the possession of a long, silky coat. And it only differs from the Balinese in the colours of that coat.
History: In America those breeders who were concentrating on developing the Balinese breed in the 1960s found that, from time to time, kittens were born with unusual colour patterns. If these colours did not conform to the basic Siamese colours, they were not accepted as true Balinese. Instead of discarding them, they were placed into a new category, that of the Javanese.

In Britain in the 1960s and 1970s attempts were being made to re-create the Angora Cat, using long-haired variants of Oriental Shorthairs. In 1989 these artificially reconstituted Angoras were given a new name to avoid confusion with the true Turkish Angoras; the name chosen was Javanese, despite the fact that the American Javanese was already well known. Adding more confusion, some breeders referred to this British form of Javanese as the Cuckoo Cat and formed a breed club called 'The Cuckoo Cat Club'. (Cuckoo was the pet name given to one of the original cats involved in this breeding programme. He had been referred to as the 'cuckoo in the nest' because he was a long-haired cat of Oriental type at a cattery full of shorthaired cats. He was about to be neutered when he was spotted by American visitors who remarked on his similarity to the Turkish Angoras that were now being seen in the United States. As a result, Cuckoo was used in the attempt to re-create the Angora artificially in Britain.) Making matters

THE ELEGANT, elongated, Javanese Cat. There has been considerable confusion about precisely
what constitutes a Javanese, and the breed is treated differently in different countries. In essence,
it is a long-haired Siamese without colourpoints.

even more complicated, when Dutch breeders Ed and Helen van Kessel acquired a blue Angora,
ie, Javanese, from the English breeder Janet Pitman, they gave it a new breed name: Mandarin.
This name has since become popular in Germany where, judging by recent publications, it is
now preferred to Javanese.

Just as the Balinese Cat had never existed in Bali, so the Javanese Cat had never seen Java –
the name was merely an exotic-sounding Oriental location.

Personality: As for Siamese.

Colour Forms: Generally speaking, the American Javanese can appear in any colour seen in the
Colourpoint Shorthair. Colours listed by the Cat Fanciers' Association are as follows:

CFA: Red Point; Cream Point; Seal Lynx Point; Chocolate Lynx Point; Blue Lynx Point; Lilac Lynx
Point; Red Lynx Point; Chocolate-Tortie Lynx Point; Blue-Cream Lynx Point; Lilac-Cream Lynx
Point; Cream Lynx Point; Seal-Tortie Lynx Point; Seal-Tortie Point; Chocolate-Tortie Point; Blue-
Cream Point; Lilac-Cream Point.

Outside America, Javanese colours are related instead to those of the Oriental Shorthair.

42

RAGDOLL CAT

A controversial American breed that acquired its name because, when held, it goes limp and becomes completely relaxed and floppy, like a feline ragdoll.

Appearance: A large, long-haired cat similar to a Birman except for certain details of its colouring and its heavier body.

Legendary History: This cat is unique in that it is a recent breed with a legendary history. All other breeds that can boast a legendary beginning are ones which have an ancient origin 'lost in the mists of time', to quote a well-worn phrase. The Ragdoll myth can only be traced back to the early 1960s, when a pregnant white Persian-style cat called Josephine, belonging to Californian Ann Baker, was involved in a road accident. She broke her pelvis when struck by a car, and it was claimed that this injury resulted in her subsequent offspring being abnormally limp and having no reaction to physical pain. Genetically this was nonsensical, but the story was retold endlessly and was believed by the gullible. Ann Baker reinforced the myth when she tossed one of her Ragdolls across the room for television cameras. As a result, the breed became notorious overnight, and many cat organizations rejected it on the grounds that it was vulnerable to abuse. If the kittens showed no response to being hurt, they were clearly at risk. The legend – which appealed to the romantic and created a wide interest in the breed – also worked against it in the world of serious pedigree breeding.

Factual History: As far as can be ascertained, this breed resulted from a 1960s mating between the white 'Persian' female Josephine and a male Birman. There is a certain vagueness about this, however. Some authorities think that the female may have been more of an Angora than a Persian, and that a sable Burmese was also involved somewhere in the early stages of the making of the Ragdoll.

According to Ann Baker, two of Josephine's sons, called Blackie and Daddy Warbucks, which were sired by different males, are to be considered as the 'founding fathers' of the Ragdoll breed. The mitted Daddy Warbucks (the epitome of the Ragdoll breed) was mated with one of Blackie's daughters to produce the kittens that were to become the first 'official' Ragdolls, called Tiki and Kyoto.

The female Josephine may well have been involved in a road accident, but that event would have had no effect whatever on the genetic constitution of her offspring. The fact that they and subsequent generations were all remarkably relaxed when being handled can only be due to what might be called an intensifying of the 'docility factor' already present in the foundation stock. Both Persian and Birman breeds are well known for their gentleness and, by bringing these two breeds together, Ann Baker, the originator of the Ragdoll, accidentally created an abnormally mild-mannered cat.

There is, however, a great difference between a cat that is tolerant of manhandling and one that is unable to experience pain. In reality the Ragdoll is an attractive breed that is genetically sound and ideal for urban, indoor living. It is excessively good-natured and makes an ideal and undemanding companion. As soon as this was realized, its popularity soared and it was gradually accepted by more and more cat societies.

Californian cat breeders Denny Dayton and his wife were responsible for developing the breed and worked hard to acquire championship status for it, which they eventually succeeded in doing. In 1981, the Norwich cat breeder Lulu Rowley purchased four Ragdolls (called Prim, Proper, Lad and Lass) from the Dayton cattery and introduced the new breed to Britain, where its numbers have since increased rapidly. By the winter of 1995 there were an estimated 3,000 Ragdolls in the country.

In the 1990s, three variant breeds have been developed from the Ragdoll Cat: the Cherubim, the Honeybear and the Ragamuffin. The Ragamuffin is already making headway (see entry), but it remains to be seen whether the other two will eventually also gain official recognition.

Personality: This is the most docile of all cat breeds. Whatever its true genetic history may prove to be, it cannot be denied that the Ragdoll is the most relaxed, mild-mannered cat in the world. To its supporters this is extolled as a virtue of the breed, but to critics it is seen as the creation of a 'living soft toy', a 'cushion cat', the 'denigration of the spirit of the cat'.

It has been reported that Ann Baker does not consider the British Ragdolls to be true Ragdolls, because they are not sufficiently 'floppy'. According to her, the 'flop-factor', which was strong in her original stock, has been diluted in the British-bred animals. (Some authorities have voiced their opinion that this is an advantage rather than a shortcoming.)

Colour Forms:

GCCF: There are three basic pattern-types: Colourpoint, Mitted and Bi-colour, and four colours: Seal; Blue; Chocolate; Lilac. The three pattern types have been defined as follows: (1) Colourpoint: dark points on mask, ears, tail, legs, feet; (2) Mitted: dark points on mask, ears, tail, legs; feet are white; (3) Bi-colour: dark points on mask, ears, tail; legs and feet are white.

Breed Clubs:

British Ragdoll Cat Club. Address: 1 Glyn Way, Threemilestone, Truro, Cornwall, TR3 6DT, England.

International Ragdoll Cat Association (IRCA). Established by Ann Baker, with strict rules about the future breeding of the Ragdoll Cat.

National Ragdoll Cat Association. Address: 9 Tadmarton, Downhead Park, Milton Keynes, Bucks, MK15 9BE, England.

Progressive Ragdoll Breed Cat Club. Formed in 1993. Address: 85a Burrows Road, Kensal Green, London, NW10 5SJ, England.

THE RAGDOLL CAT *(opposite).* The example shown here is a Bi-colour while the one on page 152 is a Colourpoint Ragdoll. Intermediate between these two types is the Mitted.

THE RAGDOLL CAT, a controversial American breed developed in the 1960s. Essentially a mixture of Birman and Persian, it is famous for its extreme docility, which some critics fear may lead to its being treated as a 'living toy'.

Ragdoll Club. Formed in 1992; publishes a quarterly magazine, *The Ragbag*. Address: 38 Faraday Road, Beechdale Estate, Walsall, West Midlands, WS2 7ER, England.

Ragdoll Fanciers Club. Address: 7320 Normandy Drive N.E., Cedar Rapids, IA 52402, USA, or 15700 Riley Street, Holland, MI 49424, USA.

NOTE: There is also a breed publication called *Rag Sheet*. Address: 18977 48th Avenue, North Loxahatchee, FL 33470, USA.

43

SNOWSHOE CAT

A recent American short-haired breed with white 'snowshoe' feet, created by crossing a Siamese with a bi-coloured American Shorthair.

Appearance: The body of this cat is halfway between the long, lean and lanky Siamese and the short, stubby, stocky American Shorthair, presenting a well-balanced, elegant compromise. The key to its success, however, lies in the combination of the two contrasting colour patterns – the pointed pattern of the Siamese and the white spotting of the American Shorthair. In a well-marked individual this shows itself as a typical Siamese colouring with dark extremities, but with contrasting white patches on the face and feet. The ideal is for the white patches to lie symmetrically on the otherwise dark points. Breeder Pat Turner sums up the perfect Snowshoe markings as follows: 'The preferred pattern is that with white to the ankles in front, white to the hocks at the back and an inverted V on the face.'

History: As with a number of recent breeds, the Snowshoe began as an 'error'. White spotted individuals would turn up occasionally in Siamese breeding programmes and then be discarded. But in the 1960s an American breeder who specialized in Siamese, Dorothy Hinds-Daugherty of Philadelphia, decided to keep some of these strangely marked individuals and consider them as a new breed. There was strong opposition to this from the more traditional Siamese breeders, and for a while it looked as though the Snowshoe Cat would prove to be a non-starter. One breeder, Vikki Olander, persisted, however, and wrote the first breed standard for the Snowshoe. By 1977 she was almost alone in her support of the new breed and it was on the verge of dying out when she was contacted by another interested party, Jim Hoffman from Ohio. Together they began a serious campaign to support and develop the Snowshoe and by the mid-eighties had succeeded, with championship status attained at last.

The British breeder, Pat Turner, who encountered the Snowshoe when judging at an international cat show in New York in 1986, was later to form a British breed club to promote the breed in Europe. It is still comparatively rare, but its visual beauty and structural elegance will undoubtedly secure its future.

When it first appeared it was rumoured that the Snowshoe was merely a short-haired version of the Birman – the Sacred Cat of Burma – but this is not true. These two white-footed breeds have completely different, separate origins. Despite this, the Snowshoe has sometimes been incorrectly referred to as the 'Short-haired Birman'.

THE SNOWSHOE CAT is another American breed. First developed in the 1960s, it is based on crosses between Siamese and Bi-coloured American Shorthairs, giving it a Siamese pointed pattern, but with the addition of white feet.

Another name that was given to the breed at one stage of its development was the 'Silver Lace Cat', but it is now universally known as the Snowshoe.

Personality: Terms used to describe this breed include: gentle, loving, affectionate, docile, inquisitive, adaptable, unflappable and happy-go-lucky. Described by owners as 'bomb-proof'.

Colour Forms: The white face and feet can be combined with any of the Siamese point patterns, although some organizations only recognize Seal and White Point and Blue and White Point. Because of the maximum contrast it affords, the Seal and White Point can be considered as the key pattern for combining with the white patches.

Breed Clubs:

The Snowshoes Cat Fanciers of America. A CFF-affiliated club.

The Snowshoe Breed Club. Address: P.O. Box 3201, Sidell, LA 70459, USA.

Snowshoes International (SSI). Formed in 1984. Address: 333 Hoyt Street, Buffalo, NY 14213, USA, or P.O. Box 121, Watkins, CO 80137, USA.

Snowshoe UK. Address: Tudor Cottage, 10 Lyncroft Gardens, Ewell, Epsom, Surrey, KT17 1UR, England.

44

DEVON REX CAT

Appeared in 1960 in the county of Devon, England. This was the second form of Rex Cat to be discovered in the West Country, the Cornish Rex having been found in the neighbouring county of Cornwall ten years earlier. The Devon Rex is sometimes referred to as the 'Pixie Cat' because of its strange head shape.

Appearance: A thin-coated, wavy-furred cat with curly whiskers and eyebrows. The hind legs are long, but the front legs are bowed and shorter. The chest is broad. The wedge-shaped head has wide cheeks and huge, low-set ears with small lynx-like tufts at their tips. There is a distinct 'stop' to the nose – giving a dip, or break in the profile of the cat's face.

Unusual Features: Despite their frail appearance, these cats are remarkably healthy and hardy animals. They cannot tolerate cold sleeping conditions because of their thin coat, but when active they will even play in the snow. As a result of their body heat-losses, they have a huge appetite with a high fat requirement.

The coat of the Devon Rex Cat is made up largely of down hairs, with a only a few guard hairs, so that what is visible is essentially the cat's undercoat. Some individuals suffer from bare patches.

The Devon Rex coat has two advantages: there are few moulted hairs; and people with cat-hair allergies are far less likely to suffer when they come into close contact with this breed.

History: The first Devon Rex Cat was a stray tom living wild in a disused tin mine near Buckfastleigh in Devon. It was hoped to breed from him, but despite many attempts to catch him, he always eluded capture. However, in 1960 he mated with a stray tortie-and-white female and she produced a litter of kittens. This female had been befriended by a Miss Beryl Cox, who lived near the tin mine, and who had been observing the strange-looking tom for some time. The litter was born in a field at the end of her garden and, taking a close look at them, she was able to see that one of the kittens, a male, had the same curly coat as the wild tom. She took this kitten and reared it carefully in her home. Named 'Kirlee', it was to become the founding father of the Devon Rex breed.

Miss Cox had seen photographs of the Cornish Rex Cat 'Kallibunker', who had been discovered nearby ten years earlier, and contacted the group who were developing that breed, with a view to a mating. They took Kirlee and mated him with several of the female descendants of Kallibunker, but to their astonishment found that all the kittens born from these pairings were straight-haired. Despite repeated attempts, the Cornish X Devon Rex cross did not produce a single curly-haired Rex Cat. They were forced to the surprising conclusion that, despite the geographical closeness, the wavy-haired gene in the Devon Rex was not the same as the one which was causing wavy hair in the Cornish Rex breed. The two recessive genes were therefore named: Gene 1 (Cornish) Rex, and Gene 2 (Devon) Rex. (They have been given the gene symbols 'r' and 're' respectively.)

Because of this difference, the only way to establish the Devon Rex as a distinct breed was to in-breed from Kirlee. A similar in-breeding programme had been successfully employed with Kallibunker. Kirlee was mated with his daughters and before long the Devon Rex Cat was safely established. Kirlee lived a long and productive life, until he was eventually killed in a road accident in 1970.

Personality: Terms that have been used to describe this breed include: friendly, lively, affectionate, playful, intelligent, mischievous, impish, enterprising, active, inquisitive, extrovert.

It has been called 'a feline comedian' and 'a monkey in cat's clothing'. Its climbing abilities are exceptional. One authority referred to it as 'an animal suited to gentle owners'.

Some authors suggest that this breed has several dog-like qualities: it retrieves; it follows its owner; it wags its tail when pleased. The dog-like tail-wagging action would be highly unusual for a cat, but closer examination reveals that it occurred in special circumstances: 'One of his [Kirlee's] favourite tricks was to walk a tight-rope, wagging his tail for approval as he did so.' On another occasion, involving a Devon Rex kitten, 'loud purring and a wagging tail were the prelude to another amorous leap'. Clearly, these were cases of tail-wagging employed for its primary function of keeping the body balanced, rather than as a social signal.

Related Breeds: The Devon Rex is superficially similar to other Rex cats, such as the Cornish and German, and was at first thought to be just another example of the same breed. But once it had been shown that its wavy coat was caused by a different gene, it was clear that it would have to be granted separate breed status.

The Devon Rex was accepted as a separate show breed from 1967, except in the United States where the CFA only accepted one 'Rex' breed, based on the Cornish Rex standard, until 1979. The fur of the Devon Rex is slightly different from that of the other Rex breeds. It contains a few guard hairs among the numerous down hairs, and is slightly harsher to the touch.

Colour Forms:

GCCF: All colours, patterns and combinations are acceptable in this breed.

CFA: All colours and patterns accepted, but specifically lists the following. (To simplify the list, the colours are grouped into convenient categories.)

SELF: White; Black, Blue; Red; Cream; Chocolate; Lavender; Cinnamon; Fawn.

SHADED: Shaded Silver; Blue Shaded; Chocolate Shaded; Lavender Shaded; Cameo Shaded; Cinnamon Shaded; Fawn Shaded; Tortie Shaded; Blue-Cream Shaded; Chocolate Tortie Shaded; Cinnamon Tortie Shaded; Lavender-Cream Shaded; Fawn-Cream Shaded; Chinchilla.

SMOKE: Black Smoke; Blue Smoke; Red Smoke Cameo (Cameo); Chocolate Smoke; Lavender Smoke; Cinnamon Smoke; Cream Smoke; Fawn Smoke; Tortie Smoke; Blue-Cream Smoke; Chocolate Tortie Smoke; Lavender-Cream Smoke; Cinnamon Tortie Smoke; Fawn-Cream Smoke.

THE REMARKABLE head-shape of the Devon Rex Cat *(opposite)* has given it the nickname 'Pixie Cat'. The gene that produces its wavy coat also endows it with characteristic curly whiskers.

THE WAVY-COATED DEVON REX CAT. It first appeared in south-west England in 1960, not far from the site of the previously discovered Cornish Rex. Despite their geographical proximity, however, the two breeds were not related.

TABBY: (Classic, Mackerel, Spotted and Patched Tabby Patterns) Silver Tabby; Brown Tabby; Blue Tabby; Red Tabby; Cream Tabby; Chocolate (Chestnut) Tabby; Chocolate Silver Tabby; Cinnamon Tabby; Cinnamon Silver Tabby; Lavender Tabby; Lavender Silver Tabby; Fawn Tabby; Cameo Tabby; Blue Silver Tabby; Cream Silver Tabby; Fawn Silver Tabby.

TORTIE: Tortie; Blue-Cream; Chocolate (Chestnut) Tortie; Cinnamon Tortie; Lavender-Cream; Fawn-Cream.

CALICO: Calico; Fawn-Cream Calico; Lavender-Cream Calico; Cinnamon-Cream Calico; Van Calico; Fawn-Cream Van Calico; Lavender-Cream Van Calico; Cinnamon-Cream Van Calico; Dilute Calico; Dilute Van Calico.

BI-COLOR: Bi-color; Van Bi-color.

Breed Clubs:

Devon Rex Breed Club. Publishes a newsletter. Address: 6251 North Sheridan, No. 18, Chicago, IL 60660, USA.

Rex Breeders United. Address: 446 Itasca Ct. N.W., Rochester, MN 55901, USA.

NOTE: There is an additional breed publication, *Devon Rex Newsletter.* Address: 32 Myer Drive, Ft. Gordon, GA 30905, USA.

45

SCOTTISH FOLD CAT

A recently discovered mutation with a unique ear shape.

Appearance: The small ears are folded downwards and forwards, giving the animal's head a smoothly rounded silhouette. The appeal of this shape is clearly that it gives the breed a more humanoid look. A stocky cat with a wide face and large round eyes, the Scottish Fold can exist in any colour and with either a short or a long coat.

The ear-shape starts to develop at about 25 days. This is the point at which the cartilage in a normal kitten's ears starts to harden and the ears stand upright. With the Scottish Fold, this change does not occur. Today there are variations in the degree of this folding, some individuals having a single fold, while others have a double fold. With the double fold, the ear tips almost touch the fur of the head.

There is also a long-haired version of this breed (see Coupari).

History: The first Scottish Fold appeared on a farm in Perthshire, Scotland, near the village of Coupar Angus 21 km (13 miles) north-east of Perth, in 1961. A local shepherd noticed that a short-haired white female cat, playing in a nearby farmyard, had strangely folded ears. He pointed this out to the cat's owners, Mr and Mrs McRae. They knew very little about the animal's ancestry, but it seemed fairly certain that the other kittens in her litter had been perfectly normal. The conclusion was that the strange one must be an isolated, spontaneous mutation. The McRaes promised the shepherd a kitten from any litter she might produce in the future.

Two years later, this cat, now called Susie, herself gave birth and produced two more folded-eared kittens. One, a male, was given to a neighbour who had it neutered and kept it as a pet. The other was a white female, looking exactly like its mother, and this one was given to the shepherd and his wife – William and Mary Ross.

Within three months, Susie herself was dead, killed by a car on the road near her home, and the survival of the breed now rested entirely with the Rosses. Fortunately, they had a special interest in pedigree cats and already owned a fine Siamese. They were fascinated by the potential of their new kitten. They named her Snooks, bred from her and began to think seriously about developing their 'new breed', which at this stage they were referring to as 'Lop-eared Cats'. A cat show judge suggested that they should contact a London breeder by the name of Pat Turner, who was interested in feline genetics. This they did in 1967 and Turner visited them at their Scottish home. She borrowed a male called Snowdrift, took him back to London,

and began a serious experimental breeding programme. It was she who persuaded the Rosses to change the name of the breed from Lop-eared to Fold, pointing out that the pendulous ears of the Lop-eared Rabbit were anatomically very different from the folded-over ears of the cat, and that the name was therefore misleading.

Snowdrift was destined to become the founding father of the breed, with 76 descendants in three years, 42 of which had the typical folded ears. He soon became famous, appearing on television and creating something of a controversy. Many experts condemned the new breed as a deformity and before long the feline authorities formally decreed that 'no applications for registration or show entries may be accepted for the Lop-eared (Fold-eared) cats'.

With opposition continuing in England, three of Snowdrift's descendants crossed the Atlantic and, in 1970, became the focus of a special study by geneticist Neil Todd in Newtontown, Massachusetts. When he eventually lost interest, a Pennsylvania breeder called Sally Wolfe Peters took on the task of developing the breed. As a result of her programme, the first Scottish Fold Cat was registered in the United States in 1973. In 1974 she formed 'The International Scottish Fold Association' and by 1978 the breed had gained championship status at American cat shows. By the 1990s, despite the disapproval it still attracts elsewhere, it ranked among the top ten most popular pedigree breeds in America.

It has been claimed that cats with folded ears have also been observed in both Germany and Belgium, but it seems that in neither country has this mutant form been developed.

Abnormalities: Sadly, the gene that causes the folded ears of this attractive breed appears to be linked to certain physical abnormalities. It is a single dominant gene that causes problems when it is present in double strength (that is, in the homozygous condition). If one Scottish Fold is mated to another Scottish Fold, the kittens all have folded ears, but they are also liable to suffer from two serious defects: (1) a thickened tail caused by the fusing of the tail vertebrae, and (2) thickened legs, with cartilage growing around the paws, making walking difficult.

As a result of this unfortunate genetic link, Scottish Fold breeders only ever put their animals with non-folded mates. The kittens resulting from such a cross have the ear-folding gene only in single strength (the heterozygous condition), and they are then free from these defects. So Scottish Fold breeders must always out-breed if they are to succeed with this unusual form of cat. Some have bred with short-haired mates and some have preferred long-haired ones, giving rise to two basic types of Scottish Fold Cat.

Because of the ever-present threat of physical abnormalities should two folded cats get together and mate, there has been strong resistance to this breed on the part of certain feline authorities and it is banned altogether, by law, in Germany.

In England the main authority, the GCCF, has refused to accept the breed for competition. The GCCF's formal objection was worded as follows: '[The ear configuration] will almost certainly lead to an increased incidence of ear disease on account of the poor natural ventilation of the ear canal and difficulty in cleaning and applying any medication'. Supporters of the breed felt that this sounded like a lame excuse for opposing the new breed. They insisted that the Scottish Fold is no more prone to ear disease than any other breed and that its ears are just as easy to keep clean. One British organization eventually agreed with them, and in 1983 the

THE SCOTTISH FOLD CAT *(opposite),* discovered in the early 1960s, has a strange ear formation. Because of this, some authorities have described it as an abnormal breed, but its many loyal supporters strongly oppose this view.

THE SCOTTISH FOLD CAT. An attractive but controversial breed discovered by a Scottish shepherd in the 1960s. Its forward-folded ears give its head a more rounded and therefore more human outline, adding to its appeal.

GCCF's rival, the Cat Association, eventually recognized the breed, and the Scottish Fold Cat is now seen regularly at their cat shows.

As with Manx Cats and other controversial breeds, careful attention to the problems of genetically linked abnormalities by responsible breeders can avoid most of the difficulties. Outright banning of these unusual and intriguing breeds seems a rather heavy-handed response, although it is easy to understand the caution of the authorities concerned.

An additional defect from which the Scottish Fold Cat has been said to suffer is deafness. This problem does not, however, have any connection with the folded ear gene. The deafness is genetically linked, not to the ear shape but to the pure white coats of some of the Scottish Fold individuals.

Personality: Terms used in connection with this breed include: affectionate, alert, intelligent, optimistic, sensible, perceptive, good-tempered, undemanding, placid, courteous, reserved, sweet, gentle, peaceable, well-balanced, soft-voiced, slow-moving, persistent, resilient, nosy and rugged.

Colour Forms:

CFA: White; Black; Blue; Red; Cream; Chinchilla Silver; Shaded Silver; Shell Cameo (Red Chinchilla); Shaded Cameo (Red Shaded); Black Smoke; Blue Smoke; Cameo Smoke (Red Smoke); Classic Tabby Pattern; Mackerel Tabby Pattern; Patched Tabby (= Torbie) Pattern; Spotted Tabby Pattern; Silver Tabby; Blue Silver Tabby (Pewter Tabby); Blue Silver (Pewter); Red Tabby; Brown Tabby; Blue Tabby; Cream Tabby; Cameo Tabby; Tortoiseshell; Calico; Dilute Calico; Blue-Cream; Bi-color (= Black and White; Blue and White; Red and White; or Cream and White).

Other colours recorded include: Black Smoke and White; Blue-Cream and White; and Tortie and White.

Breed Club:

Scottish Fold Association. Publishes a magazine: *International Scottish Fold.* Address: 12500, Skyline Drive, Burnsville, MN 55337-2920, USA.

THE LONG-HAIRED VERSION of the Scottish Fold Cat. As yet, there is no agreement on its official title, but British breeders have adopted the name Coupari, taken from the name of the village where it was discovered (see entry for Coupari).

46

BENGAL CAT

Originally christened the 'Leopardette' and referred to by some authors as the 'Bengali'. It originated from a cross between a wild Asian Leopard Cat *(Felis bengalensis)* and a domestic cat. It is therefore a hybrid cat, and one would expect all the offspring to be infertile. Surprisingly, although the first male offspring did prove to be infertile, the females did not, and it was possible to use them in a planned breeding programme to develop the new breed.

Appearance: A large cat for a domestic breed, with the females weighing 4.5-5.5 kg (10-12 lb) and the males as much as 10 kg (22 lb). It has a powerful, muscular body with high hindquarters, large feet and a characteristically spotted coat. Even the belly is spotted. The black spots are usually solid, but occasionally they appear as dark rosettes. The tail-tip is black. The main difference between the coat of the wild cat and this new domestic hybrid is found on the ear and the tail. The ear of the domestic animal lacks the vivid white patch ringed with black that is seen in the wild ancestor, and the domestic tail lacks the wild cat spotting.

History: It is believed that, over the centuries, there have been many matings between wild Leopard Cats in tropical Asia and the domestic cats taken to that region. But none of these hybrids were ever kept and developed as a special breed. Then, in 1963 an American geneticist, Mrs Jean Sugden of Yuma, Arizona, crossed a female Leopard Cat, which she had obtained from a pet shop in the late 1950s, with a black short-haired domestic male. A female offspring from this mating, called Kinkin, was then bred back to its wild father and this resulted in some plain and some spotted offspring. This could have been the start of a new, spotted breed, but the project was abandoned when Mrs Sugden was widowed.

Then, in the late 1970s, Dr Willard Centerwall, a geneticist working at the University of California, began a breeding programme that involved crossing Leopard Cats with short-haired domestic cats as part of a study of feline leukemia. Jean Sugden, now Mrs Jean Mill following her remarriage, and living in Covina, near Los Angeles, acquired eight female hybrids from Dr Centerwall in 1981 and used these as the foundation stock for a new Bengal Cat project. As before, it was her aim to combine the markings of a wild Leopard Cat with the friendly temperament of a tame domestic cat. The female hybrids were mated with a red feral domestic cat that had been found living rough in the rhinoceros enclosure of Delhi Zoo, and a brown spotted tabby found in a Los Angeles cat shelter. From these unlikely beginnings, the new breed of domesticated Bengal Cats was developed.

THE BREED called the Bengal Cat is claimed to have originated as a cross between a wild Asian
Leopard Cat *(Felis bengalensis)* and a domestic cat. It is a remarkably active cat with a
wonderfully spotted coat.

Several other American breeders were also active, and one in particular, Dr Gregg Kent, was
successful in producing crosses between a male Leopard Cat and a female Egyptian Mau. Other
domestic breeds used from time to time include the Ocicat, the Abyssinian, the Bombay and the
British Shorthair.

In 1983 TICA accepted the domesticated Bengal Cat for registration as a new breed and it
was first exhibited at cat shows in 1984–1985. It achieved National Championship status in
1990–1991.

By 1989 there were estimated to be about 200 Bengal Cats in existence. In the early 1990s
some were imported into Britain, where their value was put at £2,500 (about $3,750) each,
making them the most expensive domestic cats in the country at that time. (One British owner,

who spent £100,000 [about $150,000] assembling his family of Bengals, claimed to have refused an offer of £12,000 [about $18,000] for one particular animal). Since then, with increased interest and further breeding, the numbers have risen dramatically and the initial high values have fallen. There are now thought to be as many as 500 in Britain and, according to a TICA estimate in 1995, there are at least 9,000 domestic Bengal Cats registered with cat clubs worldwide today.

Personality: Terms used to describe this breed include: intelligent, agile, alert, active, athletic, cunning, curious, busy, powerful, determined, outgoing, social, loving, affectionate, confident and independent. They are fond of water and have been known to jump into bathtubs to join their owners. They also love climbing and indulge in endless bouts of play-hunting. Their vocalizations differ from the ordinary domestic cat, containing several 'wild' elements.

Colour Forms: Leopard; Marble; Snow Leopard; Snow Marble; Sorrel (= Golden); Mink.

Breed Clubs:

Several breed clubs already exist for the Bengal Cat, including:

Authentic Bengal Cat Club (ABC). Publishes a bi-monthly newsletter. Address: P.O. Box 1653, Roseburg, OR 97470, USA.

Bengal Breeders Alliance. Address: P.O. Box 6028, Great Falls, MT 59406, USA; or P.O. Box 2387, Park City, UT 84060, USA.

Bengal Cat Club. Address: Dovecote House, 1 Thornton Avenue, Warsash, Southampton, Hampshire, SO31 9FL, England.

Bengal Cat Club of Great Britain. Address: 15 Princes Road, Dartford, Kent, DAB 3HJ, England.

Ocicat and Bengal Cat Cub. Address: The Braes, 160 Hermitage Road, Woking, Surrey, England.

The International Bengal Cat Society (TIBCS). Publishes a bi-monthly newsletter, the *Bengal Bulletin*. Address: P.O. Box 403, Powell, OH, 43065-0403, USA; or 19726 E. Colimar Rd., Box 123, Rowlands Height, CA 91748, USA.

ALTHOUGH EXTREMELY RARE a few years ago, the spectacular, exotically spotted Bengal Cat is becoming increasingly popular, and its numbers have now risen from the hundreds to the thousands.

47

OCICAT

This American breed of spotted cat was originally a mixture of three-quarters Siamese and one-quarter Abyssinian, with later additions of American Shorthairs. The name 'Ocicat' is a combination of 'Ocelot' and 'cat'. Two other names were used in the early days of the breed: 'Ocelette' because it looked like a small Ocelot and 'Accicat' because the first one appeared as a lucky accident in another breeding programme. The breed has been described as 'a purr wrapped in polkadots'.

Appearance: A large, muscular, spotted, short-haired cat with an 'average' body shape, showing no extremes of either stockiness or angularity. In other words, a domestic cat with a 'wild-type' appearance. Despite the strong Siamese element in its original make-up, later breeding programmes, taking it away from the Siamese type of body, have meant that it has not inherited the lean, elongated Oriental look.

History: The first Ocicat appeared in 1964, bred by Virginia Daly of Michigan. It was an accidental by-product of a breeding programme that was attempting to create an Abyssinian-pointed Siamese. It resulted from a mating between a champion Chocolate Point Siamese male and a hybrid female. This female was a cross between a Seal Point Siamese male and an Abyssinian female.

Among the offspring, unexpectedly, was a golden-spotted male kitten. He was named Tonga, and was the first ever Ocicat. However, because he was not part of the official breeding programme, he was sold as a pet and was neutered. Virginia Daly's interest in the idea of developing a spotted cat grew, however, and when she repeated the mating and obtained further spotted kittens, she kept these and used them to create the foundation stock for what was to become an exciting new breed.

Another American breeder, Tom Brown, then took up the Ocicat and initiated a long-term programme. By 1970 he had seen it through five generations. Other breeders improved the type by introducing crosses with American Shorthair Cats. This increased the body size of the Ocicat and made it into the impressive animal we see today. It achieved championship status in the United States in 1987, and in the late 1980s the first ones were introduced into the British Isles, where their numbers have been growing ever since.

In the 1980s a separate line of Ocicats was developed in Germany by Karen Dupuis. The foundation animal for the European Ocicat, born in 1984, was named Nadir.

THE OCICAT is one of the new domestic breeds of spotted cat that attempt to recapture the 'wild look' while retaining the friendly domestic temperament. It was first developed in the United States in the 1960s.

Personality: Terms used to describe this breed include: affectionate, friendly, companionable, athletic, active, acrobatic, attentive, intelligent, loyal, even-tempered and sweet-natured. It is said to be unusually easy to train.

Colour Forms: The typical colouring is light brown or tawny, imitating the coat of a wild cat species. Variant colours include:

CFA: Tawny (Brown Spotted Tabby); Chocolate; Cinnamon; Blue; Lavender; Fawn; Silver; Chocolate Silver; Cinnamon Silver; Blue Silver; Lavender Silver; Fawn Silver.

Breed Clubs:

Ocicat & Bengal Cat Club. Address: Moonfleet, Bakers Lane, Shutlanger, Towcester, Northants., England.

Ocicat Club. Publishes a twice-yearly newsletter, *The Ocicat Muse.* Address: Woodlands, Mounters Lane, Chawton, Alton, Hampshire, England.

Ocicat International. Formed in 1984. Address: P.O. Box 606, Great River, NY 11739, USA, or 865 Sycamore, Boulder, CO 80303, USA.

Ocicats of North America. Address: Route 1, Box 190, Harrison, AR 72601, USA, or 1320 Hilltop Road, Susana Knolls, CA 93063, USA.

48

AMERICAN SHORTHAIR CAT

An American pedigree cat, originally called the 'Domestic Shorthair'. It was officially renamed the American Shorthair in 1966 (known as ASH, for short). This was done to raise its status and to distinguish it from the common, non-pedigree, domestic house-pets.

Appearance: A muscular, compact, heavy-bodied cat with a short, rounded face. American Shorthairs have slightly longer legs than their British counterparts. They also tend to have a denser, thicker coat.

History: According to tradition, the first American Shorthairs were ship's cats employed as pest-controllers on the *Mayflower,* arriving in America in 1620. Many more ship's cats must have followed and, before long, they were spreading out across the New World, some living wild but most continuing to act as domestic rodent-destroyers. During the great California Gold Rush these cats were so highly valued as mousers that they were selling at $50 each, a huge price to pay back in the middle of the 19th century.

By the end of the 19th century, some of the best examples of the descendants of these working cats were starting to appear at cat shows. Classified as 'Domestic Shorthairs', they included some exceptional individuals. Despite this, however, they were often relegated to a minor role, because of strong competition from the more glamorous foreign breeds that were being imported from Europe. As Ingeborg Urcia reports: 'Those who raised the new exotic breeds looked down upon the American cats. Rumours circulated that the breeders of the Domestic got their breeding stock from the animal shelter, and their cats were disdained and neglected. At some cat shows they were not even benched . . . Domestic breeders found no cages available for them at shows, and no rosettes or trophies were provided for the Domestic Shorthair class.'

In the early years of the 20th century, the breed was enhanced by the arrival in the United States of a British pedigree Shorthair named Champion Belle of Bradford. An orange tabby imported by Jane Cathcart, it was the first Domestic Shorthair to be registered as a pedigree cat in the United States. In 1904, the first home-bred, truly American, Domestic Shorthair to be registered was a male smoke called Buster Brown, which also belonged to Miss Cathcart.

After World War II, Domestic Shorthairs started winning prizes at American cat shows and it was this that eventually led to their being honoured with the new title of American Shorthairs. A group of enthusiasts met in the early 1960s and decided on this new name because they felt that the word 'Domestic' was an obstacle to the success of these cats. The strategy proved a success and by the 1970s the American Shorthairs were fully established as a major force to be reckoned with at pedigree shows all over America.

Personality: Terms used to describe this breed include: hearty, healthy, versatile, friendly, intelligent, robust, strong, good-natured and independent.

Colour Forms: The CFA in America lists the following colours for this breed. To simplify the list, the colours are grouped into convenient categories.

CFA: SOLID: White; Black; Blue; Red; Cream.

SHADED AND SILVER: Chinchilla Silver; Shaded Silver; Shell Cameo; Shaded Cameo; Blue Chinchilla Silver; Blue Shaded Silver; Cream Shell Cameo; Cream Shaded Cameo.

SMOKE: Black Smoke; Blue Smoke; Cameo Smoke (Red Smoke); Tortoiseshell Smoke; Blue Cream Smoke.

TABBY: (Classic, Mackerel and Patched Tabby Patterns) Blue Silver Tabby (Pewter Tabby); Blue Silver Patched Tabby (Pewter Patched Tabby); Cream Cameo Tabby (Dilute Cameo); Brown Patched Tabby; Blue Patched Tabby; Silver Patched Tabby; Silver Tabby; Red Tabby; Brown Tabby; Blue Tabby; Cream Tabby; Cameo Tabby.

THE AMERICAN SHORTHAIR was originally known at cat shows simply as the Domestic Shorthair, and was then little more than a common house-pet. But as the quality of the show cat improved, year by year, it was given a formal name, to set it apart.

THE DRAMATICALLY BEAUTIFUL COAT of this Silver Classic Tabby version of the
American Shorthair Cat shows just how far pedigree specialists have developed this breed from
its simple domestic origins.

SMOKE AND WHITE (including Vans): Black Smoke and White; Blue Smoke and White;
Tortoiseshell Smoke and White; Shell Cameo and White; Shaded Cameo and White; Smoke
Cameo and White.

TABBY AND WHITE: Silver Tabby and White; Silver Patched Tabby and White; Cameo Tabby and
White; Brown Tabby and White; Brown Patched Tabby and White; Blue Tabby and White; Blue
Patched Tabby and White; Red Tabby and White; Cream Tabby and White; Van Blue-Cream and
White.

PARTI-COLOR: Tortie; Chinchilla Shaded Tortie; Shaded Tortie; Dilute Chinchilla Shaded Tortie;
Dilute Shaded Tortie; Blue-Cream.

BI-COLOR: Bi-color; Van Bi-color; Calico; Dilute Calico; Van Calico.

Breed Club:

National American Shorthair Club. Address: P.O. Box 280831, San Francisco, CA 94128-0831,
 USA, or 1331 N. Wingra Drive, Madison, WI 53715, USA.

NOTE: There is a breed publication, *American Connection.* Address: P.O. Box 280831, San
Francisco, CA 94128-0831, USA.

49

AMERICAN WIREHAIR CAT

The American Wirehair Cat appeared in 1966 on a farm in the state of New York.

Appearance: The fur of this breed is unique among cats. Each hair is bent or hooked, giving the animal a harsh, dense, springy coat. Apart from this special feature, the cat is similar to the American Shorthair, with its typically strong, muscular body. In some individuals the whiskers are curly – a similarity to the Rex Cats.

History: This breed began as a single, spontaneous mutation in a litter born to a pair of farm cats called Bootsie and Fluffy, in a barn near Vernon (not Verona, Vermont or Utica, as quoted by various authors) in upper New York State. Among the litter of six, a red and white male kitten was seen to have a strange, wiry coat, unlike its litter-mates. The farmer contacted Mrs William O'Shea, a cat breeder living nearby, who kept Rex Cats and was familiar with strange feline hair patterns. She immediately recognized the importance of this kitten and acquired it (for $50) to start a serious breeding programme. With a view to in-breeding, she also purchased a normal-coated female from the same litter. The male was called Adam and the female Tip-Toe (full names: Council Rock Farm Adam of Hi-Fi and Tip-Toe of Hi-Fi).

Subsequent breeding successfully produced a number of Wirehair kittens. Some of these were acquired by other breeders in the United States and word soon began to spread about this remarkable new type of feline. Before long kittens were being exported to breeders in Canada and Germany. As early as 1969, a true-breeding American Wirehair had been developed and the breed was secure for the future. It was officially recognized by the CFA in 1977, and by the 1990s it had achieved championship status throughout the United States. It has also appeared at cat shows in Canada, Germany and Japan. Worldwide, however, it remains a rare breed.

Whereas the Rex gene proved to be recessive, the Wirehair gene is dominant to normal coat. It has been given the gene symbol 'Wh'.

Unlike the Cornish Rex gene, the Wirehair gene has not been preserved from more than one source, and this means that every American Wirehair Cat in existence today can be traced directly back to the aptly named Adam. There were rumours of harsh-haired cats being seen on derelict bomb sites in London at the end of World War II, but these cats were never used for breeding purposes. Two of them were apparently exhibited at the National Cat Club Show in England, some years before Adam's discovery in America, but they were treated as a mere curiosity and not developed.

THE AMERICAN WIREHAIR was first discovered on a farm in New York State in 1966. It is characterized by its uniquely harsh, wiry coat.

Personality: Terms that have been used to describe this breed include: friendly, intelligent, adaptable, sweet-tempered, affectionate. There is some contradiction – one authority describes this cat as quiet and reserved, while others say it is playful, zany, independent and inquisitive. Because its hair stands on end, it has been described as 'the punk of the feline world'. It has also been said to 'rule its home and other cats with an iron paw'.

Colour Forms: Almost any colour is acceptable in this breed. The Cat Fanciers' Association in America lists the following colours:

CFA: White; Black; Blue; Red; Cream; Chinchilla Silver; Shaded Silver; Shell Cameo (Red Chinchilla); Shaded Cameo (Red Shaded); Black Smoke; Blue Smoke; Cameo Smoke (Red Smoke); Classic Tabby Pattern; Mackerel Tabby Pattern; Silver Tabby; Red Tabby; Brown Tabby; Blue Tabby; Cream Tabby; Cameo Tabby; Tortie; Calico; Dilute Calico; Blue-Cream; Bi-color.

50

EXOTIC SHORTHAIR CAT

The short-haired version of the Persian Cat, first developed in the 1950s. The name 'Exotic' was introduced by American breeders in 1966.

Many people wished to own a cat with the docile, serene personality of the Persian, but without having to suffer the endless grooming problems created by their exceptionally long fur. The solution was to shorten the hair genetically, but without altering the character of the cat. Once this had been done, the new breed quickly became immensely popular. It has sometimes been referred to as the 'Easy-care Persian'.

Appearance: A 'chunky' cat, it retains the heavy head, the flat face, the stocky body and the short legs and tail of the Persian, but it has a thick, soft, plush, luxuriant, short coat, giving it an appealing 'teddy bear' look.

History: The breed originally arose because of attempts to strengthen the quality of the American Shorthair Cat. This was done by introducing Persians into Shorthair breeding programmes in the United States. This soon gave rise to a new, 'improved' American Shorthair which was so different from the traditional Shorthair that it was decided to give them two separate breed names. In 1966, Jane Martinke suggested the title 'Exotic Shorthair' for the newer type. The first 'Exotic' was shown under that name in 1967. Two years later, two Americans, Bob and Nancy Lane, started the first Exotic Breed Club, and began more carefully orchestrated breeding programmes.

Various other short-haired breeds were occasionally involved in the crosses in the early days, including Abyssinians, Burmese and Russian Blues, but once the Exotic Shorthair breed had been firmly established, only out-crosses using American Shorthairs and Persians were permitted.

Similar crosses were made in Britain, using British Shorthairs, where the results were sometimes referred to as 'British Exotics' to distinguish them from their American counterparts. Two clubs were formed: the 'Exotic Cat Club' in 1983 and then the 'Exotic Shorthair Breeders Society' in 1984.

The arrival of this breed has caused some controversy, since some cat organizations classify them as short-haired cats (because of their fur) and others as long-haired (because they are Persian in every other respect). This difference of opinion serves to underline the unfortunate state in which pedigree cat classifications find themselves today.

THE EXOTIC SHORTHAIR CAT is essentially a short-haired version of the Persian Cat. For those who want a docile cat that does not require endless grooming, this is the ideal breed.

Personality: Terms used to describe this breed include: quiet, placid, tranquil, home-loving, hardy, intelligent, alert, bright, inquisitive and playful.

Colour Forms: Almost all colours are known in this breed. In fact, no fewer than 96 different colour forms are listed by the Exotic Shorthair Breeders Association.

Breed Clubs:

Exotic Cat Club. Address: 6 Oakwell Crescent, Ilkeston, Derbyshire, DE7 5GX, England.

Exotic Shorthair Breeders Society. Founded in 1984. Issues a half-yearly *Journal.* Address: The Cottage Cattery, Mill Road, West Walton, Nr. Wisbech, Cambs., PE14 7EU, England.

NOTE: There is an additional breed publication, *Exotic Thoughts.* Address: P.O. Box 52, Verona, PA 15147, USA.

51

SPHYNX CAT

The most controversial of all modern cat breeds, the nearly naked Sphynx Cat is a recent Canadian discovery. It has also been called the Canadian Hairless Cat and the Moon Cat, and has been nicknamed the Wrinkled Cat and the Birthday Suit Cat. In France it is known as the *Chat sans Poils.* It has been said that it is 'so ugly that it is beautiful'.

Appearance: A slender, elongated cat with suede-like, almost hairless skin, and a long, pointed tail. Its wedge-shaped head has very large ears and no whiskers. It is hot to the touch, and has sometimes been referred to as 'a suede hot-water bottle'. Its skin 'should look like velvet and feel like moss'. It has been likened in appearance to E.T., the extra-terrestrial in Steven Spielberg's 1982 film.

History: On 31st January 1966, a black and white pet cat called Elizabeth, belonging to a Mrs Micalwaith of Toronto, gave birth to a mutant hairless male kitten which was given the name of Prune. A young science student from the university heard of this strange new arrival. His mother, Mrs Yania Bawa, happened to be a breeder of Siamese Cats and together they acquired both the naked kitten and its mother. When the kitten became adult it was mated back to its mother to produce more hairless kittens. A serious breeding programme was planned, involving a complicated series of crosses with American Shorthair females and hairless males. It was decided to name the hairless progeny as a new breed, the Sphinx, later changed to Sphynx, and to develop it further as a pedigree cat for show competition. Championship status was obtained by 1971 but concern about difficulties in rearing the kittens, especially the female ones, soon led to a decline in interest and, indeed, some strong opposition to it.

Its championship status was later revoked and the breed was in danger of dying out altogether, but a few specimens were exported to Europe, where the Sphynx found new supporters. Breeding programmes were begun in both Holland and France and the 'naked cat' eventually arrived in Britain. Even today it remains a rare breed, but its future survival now seems reasonably secure. In the early 1990s TICA granted it championship status.

An interesting feature of this cat is that the recessive gene which causes the hairlessness also appears to modify the body shape. The domestic cat that gave birth to the first hairless kitten was of 'average' shape, but the Sphynx Cat is exceptionally elongated and angular. In this respect it is reminiscent of the Rex breeds, where the sparse coat is again apparently linked to a lanky, angular body-shape.

176

Although this breed has the obvious disadvantage that it cannot stand a cold climate and must always be thought of as an 'indoor cat' needing special protection from its owners against the cold, it does have one particular advantage, namely that it does not cause allergic responses in those sensitive to cat fur. (However, it has now been reported that, in cases of extreme allergy, even this cat may cause problems because of the very fine 'peach-fuzz' of down hair which is present on its skin.)

Personality: As anyone who has encountered this cat in the flesh will testify, its sensitivity and loving nature more than compensate for its bizarre appearance. It is unusually sociable and affectionate. It has been described as 'part monkey, part dog, part child and part cat'.

Those who have only seen the cat in photographs sometimes take a less flattering view of it. It has also been described as 'the ugliest cat alive' and 'a creature with a hairless body, a snake's head, a rat's tail, and ears like bats' wings'.

Colour Forms: Any colours accepted.

Breed Clubs:

International Sphynx Breeders and Fanciers Association. Address: HC66, Box 70035, Pinetop, AZ 85935, USA.

Sphynx Cat Club. Address: 10 York Road, Waltham Cross, Herts., EN8 7HW, England.

THE EXTRAORDINARY, naked Sphynx Cat from Canada. No domestic breed has caused more heated debate than this amazing-looking feline, which is either loved or hated but is rarely ignored.

52

Somali Cat

The long-haired version of the Abyssinian Cat. The ticked coat is not only longer but also softer, silkier and with more colour-bands per hair. Apart from its coat, the breed is essentially the same as the Abyssinian.

Its name has no historical significance. It is doubtful whether any Somali Cat has ever trodden on Somali soil. It was given to the new breed simply because Somalia is close to Abyssinia (now Ethiopia) and the Somali Cat is close to the Abyssinian Cat. It has been referred to as a 'soft orange cloud' and a 'striking red fox', or simply the 'fox cat'.

Appearance: As for the Abyssinian Cat except for the semi-long hair on its body, the ruff and the thickly plumed tail. Often described as a 'wild-looking cat'.

History: The Somali began as unwanted accidents in the 1950s and 1960s, with long-haired kittens turning up unexpectedly in short-haired Abyssinian litters. Initially, they were given away as pets and excluded from future pedigree breeding plans, but then it was decided that they had a special appeal of their own and were treated more seriously, leading eventually to the establishment of a new breed. Long-haired Abyssinians from the United States, Australia and New Zealand were exchanged to improve the quality of the foundation stock.

The moving force in developing the Somali was the American breeder Evelyn Mague, from Gillette, New Jersey. It was she who named the breed and whose male kitten, George, became its 'founding father'. He was born in 1967 and heralded a long-term breeding programme. It was successful and eventually, in 1972, a breed club was formed – The Somali Cat Club.

In 1978, the new Somali Cat achieved championship status with the CFA in the United States. A year earlier, in 1977, Somalis had been exported to continental Europe, where breeding programmes were quickly instigated. Matters moved more slowly in Britain. British breeders have always been more resistant to novelties and were reluctant to accept the Somali. As early as 1971, two long-haired Abyssinians had been exhibited at a cat show in London, but they were badly received and were ignored as potential pedigree cats for the future. It was not until 1981, when the breed was already fully accepted elsewhere, that the first imported pair arrived in Britain and were given due attention. The breed was recognized by FIFe in 1982.

In Australia it is reported that the Somali has almost eclipsed its ancestor, the Abyssinian.

It should be noted that there has been considerable controversy over the true source of the original 'accidents' that led to this breed. Some have claimed that a long-haired breed must have

THE SOMALI CAT — the long-haired version of the Abyssinian, first seriously developed as a new breed in the late 1960s in the United States. It arrived in Continental Europe in the 1970s and in Britain in the 1980s.

been introduced into the Abyssinian stock at some early stage in the development of that breed (a Persian in 1900 is specifically mentioned), and that these elements then re-emerged years later. Others feel strongly that such a crossing played no part and that the recessive long-haired gene cropped up naturally, as a simple mutation in otherwise pure Abyssinian stock. The latter explanation seems to be more likely because, apart from its longer hair, the Somali does not show any non-Abyssinian features.

Personality: Terms used to describe this breed include: extrovert, active, alert, aware, athletic, shrewd, lively, friendly, good-tempered, affectionate, playful, intelligent, demonstrative and gentle. Requires considerable freedom.

Colour Forms: To simplify this list, the colours are grouped into convenient categories.

GCCF: Usual (= Ruddy); Sorrel; Chocolate; Blue; Lilac; Fawn; Red; Cream.

TORTIE: Usual Tortie; Sorrel Tortie; Chocolate Tortie; Blue Tortie; Lilac Tortie; Fawn Tortie.

SILVER: Usual Silver; Sorrel Silver; Chocolate Silver; Blue Silver; Lilac Silver; Fawn Silver; Red Silver; Cream Silver.

TORTIE SILVER: Usual Tortie Silver; Sorrel Tortie Silver; Chocolate Tortie Silver; Blue Tortie Silver; Lilac Tortie Silver; Fawn Tortie Silver.

CFA: Ruddy (= Usual); Red; Blue; Fawn.

Breed Clubs:

The Grand Somali Society. Address: 238, Church St., Poughkeepsie, NY 12601, USA.

International Somali Club. A CFA-affiliated club, formed in 1975. Address: 10 Western Blvd., Gillette, NJ 07933, USA.

Somali Cat Club (UK) Formed in 1981, it issues a twice-yearly *Journal.* Address: 21 Norman Road, Sutton, Surrey, SM1 2TB, England.

Somali Cat Club (USA). Formed in 1972. Address: 10 Western Blvd., Gillette, NJ 07933, USA.

Somali Cat Club of America, Inc. Address: 5027 Armstrong, Wichita, KS 67204, USA.

THE DELICATE Blue Silver colour form of the Somali, emphasizing the sleek elegance of the long-haired version of the popular Abyssinian Cat.

53

TIFFANY CAT

Often mistakenly referred to as a 'Long-haired Burmese', this American breed has a different origin from the British cat called the Tiffanie (see entry), and should not be confused with it. Attempts to avoid this confusion have led some authorities to rename the Tiffany as the Chantilly.

Appearance: A medium-sized cat with golden eyes and a rich, lustrous brown coat which is long and silky. There is a pronounced neck ruff and a plumed tail.

History: The genetic origin of the American breed known as the Tiffany is something of a mystery. The founding cats were a pair of golden-eyed, chocolate-coloured, long-haired cats of unknown background. They were bought from an estate sale by American breeder Jennie Robinson of New York in 1967. The male, Thomas, was a little over a year old and the female, Shirley, was only about six months old. It is probable that they had the same parents, but they were clearly not litter-mates. Two years later, in May 1969, they produced their first litter. To the breeder's surprise, all six kittens had identical, rich chocolate-brown coats, and this prompted further breeding. In the early 1970s the cats from this programme were registered with the ACA under the name of Foreign Longhairs.

Several breeders guessed that these must be Long-haired Burmese, or that at the very least they must have had elements of Burmese in their ancestry. Close examination of the finer details of their coat-colouring and their paw-pads (which were pink instead of brown) revealed that 'none arose from nor were bred to Burmese'.

The history of the breed then took a misleading turn. Some of the Robinson kittens were bought by a Florida breeder, Sigyn Lund, who was well-known for her Burmese stock. She became the new champion of the Foreign Longhairs and it was she who devised the new name of Tiffany for them. They were given this name after a Los Angeles theatre and it was meant to suggest a classy elegance – much more appropriate than the colourless title of Foreign Longhair. Unfortunately, not knowing of their mysterious New York beginnings, many people naturally assumed that these delightful animals must be long-haired versions of the Lund Burmese stock. And so the myth of the 'Longhair Burmese' began.

Book after book repeated the error that the American Tiffany Cat was a Longhair Burmese. As recently as 1995, one stated bluntly: 'Tiffany – This new breed, the result of crossing a Burmese with a Persian, was developed in the United States.' Another describes it as resulting from 'a cross between a Burmese and a self longhair'.

Yet another comments: 'In the United States the Tiffany was developed from long-coated cats which appeared in litters of normal Burmese.'

Like a game of Chinese Whispers, the error was repeated and repeated until it became firmly entrenched. Only one recent book, the diminutive *Letts Pocket Guide to Cats,* by David Burn and Chris Bell, avoided this mistake. They correctly state: 'Documentation of the true origins of the US Tiffany seems to have been lost . . . Burmese brown is the most common Tiffany (US) colour but the gene that gives rise to it is independent of the Burmese type and there is now doubt as to whether the American breed of this name has any Burmese (breed) ancestry at all.' Quite so. As stated at the outset, the origin of this breed must remain a mystery, a mystery that began with two unidentified brown cats at a New York estate sale.

To confuse matters further, in the 1980s British breeders working on variations of the new Burmilla breed accidentally created a long-haired brown cat that really did have some Burmese blood in its veins. At first it was known as the Asian Longhair, but then, when it was wrongly assumed that the American Tiffany was also a long-haired Burmese, the British breeders decided to call their animals by the same name. By a lucky chance this was not possible because in Britain the word 'Tiffany' was already registered as a breeder's prefix and was therefore unavailable as the title of a new breed of cat. Wishing to keep the UK/USA link alive, it was then decided to call the British long-haired cats by the name of 'Tiffanie'.

Needless to say, this only added further confusion, with many authors talking about the 'American Tiffanie' and others referring to the 'British Tiffany', neither of which existed.

As if this were not enough, to make matters worse, a third plot had been quietly unfolding, this time in Canada. This story had a beginning as mysterious as the New York estate sale. In 1973, a pregnant, golden-eyed, long-haired, chocolate brown cat walked unannounced into the home of a Canadian land-owner and promptly presented him with a litter of identically coloured kittens. Canadian breeders eventually acquired some of the offspring of these cats and began to develop them. By the late 1980s, in co-operation with their American counterparts, they had managed to boost the fortunes of the Tiffany breed, which at one point had been in danger of disappearing. In the meantime, however, word had spread across the Atlantic about the British Tiffanie and, in order to avoid further confusion, it was decided to give the North American breed a new name. The one chosen was 'Chantilly'. However, in the world of pedigree cats, matters are never that simple. Some cat associations accepted the new name, others retained the original 'Tiffany' and still others went for a safe compromise with the clumsy title of 'Chantilly/Tiffany'. Danette Babyn, writing in 1995, comments: 'The former "Foreign-Longhair" is registered in North America as "Chantilly", "Tiffany", or "Chantilly/Tiffany", depending on the association; some registries felt the breed was entitled to use the original "Tiffany" name, so the breed has a dual designation.' And that is how the situation stands at the present time.

Personality: Terms used to describe this breed include: loyal, affectionate, gentle, sociable, devoted, outgoing, inquisitive, friendly. The voice includes 'quiet chirps or trills'.

Colour Forms: Traditionally, the self-coloured Tiffany coat is a rich, dark brown colour, but already there are a number of dilutions and variations of this, including blue, cinnamon, lilac and fawn, in both solid and tabby patterns.

54

CALIFORNIA SPANGLED CAT

An American spotted breed deliberately created by a carefully planned breeding programme. Sometimes called the 'California Spangle'.

Appearance: The special feature of this short-haired cat is that its coat is covered in distinct, conspicuous, round, black spots. Its long, well-muscled body is carried low, as if the animal is permanently on the hunt. In a strange way, this low-slung walk makes the cat reminiscent of a much larger feline species. The blunt tail always has a black tip.

History: When American screen writer Paul Casey of Burbank, California, was on an assignment to the Olduvai Gorge in Africa in 1971, he was horrified at the wanton destruction of African leopards that was still taking place. He commented later: 'While I was there, we received word that a poacher had just killed and skinned the last remaining breeding leopard in the area. This, to me, seemed a sad signal of things to come.'

He resolved to create a domestic breed of cat to serve as a reminder of the beauty of all spotted felines. On returning home, he drew up an elaborate and ambitious eleven-generation blueprint for a breeding programme that would, in theory, give him the new breed he wanted. The idea was to create a wild-looking cat by using a combination of purely domestic stock. The foundation stock was chosen personally by him from four continents. Eight different lines were involved, including an Abyssinian/domestic cross-breed, an American Shorthair, an Angora-type silver spotted tabby, a British Shorthair, a feral Egyptian cat (a Cairo street cat), a domestic shorthair from Malaysia (a house-cat), a spotted Manx and a traditional Seal Point Siamese. The project was a success. With the 11th generation, the first true Spangled Cats arrived on cue. By 1991, the breed had been accepted by two American associations (TICA and the ACA). A California Spangled Cat Association has been formed, with Paul Casey as its president.

A unique feature of this breed, and one that has caused severe criticism in some quarters, is that it was introduced to the world, not at a major cat show, but on the pages of the Neiman Marcus department store's 1986 Christmas mail-order catalogue. Spangled kittens were offered for sale at $1,400 in a 'his and hers Xmas surprise present package'. This unusual debut saw it branded by many as a purely commercial cat – a designer cat for the rich. The catalogue made it clear that kittens could be bought 'in any color clients may desire to match their clothes or their house decorations'. A humane society called for a boycott of Neiman Marcus, and it is reported that there was protest picketing. One author described the new breed as 'an exclusive

West Coast feline starlet'. Another commented sternly: 'Living things are not appropriate catalogue items to be bred for a luxury market and sold as high-priced toys.'

Defenders of the breed retort that it was 'an environmental symbol for the protection of endangered species of spotted wild cat', and it would seem that they eventually won the day because, by 1992, the price of California Spangled kittens had risen to $3,600 and there was a long waiting-list of would-be owners. In a 1994 interview, Paul Casey stated that he had originally intended 'to provide only five cats. Instead they took in orders for over 350 in the first month alone. We never even came close to filling all the orders.' He saw the value of the publicity surrounding the launch of the Spangled Cats as giving him a launching platform to further his original aims, namely 'to draw attention to the plight of the wild cats'. And he has since been active in trying to stamp out the illegal hunting and slaughter of Central and South American wild cats.

Personality: The following terms have been used to describe this breed: expressive, good-tempered, active, athletic and unusually intelligent.

Colour Forms: Nine colours have been recorded: Black; Blue; Bronze; Brown; Charcoal; Gold; Red; Silver; White.

Breed Club:

The California Spangled Cat Association. Address: P.O. Box 386, Sun Valley, CA 91352, USA.

THE CALIFORNIAN SPANGLED CAT, a recently created spotted breed which has caused considerable controversy because it was launched, not at a major cat show, but in a mail-order catalogue.

55

SINGAPURA CAT

A recently acknowledged cat from Singapore. A small, short-haired breed that was known locally as the 'Drain Cat of Singapore' (because it is reputed to take shelter in the city drains, during the dry season, when suffering from human persecution), or the 'Singapore River Cat' (because it is supposed to have originated on the banks of the river system there).

There is no mystery over its internationally recognized name, Singapura: it is simply the Malay term for Singapore. This was the title originally given to the city in 1299, by a visiting Sumatran Prince.

Today this cat is known by yet another name in Singapore. It is called 'Kucinta, the Love Cat of Singapore'. This is not, however, an old traditional name, but a recently promoted one. It was introduced in 1991 by the Singapore Tourist Board as part of a worldwide promotional campaign for the city.

In 1993 the Singapura Cat became the official symbol of Singapore and two pedigree specimens were returned there to act as models for statues of 'Kucinta' that will be positioned on the Singapore River, where the breed supposedly began its existence.

Appearance: This is one of the smallest of all the pedigree breeds. It is a muscular cat with a very short, fine, satiny coat that lies close to the body. The ground colour of the breed is ivory, each individual hair being ticked with two or more bands of dark brown. (The only other pedigree cats with ticked, or agouti, hair are the Abyssinian, the Somali, the Wild Abyssinian and the Ceylon.) The tail tip is black. The eyes and ears are large. The legs are strong, but the feet are small.

History: There has been considerable controversy about the origins of this attractive breed. The usual story, as reported in most cat publications (but now known to be incorrect in several respects), goes as follows:

The founders of the breed, an American couple called Hal and Tommy Meadow, discovered it in Singapore in 1974. There they heard about an unusually small breed of cat that lived in the streets and sewers of the city. They acquired a kitten which they called 'Pusse' and later an adult pair called 'Tickle' and 'Tessa'. They started breeding from these cats while still in Singapore and then, in 1975, took five of them, including the original three, back to the United States. There they set about establishing the Singapura Cat as a new addition to the list of pedigree cat breeds.

In a 1988 interview, Mrs Tommy Meadow added the following details to this version of the Singapura's origin: 'In April [1975] Saigon fell and in July I was moving back to the United States, with my husband Hal following a few days later. With me I brought my orchids, ten hooded rats . . . and six cats. Of the six cats, five were cats that acquired the breed name of Singapura while in Singapore and had been registered with the Singapore Feline Society . . . the oldest one was Pusse who had been found near the Goldhill Building in the centre of the 225 square mile island. The next in age were a male, Tickle, and his little sister Tessa found near the waterfront. George and Gladys, named after members of the Singapore Feline Society, were 4 month old kittens travelling with mum Pusse and had been sired by Tickle. These 1975 immigrants into the United States were joined in 1980 by a cat named Chiko who had been located at the SPCA by another American cat breeder vacationing in Singapore. Subsequently Chiko was shipped to a Singapura breeder [Barbara Gilbertson] in the State of Washington.'

That was the official story of the origin of the new breed and was accepted by everyone until, a few years later, another American breeder, Jerry Mayes, visited Singapore in search of new blood, only to make a surprising discovery. To his astonishment he found that there was documentary evidence to prove that Mr and Mrs Meadow had *imported* Pusse, Tickle and Tessa into Singapore from the United States.

The story of them being found 'near the Goldhill Building' and 'on the waterfront' was an elaborate deception. But why?

One theory was that Mrs Tommy Meadow had deliberately concealed the true origin of the Singapuras in order to give them a more romantic heritage. It was pointed out that she had previously owned both Burmese and Abyssinians, and that a cross between those two breeds can look remarkably like a Singapura. If she had created such a cross in America, taken the progeny to Singapore, 'discovered' them in the streets of the city, and then brought them back to the United States as an exotic new breed from the Orient, she would have pulled off a remarkable subterfuge to become the founder of a delightful 'Eastern' breed that was rapidly gaining popularity on the show benches. Critics of the original version of the Singapura 'history' felt that this was the true story of what had happened, and their scepticism forced Tommy Meadow to make a new statement, correcting her earlier comments.

In a 1994 interview, she admitted that there were inaccuracies in the way she had told the original version of the story. Her new account ran as follows:

During a previous marriage, she had been a successful exhibitor of Siamese, Burmese and Abyssinian Cats. In 1970 she had met Hal Meadow, a geophysicist whose work for an oil company took him repeatedly to the Far East, including Singapore. Hal had always been fascinated by cats, and through Tommy he developed an interest in the cat fancy and pedigree breeds. When he was on one of his trips to Singapore, in 1971, he spotted some local cats that he realized at a glance were unusual. He was particularly struck by the fact that they had a ticked coat like an Abyssinian's, but with a more silvery colour. Never having seen such a colouring before, he arranged to have four of these 'strange coloured Abys' shipped back to his wife in the United States. The group consisted of a male and three females, and in Tommy's care they soon began breeding.

Then in 1974, after Hal and Tommy had married, they travelled to Singapore together, accompanied by a group of her cats, including three grandchildren of the original quartet. These three were called Pusse, Tess and Ticle. (Slightly different spellings are given in this version of the story.) The Meadows continued breeding from these cats while still in Singapore. They had

THE EXQUISITELY DELICATE Singapura is one of the smallest of all breeds of domestic cat.
Incorrectly described as 'Singapore drain cats', they were in reality ships' cats discovered in the
harbour of Loyang in the north-east of Singapore.

intended to stay there for ten years but, following the fall of Saigon in July 1975, and the collapse of the American involvement in Vietnam, they returned earlier than expected to the United States. They took five Singapuras with them, including the original three, plus Gladys and George, who had been born there in the meantime. Once back home, they set about firmly establishing the new breed and gaining official recognition for it.

From this point onwards there is no controversy about what happened. In late 1975, Tommy Meadow started exhibiting her Singapuras at American cat shows. In the years that followed, the Singapura was formally recognized by more and more cat societies in America and in 1980 a United Singapura Society was formed to support the breed. By 1988 it was estimated that there were over 500 of these cats in North America and by the mid-1990s this had risen to about 2,000.

The first Singapura in Britain was a pregnant female called Faye Raye, who arrived on 25th July 1988 and gave birth a few weeks later, while still in quarantine. British interest in the Singapura developed in the 1990s and a Singapura Cat Club was formed to promote the breed. By 1995 there were an estimated 30 cats of this breed in the British Isles.

The question remains as to what drove Tommy Meadow to 'simplify' the history of the breed by pretending that she and her husband had picked up Pusse, Tessa and Tickle in the streets of Singapore. Were these three cats, as some critics were now suggesting, American-born hybrids between Abyssinians and Burmese, or were they truly the grandchildren of those original Singapore cats discovered by Hal Meadow in 1971? When this question was put to Tommy Meadow, she defended her 'revised' version of events in the following way:

It had been necessary to conceal the information about the original quartet of cats sent to her from Singapore by Hal Meadow in 1971, because at the time (to quote her) 'he was involved in "sensitive" work and his presence in Singapore could not be revealed'. The cats were perfectly genuine and had originated in Singapore, but for reasons quite unconnected with the animals themselves, it had been advisable to omit the earliest phase of their discovery.

Additional information obtained directly from Hal Meadow himself in 1996 confirms this. He was in Singapore to carry out confidential marine surveys for an oil company and was operating out of a port called Loyang in the north-east of the island. One day he noticed three ships' cats on one of the marine survey vessels and was surprised by their unusual appearance. They looked to him like odd-coloured Abyssinians and, as he had never seen anything like them before, he arranged for them to be shipped back to Houston on one of the work boats. About six months later, he saw a fourth cat of this type, also in the harbour at Loyang, which he managed to obtain from a local sailor. This, too, he had shipped back to the United States. Tommy took in all four cats and began to breed from them. When the Singapore cats arrived, her other cats were all neuters and she was not at that stage engaged in breeding programmes with anything else. She kept the Singapore cats pure and took them through two generations before she set off for Singapore with Hal in 1974, taking with her the soon-to-be-famous trio of Pusse, Tessa and Tickle.

The fact that, in July 1975, when Saigon fell, the Meadows returned unexpectedly to the United States was due to the rapid change in the economics of oil company activities in the Orient, caused by the sudden ending of the war in Vietnam.

Based on this more detailed explanation, it is safe to assume that the Singapura is, after all, a true-blue Eastern cat that developed naturally over a long period in the streets of Singapore. Certainly, it is the general view among most Singapura breeders that a cat of this type has been present in Singapore for at least 300 years, and that it is a well-established, ancient breed.

Furthermore, supporters of this 'ancient Singapura' view believe that there is a perfectly good explanation as to why some critics have favoured the rival idea that the breed is a more recent hybrid between Abyssinian and Burmese Cats. They point out that attempts by unscrupulous dealers to mass-produce inexpensive 'fake Singapuras' using crossings of this type, could easily have led to the incorrect belief that all Singapuras were created like this. It is pointed out that Mrs Meadow has been quite open about the fact that she did introduce other breeds in the early days of her Singapura breeding programme, but that these crossings were merely 'test-matings to eliminate known recessive genes from Singapura breeding stock'.

The best way to settle the matter of the breed's origin is for a detailed check to be made of the feral cat population of Singapore today, to see if pockets of typical Singapuras are still present there. A recent attempt to do this by Sarah Hartwell, during a brief stay in the city, proved inconclusive. She scoured the streets for pure specimens, but reports that 'although I saw numerous nervous cats of Oriental or Bobtail type, I found no Singapuras . . . During my stay I saw tabbies, bi-colours and self-colours, but not a single cat with "ticked fur the colour of old ivory", though this might simply mean that Kucinta is a shy and elusive creature. Having scoured the river area and not managed even a glimpse of Kucinta, I eventually began to wonder "are there any Singapuras in Singapore?".'

It seems likely that she was looking in the wrong districts. Perhaps if she had searched in the harbour region in the north-east of the island, where Hal Meadow discovered the original foundation stock for the breed in 1971, she might have been more successful. Obviously, a more careful search is indicated, although it must be borne in mind that, according to a new report, the Singapore authorities have recently introduced a policy of 'clearing the streets of stray cats', so it may already be too late.

Personality: Words used to describe this breed are slightly contradictory and include: playful, sociable, lively, responsive, undemanding, calm, even-tempered, quiet, gentle, alert, good-natured, placid, inquisitive, mischievous, active, intelligent, friendly and fearless. Some describe them as outgoing, but this is denied by others who say they are shy, demure and reserved. They have also been called 'aggressively affectionate'.

Colour Form: Only one colour is accepted: Sepia Agouti (sometimes called Brown Ticked).

Breed Clubs:

International Singapura Alliance. Address: P.O. Box 32218, Oakland, CA 94604, USA.

Original Singapura Breeder's Network. Address: P.O. Box 1457, Solvang, CA 93464, USA.

Singapura Cat Club. Issues a quarterly *Mewsletter.* Address: 437 Whippendell Road, Watford, Herts., WD1 7PS, England.

Singapura Fanciers' Society. Address: 82 W. Catalina Drive, Oakview, CA 93022, USA.

United Singapura Society. Address: 2135, Edison, Santa Ynez, CA 93460, USA, or 5520 Dublin Avenue, North Little Rock, AR 72118, USA.

IT IS THE REFINED DELICACY of the tiny Singapura Cat that has given this cat its great appeal to a growing band of fanatical supporters.

SPOTTED MIST CAT

The Spotted Mist Cat is an experimental breed from Australia developed in Sydney in the late 1970s from crosses between Burmese and Abyssinian, with the addition of domestic tabby. The result is a cat with a short, fine, spotted coat. This is Australia's first important home-grown pedigree cat breed and has recently been included in a CD-ROM listing 'Australian Innovations'.

THE SPOTTED MIST is the first truly Australian breed of domestic cat. It was developed in Sydney, starting in the late 1970s with a carefully planned, ten-year breeding programme using 30 foundation cats, including Burmese, Abyssinian and domestic tabbies.

Appearance: The short coat is described as glossy, dense and resilient. The spots occur over the sides, flanks and belly, and are seen against a misty ground colour, which gives the breed its name. The legs and tail are marked with dark rings and the face shows a typical tabby pattern. The rounded head has large, green eyes.

History: In 1976 a Sydney ecologist, Dr Truda Straede, began a ten-year breeding programme to create a spotted Australian breed. In order to avoid a narrow gene pool, no fewer than 30 foundation cats were involved. Half of these were Burmese, a quarter were Abyssinian and a quarter were domestic tabbies. The Burmese were used to provide temperament, size, conformation and colour dilution; the Abyssinians provided intelligence, colours and ticking; and the domestic tabbies provided vigour, health and reproductive qualities. All three types contributed to the creation of the spotted coat.

The result is a well-balanced cat, lacking in extremes and with a friendly temperament. It is claimed that Spotted Mists suffer little distress at being kept indoors. This is a significant feature in a new breed that is being developed in a country where government rules often demand a 'feline curfew', in order to protect the native wildlife.

In 1986 the breed was accepted for registration by the Royal Agricultural Society Cat Control of New South Wales. 1988 saw the first Spotted Mist Champion, and 1989 the first Grand Champion.

Colour Forms: Already five colour forms are recognized: Brown (Seal brown markings on silvery fawn); Blue (bluish-grey markings on silvery cream); Chocolate (chocolate markings on creamy-fawn); Lilac (dove grey markings on pinkish-grey); Gold (old gold markings on rich cream); Peach (salmon pink markings on pinkish-cream).

Breed Club:

The Spotted Mist Breeder's Association. Address: P.O. Box 384, Epping, New South Wales 2121, Australia.

SOKOKE FOREST CAT

Originating from the Sokoke district of eastern Kenya in East Africa, this breed is now being developed in Denmark. It has an unusual form of tabby coat pattern resembling a wood-grain effect, and there is still some disagreement as to how it acquired this. One theory suggests that it is a local, spontaneous mutation of an ordinary domestic cat. Another prefers to see it as a

THE SOKOKE FOREST CAT, is a rarity – a new domestic breed originating from tropical Africa.
Its appeal lies in its modified tabby pattern, now described as 'African Tabby', which gives
it a 'wood-grain' appearance

local subspecies of wild cat, while a third theory views it as a cross between a Kenyan domestic cat and a wild cat.

Appearance: The Sokoke Forest Cat, or Sokoke Cat, has a tabby pattern that has been designated 'African Tabby' to distinguish it from the other types. It is similar to Blotched or Classic Tabby, but with a 'wood-grain' look. Pat Turner has accurately described the way in which it differs from the typical Blotched Tabby: 'The differences are really only in the shape of the "oysters" which can easily be accounted for by a modifying gene or genes extending the central spot. The remainder of the pattern is as found in other blotched breeds with bonnet strings, eye liner, necklaces (Alderman's chains), butterflies and black dots at the whisker roots.'

As might be expected with a tropical feral cat, the Sokoke Cat has an elegant, slender body and a long, pointed, tapering tail.

History: In 1977 a female cat with a litter of kittens was discovered in a hollow under a dead bush during land clearance at the edge of the forest. The owner of the land, wildlife artist Jeni Slater, inspected the family and realized that they all had unusual markings of a kind she had not seen before. She took a male and female kitten home with her, hand-reared them, and later started breeding from them.

The ease with which they became tame suggests that they were, in fact, domestic cats that had gone wild, rather than true wild cats. It is perhaps significant that no further 'wild' specimens have been seen since that first encounter in 1977. This points to the likelihood that the Sokoke cats were a very restricted phenomenon, probably resulting from a few escaped domestic cats (belonging to Europeans resident in Kenya) that began breeding and at some point developed the novel coat pattern through a mutation in the small local population.

When Danish cat enthusiast Gloria Moldrup visited Jeni Slate in Africa, she was given a pair of Sokoke kittens and took them home with her to Denmark. There they were exhibited at the JYYRAK Show at Odense, and became the foundation pair for the breed in Europe. Jeni Slater has refused to allow any Sokoke Cats to go to Great Britain because of Britain's strict, six-month quarantine laws.

58

AMERICAN LYNX

A breed of stump-tailed cat that has recently appeared in the United States. In Germany it is known as the *Amerikanische Luchskatze*. It was developed in the 1980s by American breeders Joe Childers of North Carolina and Robert Mock of Seattle. There are both short-haired and long-haired versions. Coat patterns include two tabby variants known as Leopard and Tawny.

COLOURPOINT BRITISH SHORTHAIR CAT

A recently created breed in which a typical British Shorthair Cat has been enhanced by the addition of a characteristic Siamese coat pattern. It should not be confused with the American cat referred to as the 'Colorpoint Shorthair'. The latter is essentially a Siamese Cat with unusual colouring on its points.

Because of this confusion and because the Colourpoint British Shorthair Cat has such a cumbersome name, a new title will no doubt be forthcoming for this attractive breed.

Appearance: The same as for the British Shorthair Cat, except for the coat pattern. The dark extremities – the Siamese points – may be present in any of the usual colours. The short body has a stocky, cobby shape, with strong, thick legs, rounded head, large feet and heavy tail.

History: This breed was artificially developed by careful crossing experiments. The programme was started in England in the 1980s but the breed was not formally recognized until 1991. The aim was to 'borrow' the pointed coat pattern of the Siamese without any of the other Oriental qualities, such as angular body shape.

Personality: This cat remains essentially a typical British Shorthair, with a personality to match. Despite gaining the Siamese colouring, it has not acquired the Siamese character.

Colour Forms: All the various Siamese point colours are acceptable, and many have already appeared, including the following: Blue-Cream Point; Blue Point; Chocolate Point; Cream Point; Red Point; Seal Point; Seal Tortie Point.

Breed Club:

The Colourpoint British Shorthair Cat Club. Address: 77 Hallsfield Road, Bridgewood, Chatham, Kent, ME5 9RT, England.

THE COLOURPOINT BRITISH SHORTHAIR CAT, a 1980s breed in which Siamese markings have been added to a typically British Shorthair body. Although it has acquired the Siamese coat pattern, it has retained the personality of the Shorthair.

COUPARI

The name given to the long-haired version of the Scottish Fold Cat by British breeders. One American cat society introduced the name Highland Fold for this breed, but British breeders, knowing that it originated in the Lowlands of Scotland, preferred a more appropriate name based on its true home – the village of Coupar Angus, 21 km (13 miles) north-east of Perth.

There were long-haired individuals in the Scottish Fold stock from the very beginning of the breed in 1961, but when the official standard was written it referred only to the short-haired version. That became the dominant form, but no attempt was made to eliminate the long-haired gene.

The short-haired version was preferred because the long-haired individuals 'looked earless'. But then, in the early 1980s, an American exhibitor by the name of Hazel Swadberg started showing the Longhair Fold Cat for the first time. It was confined to the household-pet classes, but its presence began to make an impact and, in 1986, it was at last taken seriously when TICA officials voted by 39 to 1 to accept it as a separate breed in its own right.

Although the breed quickly became established, its name did not. TICA called it the Scottish Fold Longhair, as did the CFA. Then the CFF gave it the name of Longhair Fold when they accorded it championship status in 1991, while the ACFA preferred the more colourful title of Highland Fold when according it championship status in that same year. British breeders chose Coupari. It remains to be seen which of these four names will eventually win through to become the internationally accepted form.

Breed Club:

The Longhair Clan – Longhair Scottish Fold Breed Club. Address: 49 Hancock Street, Salem, MA 01920, USA.

COUPARI IS THE British name for the appealing long-haired version of the
Scottish Fold Cat *(opposite)*.
It was discovered at the Lowland Scottish village of Coupar Angus.

TIFFANIE CAT

The Tiffanie Cat is, essentially, a long-haired Burmese. A recent British breed, it is frequently confused with the superficially similar American breed called the Tiffany (see entry for Tiffany Cat). The Tiffanie was a long-haired by-product of the Burmilla breeding programme instigated in the 1980s. It is a member of the Asian group and was originally called the 'Asian Longhair'.

THERE HAS BEEN CONSIDERABLE confusion over the distinction between the British Tiffanie (pictured here) and the American Tiffany. The Tiffanie is essentially a long-haired Burmese. The Tiffany is superficially similar but, contrary to widespread published statements, does not have Burmese origins.

60

It was renamed the Tiffanie when it was wrongly believed to be closely related to the American Tiffany Cat.

Appearance: A golden-eyed cat with a long, silky coat, a ruff and a full tail. Otherwise it has the body proportions of a Burmese. Typically, the coat is brown but may also be in a variety of other colours.

History: During the 1980s Asian Shorthair breeding programmes, producing variations on the Burmese theme, several breeders accidentally began to produce long-haired kittens. The first to do so was Jeanne Bryson of Droitwich in Worcestershire, England. The Longhairs were often neutered and sold as pets, but some were kept and formed the basis of the new breed.

Colour Forms: The Tiffanie can be in any colour or pattern found in the Asian group.

62

WILD ABYSSINIAN CAT

Despite its name, this is not a wild feline, but a recent attempt on the part of pedigree cat breeders to recreate the original version of the Abyssinian, as it was back in the 19th century.

Appearance: This short-haired breed is similar to the modern Abyssinian except for the following features: it has a larger body, dark ring-markings on the tail, dark bars on the legs, a dark, M-shaped 'frown' marking on the forehead and dark rings on the neck. It is also slightly larger than the Abyssinian. It gives the impression of being a cross between an Abyssinian Cat and a Tabby Cat.

History: In the 1980s cats of this type were found living wild in Singapore and some were taken to the United States where Tord Svenson of Massachusetts has been developing and promoting the breed.

Personality: This cat has been referred to as independent and friendly.

63

MALAYAN CAT

An alternative name for certain types of Burmese Cats. Some cat organizations have accepted the whole range of Burmese colour forms as 'Burmese'. Others have refused to include the more recent colour forms, such as blue, champagne and platinum, under the title of Burmese. Purist breeders felt that a Burmese Cat is, by definition, a brown cat, and that any other colour must therefore be classified separately. To satisfy them, the name 'Malayan Cat' was introduced in 1980 to cover all non-traditional Burmese colour variants.

64

AMERICAN CURL CAT

A recently discovered American breed which has strongly curved ears.

Appearance: This breed is identified by the shape of its ears, which are curled back on themselves, exposing hairy ear-tufts. The ears feel rigid and stiff to the touch. This was a chance mutation, discovered accidentally. It involves a simple dominant gene which will give 50 per cent curly-eared kittens in litters resulting from crosses between curled cats and plain ones. It is quite different from the ear-curling that occurs with the Scottish Fold Cat. The American Curl's ears curl up, while the Scottish Fold's ears fold down. The kittens are born with straight ears, which then curl up tightly within 24–72 hours. During the next four months, the tight curling starts to relax until finally the ears settle into their typical adult, semi-curled condition.

There are both long-haired (the original cats) and (later) short-haired forms of this breed.

History: This breed first appeared as recently as 1981, in Lakewood, California. In June 1981 John and Grace Ruga found two stray kittens on their doorstep. One of them, a silky, long-haired, black female, stayed with them and they called her 'Shulamith' (not 'Shulasmith', as is sometimes reported). The name means 'black but comely'. The Rugas noticed that she had strangely shaped ears, and they decided to keep her. Later that year, on December 12th, she gave birth to a litter of four kittens. Two of these kittens showed the same curled ears as their mother and it was clear that there was a possibility of using these cats as the foundation stock of a new breed. An acquaintance of the Rugas, Nancy Kestrel, encouraged them to exhibit Shulamith and her two curly-eared kittens in a cat show being held at Palm Springs in California in October 1983. This was the first time this new breed had been shown in public. The reaction was favourable and in a matter of only a few years it became an officially registered breed with certain of the American Cat Societies. In 1985, TICA formally recognized it as 'The American Curl' and in 1986 the CFA followed suit.

Although the unusual shape of the ears of this cat does not appear to cause the animal any problems, some critics nevertheless see the curl mutation as a 'deformity' and the breed is not yet universally accepted. It remains a comparatively rare breed. In 1993 it was estimated that, even after 12 years of breeding, there were fewer than 1,000 American Curls in existence.

Personality: Terms used to describe this breed include: mischievous, curious, placid, playful, even-tempered, amusing, lively, whimsical, adaptable, friendly, sturdy, affectionate, intelligent and thieving. They are said to 'think like kittens all their lives'.

THE AMERICAN CURL, with its uniquely curved ears, is a new breed, not discovered until 1981. It first appeared in the form of a stray kitten on a doorstep in Lakewood, California, and was soon developed into a popular pedigree show-cat.

Colour Forms: All colours are acceptable in this breed. The CFA in America lists the following colours for this breed. To simplify the list, the colours are grouped into convenient categories.
CFA: SOLID: White; Black; Blue; Red; Cream; Chocolate; Lilac.
SHADED, SILVER AND GOLDEN: Chinchilla Silver; Shaded Silver; Chinchilla Golden; Shaded Golden; Shell Cameo; Shaded Cameo (Red Shaded); Shell Tortie; Shaded Tortie.
SMOKE: Black Smoke; Blue Smoke; Cameo Smoke (Red Smoke); Chocolate Smoke; Lavender Smoke; Cream Smoke; Smoke Tortie; Chocolate Tortie Smoke; Blue-Cream Smoke.
TABBY: (Classic, Mackerel, Patched, Spotted and Ticked Tabby Patterns) Brown Patched Tabby; Blue Patched Tabby; Silver Patched Tabby; Silver Tabby; Red Tabby; Brown Tabby; Blue Tabby; Cream Tabby; Blue Silver and Cream Silver Tabbies; Chocolate Silver Tabby; Lavender Silver Tabby; Cameo Tabby.
PARTI-COLOR: Tortie; Blue-Cream.
BI-COLOR: Bi-color; Van Bi-color, Calico; Dilute Calico; Van Calico; Van Dilute Calico.
TABBY AND WHITE: Seal Point; Chocolate Point; Blue Point; Lilac-Lynx Point; Lilac-Cream Point; Lilac-Cream Lynx Point; Flame (Red) Point; Cream Point; Cream Lynx Point; Tortie Point; Chocolate-Tortie Point; Chocolate-Tortie Lynx Point; Blue-Cream Point; Blue-Cream Point; Chocolate Lynx Point; Seal Lynx Point; Blue Lynx Point; Tortie-Lynx Point; Blue-Cream Lynx Point.

Breed Clubs:
American Curl Cat Club. Address: 100 Westmont Road, Syracuse, NY 13219, USA.
United Society of American Curls. Address: 11691 Kagel Canyon, Lake View Terrace, CA 91342-7422, USA.

65

BURMILLA CAT

A recent British breed resulting from an accidental mating between a male Silver Chinchilla and a female Lilac Burmese.

Appearance: In appearance, this cat is essentially a silver Burmese. The combination of the Burmese body-type with a soft, dense, delicately tipped-silver, short-haired coat, gives it a special appeal. In addition it has dark pencilling around the eyes, as though wearing eyeliner.

History: The Burmilla was accidentally created by the Baroness Miranda von Kirchberg in 1981. A male Silver Chinchilla called Sanquist and a female Burmese called Fabergé were awaiting mates of their own respective breeds, but began to demonstrate an unusual degree of interest in one another. When Fabergé came into season she was immediately isolated in preparation for a journey to a Burmese stud male. Before this could happen, however, Sanquist was accidentally given brief access to her by a cleaner who did not realize the consequence of her actions. In the Baroness's own words: 'A kind lady, passing the door and seeing the dejected Sanquist, took pity on him and let him into Fabergé's room, just to say a last farewell.' Fabergé was then sent away for her official mating with another pedigree Burmese. When she returned, her litter was not Burmese as expected, but from their appearance had clearly been fathered by Sanquist, who now took a strong paternal interest in them, grooming them and protecting them.

The litter consisted of four female kittens and they were named Galatea, Gemma, Gabriella and Gisella. They were so attractive that, instead of neutering them and disposing of them as pets, as usually happens with 'accidents', the Baroness decided to keep them and develop them as the foundation stock of a new breed. They were back-crossed to Burmese and it was found that their appealing characteristics were maintained in the next generation. Further breeding helped to fix the Burmilla as a distinct new type of pedigree cat and the Baroness was soon to form the Burmilla Association, with a view to promoting the breed.

Another breeder, Therese Clarke, who acquired Gemma from the original litter, launched the Burmilla Cat Club in 1984, with a regular publication called the 'BCC Mews'. Within four years the club had 50 active members and more recently this figure has risen to 70.

With the two groups of breeders both actively developing the Burmilla, it was soon safely established as an important new breed. The first (Kirchberg) group made efforts to improve the body shape, while the second (Clarke) group concentrated on improving the tipped coat.

The Burmilla was granted preliminary championship status in Britain in 1990.

THE BURMILLA CAT, an elegant breed developed in England during the 1980s. It began as an accidental mating between a male Chinchilla and a female Burmese, but rapidly became established as an attractive new show cat.

Personality: Terms used to describe this breed include: playful, outgoing, sociable, friendly, affectionate, sweet-tempered and gentle.

Colour Forms:

GCCF: The agouti coat, which appears in both standard and silver versions, may either be tipped or shaded, in the following colours: Black; Blue; Chocolate; Lilac; Red; Caramel; Apricot; Cream; Black Tortie; Blue Tortie; Chocolate Tortie; Lilac Tortie; Caramel Tortie.

Breed Clubs:

Burmilla–Asian Association. Address: 1 Thistlecroft Rd, Hersham, Surrey, KT12 5QT, England.

Burmilla Cat Club. Address: Mill House, Letcombe Regis, Oxon, OX12 9JD, England.

COLOURPOINT EUROPEAN SHORTHAIR CAT

A similar development to the Colourpoint British Shorthair (see entry). Created in Italy in 1982, the typical European Shorthair was successfully given a Siamese pointed coat pattern, without altering its character or anatomy in any other way. Despite its Oriental colouring, the breed remains a stocky, quiet Shorthair Cat.

THE BLUE POINT VERSION of the stocky Colourpoint European Shorthair Cat, developed in Italy in the early 1980s.

EUROPEAN SHORTHAIR CAT

The modern pedigree European Shorthair has been developed from the ordinary working cats and pet cats of Continental Europe, with careful, selective breeding replacing the casual breeding that had been going on for centuries.

Appearance: A stocky cat with a round, longish head, rather thick, strong legs and a medium-length tail. In fact, this is generally a rather 'medium' breed in most respects, which is not so surprising, bearing in mind its incredibly mixed ancestry.

THE EUROPEAN SHORTHAIR CAT. Until 1982 this pedigree cat was not separated from the very similar British Shorthair, but in that year a distinction was made for show purposes.

BECAUSE MOST non-pedigree house-pets have short hair, a special name was required to distinguish their carefully bred, pedigree show-cat relatives. The solution was to give the latter the name European Shorthair (pictured here), British Shorthair or American Shorthair.

History: Until 1982 no distinction was made between the British Shorthair and the European Shorthair, but then they were formally separated for show purposes. Since then they have been diverging slightly, although it is still easy to confuse them. The European breed has a less stocky body, longer legs, a slightly longer head and larger ears.

The most confusing aspect of this breed is that it is possible to find three separate definitions of it, according to the kind of author writing about it. It has been defined as:

1 Any domestic short-haired cat living as a household pet in Europe (by authors writing about the history of cats in general).
2 Any British Shorthair Cat living on the mainland of Continental Europe (by British authors writing about British pedigree breeds).
3 A distinct breed of pedigree cat not to be confused with the British Shorthair Cat (by authors writing about international breed classifications).

Personality: Terms used to describe this breed include: hardy, rugged, quiet, untemperamental, adaptable, moderate, sensible, active, intelligent, shrewd, inquisitive, brave and lively.
Colour Forms: Essentially the same as the British Shorthair. A huge variety of colour forms is available. (For details see British Shorthair.)

68

YORK CHOCOLATE CAT

The York Chocolate Cat is a new American cat that takes the first part of its name from the state of New York, where it originated, and the second part from the rich chocolate brown colour of its coat.

Appearance: The body proportions are similar to those of the Siamese, but it is bigger. The long coat comes in a variety of chocolate colours and patterns.

History: This recent breed arose in 1983 on a farm belonging to Janet Chiefari. The foundation stock consisted of a pair of house cats of uncertain ancestry. The male was long-haired and black; the female was long-haired and black and white. Somewhere in their past lurked a trace of Siamese.

Because of the confused genetic background of this breed, it is generally frowned upon by the official feline organizations. As a result it remains a rare breed, and as recently as the 1990s there were no more than 100 specimens in existence.

Personality: Terms used to describe this breed include: energetic, lively, playful, enthusiastic, agile and cheerful.

THE AMERICAN BREED known as the York Chocolate *(opposite)* dates from 1983. It appears in many patterns, the dark areas being a rich, dark chocolate brown. Some are predominantly brown; others, like this one, show large areas of white.

OJOS AZULES

A recent American discovery from New Mexico. The Spanish name means, literally, 'Blue Eyes'.

Appearance: A tortoiseshell cat with intensely blue eyes. The colouring of the eyes is even more intense than that found in Siamese. There is no deafness or squint associated with this particular blue-eyed gene.

History: The first example of this new breed was found in New Mexico in 1984. She was a tortoiseshell female called 'Cornflower'. Her vivid blue eyes were a spontaneous mutation and subsequent breeding from her has proved that the blue-eyed gene is dominant. All her kittens displayed the same dramatic eye colour.

The Ojos Azules remains a rare breed. As recently as 1992 only ten had been registered.

A NEW BREED OF CAT *(opposite),* the Ojos Azules, meaning 'Blue Eyes'. The extraordinary, intense blue eyes have no squint and are not linked to any problems with deafness, as has happened in other cases in the past.

SEYCHELLOIS CAT

An experimental breed created in England in the 1980s.

Appearance: Oriental build, with slim, elegant body, long neck and legs, and wedge-shaped head with large ears. The coat is white with splashes of colour. There are both short-haired and long-haired versions. The eyes are blue.

THE SEYCHELLOIS is a comparatively new breed, displaying a white coat splashed with colour. It was developed in England in the 1980s.

The markings are divided into three types:

SEYCHELLOIS SEPTIÈME: White, with a coloured tail, and large patches of colour on the head, body and legs.

SEYCHELLOIS HUITIÈME: White, with a coloured tail, and small patches of colour on the head and legs.

SEYCHELLOIS NEUVIÈME: Almost entirely white, with a coloured tail and only small patches of colour on the head.

History: A report on the cats of the Seychelles was the inspiration for this breed. British breeder Pat Turner of Milton Keynes, Buckinghamshire, set about re-creating the Seychelles coat pattern which consisted of a white ground colour with small splashes of colour and a fully coloured tail. Her breeding programme began in 1984, in co-operation with another British breeder, Julie Smith. As foundation stock, they used two female tortie and white Persians and two male Siamese. By back-crossing the offspring of these matings to Siamese and Oriental cats, the Seychelles pattern was improved, and has been further strengthened with each subsequent generation. The first fully developed Seychellois Cats in the programme were named Félicité, Victoria, Amirante and Thérèse and the first two of these were used to introduce the breed at a cat show in 1988 – the first to be exhibited under the new name. In 1989 a Seychellois Cat Society was formed and the future of the breed was assured.

Personality: Terms used to describe this breed include: athletic, scatter-brained, demanding and demonstrative.

71

DUTCH REX CAT

One of the later breeds of Rex Cat.

Appearance: Said to have a coarser wavy coat, with a more bristly texture, than the better-known Rex Cats.

History: First reported from Holland in 1985.

LA PERM CAT

A new, curly-coated breed from the United States. Its full title is 'The Dalles La Perm', after the place in Oregon where it was discovered as an isolated mutation.

THE DALLES LA PERM from the United States is a new breed of curly-coated cat that is destined for a great future because of its exceptionally attractive, shaggy appearance. It was discovered among Oregon barn-cats in 1986.

Appearance: A cat with 'a distinctive coat that falls in loose ringlets, reminiscent of the Komondor or Puli Dog'. In short-haired examples it has an 'Afro' look, but in longer-haired versions the coat forms into very tight ringlets. Referred to as 'The Cat with the Permanent Curl', it has also been called the Alpaca Cat.

History: Described by its discoverer as 'The Cat for the '90s', the first example of this exciting new breed was found among ordinary, short-haired American barn-cats by Linda Koehl of The Dalles, Oregon, in 1986. She noticed that one of the kittens had been born bald and she thought it would die. But it survived and two months later began to grow a unique, curly coat. This animal – a brown tabby female, predictably named 'Curly' – became the foundation cat of a breeding programme to foster the unusual hair mutation. The La Perm has already gone though seven generations and in September 1995 was accepted as a New Breed by TICA. All colours are allowed. Bald kittens still appear occasionally but are no longer common. It is estimated that by early 1996 there were about 60 cats of this breed in existence. In personality it is described as extremely affectionate and easy-going.

Breed Club:

There is as yet no breed club, but until one is formed, enquiries are directed to 2945 Dry Hollow Road, The Dalles, OR 97058-9551, USA.

SI-REX

This is a recent form of Cornish Rex Cat, with a coat pattern showing Siamese points. For some years it was ignored as a distinct breed, but was eventually recognized by the CFA in America and given championship status in 1986. The Si-Rex was created by crossing Cornish Rex Cats with Siamese Cats.

THE DRAMATICALLY proportioned Si-Rex, a recently developed cross between Cornish Rex Cats and Siamese, now becoming established as a new breed in its own right.

SELKIRK REX CAT

Appeared in Wyoming in 1987 and quickly developed as a new Rex breed. Aptly described as 'The Cat in Sheep's Clothing', or a 'Sheepcat'.

Appearance: It has the characteristic curly coat and curled whiskers of a Rex Cat, but unlike the other Rex breeds, the Selkirk has a bulky appearance with a rectangular, muscular body. The head is wide and rounded with a short muzzle. The ears, which have ear-tufts, are smaller than those of a typical Rex Cat. Coarse guard hairs are present and these, as well as the awn and down hairs, are curled. Selkirk kittens are born with curly coats, but these disappear at about six months, to be replaced by a temporary covering of sparse, wiry hair. Then, at about ten months, the plush, thick, curly adult coat appears.

History: The first Selkirk Rex was spotted in 1987 as a curly-coated, dilute calico female kitten in an otherwise normal, straight-haired litter of non-pedigree cats. This litter, along with their straight-haired mother, had been deposited in an animal shelter as unwanted pets.

The curly kitten was noticed as something out of the ordinary by Peggy Voorhees of the Bozeman Humane Society in Wyoming. Because the animal's coat was so unusual, she was adopted by Jeri Newman, a Montana breeder of pedigree Persian Cats. When 14 months old, this young female, now known as Miss De Presto, was mated with Newman's champion Black Persian called Photo Finish, and on 4th July 1988 produced a litter of six kittens. Half of these displayed their mother's curly coat. One was a black and white male, another was a black female and a third was a tortie female.

It was soon clear to those involved that they were witnessing the birth of an exciting new breed and it was decided to give it the name of Selkirk, after the Selkirk Mountains in Wyoming, which were near to the spot where the foundation cat, Miss De Presto, had been discovered.

Further matings, including back-crosses to Miss De Presto, were organized. There were also out-crosses to various short-haired breeds as well as long-hairs. Other Rex breeds are not, however, to be introduced into the Selkirk development programme, because it is clear that the Selkirk is the only type of Rex that is genetically dominant. This means that the Selkirk Rex cannot be related to any of the other Rex genes, and there is therefore no point in mixing them.

Encouraged by the success of the Selkirk programme, the breeders involved formed a Selkirk Rex Society and in August 1990 two American cat associations agreed to give official recognition to this new breed. There is now also a Selkirk Rex Breed Association in Canada.

THE SELKIRK REX, a shaggy-coated cat discovered in 1987. It has a heavier build than the more familiar, long-established Rex Cat breeds. It acquired its name because it first appeared near the Selkirk Mountains in Wyoming.

Personality: Terms used to describe this breed include: patient, tolerant, laid-back, cuddly, playful.

Colour Forms: Those recorded so far include: Black Tortie Smoke; Blue-Green; Tortie. Pointed coats are known, inherited from the foundation cat, and Burmese and 'mink' colours have also been recorded.

Breed Clubs:

Selkirk Rex Breed Club. Publishes a quarterly newsletter, *Woolgathering.* Address: 3555 South Pacific Highway No. 3, Medford, OR 97501, USA.

Selkirk Rex Breeders. Address: P.O. Box 21282, Concord, CA 94521-0208, USA.

Selkirk Rex Society. Address: 231 South D Street, Livingston, MT 59047, USA.

75

REXED MAINE COON CAT

A wavy-haired mutation of the long-haired Maine Coon Cat. Also known as the Maine Wave. The Rex gene was first reported in the Maine Coon by British breeder Di Everett. In 1994 she commented: 'The first Rexed Maine Coon in Britain was born, as far as we know, in our household in 1988 . . . We have produced a total of four rexed kittens, from three different

THE REXED MAINE COON CAT, or 'Maine Wave'. It is reported that the Rex gene occurs in about one in every 200 Maine Coon births. Some breeders reject Rexed kittens, but others are encouraging them.

mothers, all mated to the same male.' Tests proved that the mutation concerned was neither the Devon Rex gene nor the American Wirehair gene, and there were some indications that the Cornish Rex gene was probably not involved either.

She investigated the occurrence of the Maine Coon Rex gene and found that 'out of some 4,000 registrations in Britain, we only have approximately 20 rexed kittens.' Because some of the rexed animals died young she feared that it might be a semi-lethal gene in this breed, but other Maine Coon breeders disagreed, pointing out that their own rexed animals were 'bounding with health', and suggesting that the early deaths were probably not related to the special hair condition.

Some Maine Coon breeders see the Rex gene as a problem to be eliminated, while others consider it to be an intriguing new variant. Breeder David Brinicombe reported positive reactions: 'I exhibited my three recently (billed as 'Maine Waves' or just 'Waves') and received an overwhelmingly positive reaction to them with very few adverse comments. I have just heard there is interest being shown in them from Italy, so this may not be the end of the story.'

76

NEBELUNG CAT

A new American breed, the recently developed long-haired version of the Russian Blue.

Appearance: Similar in all respects to the Russian Blue, except for the coat length which is long and soft to the touch. The blue-grey double coat has guard hairs that are silver-tipped, giving the cat a lustrous look.

History: This new long-haired cat was developed in the 1980s by American breeder Cora Cobb from a foundation pair called Siegfried and Brunhilde. Their ancestry can be traced back to a black female called Terri who produced a litter that appeared to be carrying Angora genes. One of her daughters, named Elsa, was mated to a Russian Blue male. They produced two litters

THIS BEAUTIFUL new American breed, the Nebelung, is the long-haired version of the well-known Russian Blue. This is the Blue colour form, although this particular example appears to be unusually dark.

including the male Siegfried in the first litter and the female Brunhilde in the second. These were then acquired by Cora Cobb and used for further careful breeding to stabilize the new 'Long-haired Blue'. In 1987 it was finally given official recognition by TICA and looks set for a successful future.

Personality: Terms used to describe this breed include: calm, reserved, gentle, quiet, timid, affectionate, loving, adaptable and intelligent.

Colour Forms: Only two are recognized so far: Blue (blue-grey, with a slight silvery sheen); White (pure, glossy white).

SUQUTRANESE CAT

A dazzling white, unticked version of the Somali (the long-haired form of the Abyssinian), recently developed in Britain. It was first exhibited at a Cat Association show in England in 1990.

MUNCHKIN CAT

A short-legged American cat discovered in the 1990s. Viewed as a freak by most cat societies. Also referred to as the American Munchkin, the Munchkin Mutant, the Wiener Cat, the Dachshund Cat, the Minikat, or the 'Ferret of the Feline World'. It was named after the 'little people' who appear in *The Wizard of Oz*.

Appearance: This is a short-haired cat with a dominant gene for reduced leg-length, the front legs being even shorter than the back legs. The length of the front legs is no more than 7.5 cm (3 inches).

History: This unusual mutant feline is the first short-legged cat to be taken seriously as a breed. It parallels the Dachshund and the short-legged terrier breeds of dog, but there is a fundamental difference between them. The Dachshund and the short-legged terriers were bred for a specific

THE STARTLING NEW, short-legged breed called the Munchkin Cat has caused an uproar in the cat world. Many see it as a degradation of feline grace, while others argue that it is no more unusual that a Dachshund or any other short-legged breed of dog.

purpose – to go to earth. Their short legs were an advantage to them in entering burrows. But the Munchkin Cat has been developed purely as an oddity, whose modified legs offer the animal no serious, practical advantage.

It emerged as a chance mutation in the United States in 1983, when a short-legged stray cat was discovered and became the foundation stock for the breed. Despite its clumsy appearance, it appears to have found favour among those who prefer to own an undemanding indoor cat. It first came to the notice of American cat breeders at a TICA show in Madison Square Garden in 1991. The original Munchkin was a black female called 'Blackberry' and the early examples came from Lousiana.

The breed has been developed in Virginia Beach, Virginia, by the American breeder Penny Squires, who insists that they are not deformed. She points out that, for their owners, they offer the advantage that 'they can't jump on to kitchen counters'. The only benefit she can envisage for the cats themselves is that 'they can chase things under the bed'.

According to one report, the Munchkin is capable of turning faster than longer-legged breeds and is able to run backwards.

Critics of this breed, and there are many, point out that, apart from its lack of lithe feline grace, the Munchkin has great difficulty in grooming itself and also runs the risk of suffering from premature ageing of its unnaturally long spine. Despite the claims made for it by Penny Squires, these critics feel it is unlikely that this new breed will ever obtain wide popularity as a pedigree show cat.

Short-legged cats have appeared before, the first in England in the 1930s. They lasted for several generations but apparently died out during the chaos of World War II. After the war, one was reported in Russia in Stalingrad (now St. Petersberg) in 1953, but, like the English ones, this line did not survive.

Breed Club:

The International Munchkin Society. Tel (USA): 413-736 6381.

79

URALS REX CAT

According to a recent report, a new example of the wavy-haired Rex gene was discovered in the Urals in Russia in 1991.

80

RAGAMUFFIN CAT

A very recent American breed, similar to the Ragdoll Cat (see separate entry), but in a new range of colours.

Appearance: A luxuriant, long-haired breed, the Ragamuffin is described as 'the new rag-type cat with the coat of many colours . . . [a] large cat with silky, plush non-matting fur and large, expressive oval eyes'.

THE RAGAMUFFIN CAT, an American breed developed in the 1990s, is in essence a Ragdoll Cat in unusual colours. It appears to signal a split between two groups of breeders, with one camp supporting Ragdolls and the other favouring Ragamuffins.

History: One of the newest of all breeds, the Ragamuffin was created in 1994. Pat Steckman describes how this came about: 'Ann Baker founded an organization, the International Ragdoll Cat Association, whose cats are not shown. In early 1994 a group of breeders from IRCA formed a new group and breed called the Ragamuffin, which has been accepted as an experimental breed by ACFA.' According to another source, the Ragamuffin is already recognized for competition by the United Feline Organization in America and can be registered with the American Cat Fanciers' Association, although not, as yet, shown with them.

Personality: Terms used to describe this breed include: docile, quiet, affectionate, intelligent, playful, placid and loving.

Colour Forms: On the subject of Ragamuffin colour, Judy Thomas, writing in 1996, comments: 'The conformation and pattern standards for the Ragamuffin are virtually identical to that of the Ragdoll, but Ragamuffins include many more colors. All varieties of pointed color, including Lynx Point, Tortie Point and Red Point, all the Mink and Sepia colors produced by the introduction of the Burmese gene and all the colors of the Persian Cats are accepted in Solid, Mitted and Parti-color varieties . . . Seal, Blue, Chocolate and Lilac Pointed, Mitted and Parti-color Ragamuffins are virtually indistinguishable from Ragdolls; the other colors resemble Ragdolls in conformation but differ in color.'

Breed Clubs:

Ragamuffin Associated Group. Describes itself as 'the parent club of the Ragamuffin'. Address: 5759 Cypress Cir., Tallahassee, FL 32303, USA.

Ragamuffin Fanciers Association. Address: RR 1, Box 185, LeRoy, IL 61752, USA.

EXPERIMENTAL BREEDS

New breeds are named from time to time, and sometimes little or nothing is known about them beyond the fact that they exist. Brief references to them provide no details beyond their name. For the sake of completeness, however, they are included here because, although some of them will no doubt vanish without trace, others may eventually go on to become serious, recognized breeds.

ASIAN SMOKE

A recent British breed created by mating Burmilla with Burmese. A member of the Asian Group, it was formerly called the Burmoiré Cat but has now been renamed the Asian Smoke. Ghost tabby markings on the body give the fur the look of rippling, or the moiré pattern of watered silk. In its anatomy and the texture of its fur it resembles the Burmese Cat, but its colour and markings are like those of the Oriental Smoke.

BRISTOL CAT

A new experimental breed.

CEYLON CAT

A cat developed by the Cat Club of Ceylon (now Sri Lanka), which looks like an early form of the Abyssinian. Also known as the 'Ceylonese Cat' or 'Celonese Cat'.

Appearance: It has the typical ticked coat of the modern Abyssinian, but with the addition of the barred leg-markings common in that breed at the turn of the century. It is very similar to the so-called 'Wild Abyssinian' developed in the 1980s from feral stock found in Singapore.

History: In recent years it has found favour among Italian breeders. In January 1984, Dr Paolo Pellegatta, a Milanese veterinary surgeon, was exploring some of the smaller villages in Sri Lanka, when he came across an unusual and delightful form of local cat. Although feral, the animals in question were remarkably friendly and Dr Pellegata decided to take a small group of them back to Italy. There were two males, Tisa and Serendib, and two females, Taranga and Aralyia. They were later to be joined by a few more, and together formed the European nucleus of the breed. They made their first public appearance in the West a few months later, in May 1984, at the Como Cat Show in Italy, and were an immediate success. There followed four years of carefully planned breeding and then, in May 1988, the Ceylon Cat was submitted to

FIFe, and started on the first phase of its official recognition as a new form of pedigree cat.
Colour Forms: The traditional colouring is a sandy-golden background with black markings. This is known as the Manila. There are also Blue, Red, Cream and Tortoiseshell variations.
Breed Club:
Club Amatori Gatto di Ceylon (The Ceylon Cat Lovers Club) was formed by Dr Pellegatta at Verigate and is based at Corgeno, near Milan, Italy.

CHERUBIM CAT

This is a new, experimental breed developed as a variant of the Ragdoll Cat. It has not, as yet, been accepted by any official cat organization.

CHINESE HARLEQUIN CAT

A new type of short-haired black and white cat. A predominantly white cat, but with a black tail and black patches on the head and body. It is now recognized by TICA. It is said to have been an attempt to re-create an ancient Chinese cat.

CORNELIAN CAT

An experimental breed referred to as 'a self red short-haired cat of Burmese type; it can be regarded as the red equivalent of the Bombay. The name was adopted because it perfectly describes the beautiful rich russet red coat, just the colour of the cornelian gemstone.' It arose more or less accidentally during breeding programmes intended to improve the colouring of certain types of Burmese Cat, but now looks as though it may end up being officially recognized in its own right.

HIMBUR CAT

A new experimental breed based on a cross between Himalayan and Burmese Cats. This is a long-haired cat with Tonkinese markings (the Tonkinese itself being a cross between Burmese and Siamese, displaying a dark brown body with even darker extremities).

HONEYBEAR CAT

This is an experimental breed developed as a variant of the Ragdoll Cat. It is not, as yet, accepted by any official cat organization.

KARELIAN BOBTAIL CAT

Similar to the Japanese Bobtail Cat, but with a longer coat. Little is known about this breed. In 1995 international judge Alan Edwards commented: 'In Germany last year, I encountered a new variety called the Karelian Bobtail, a semi-longhaired cat from Russia. Its Standard of Points includes: "as many bents in the tail as possible".'

KHMER CAT

A rare, long-haired breed with Siamese colouring similar to the Birman but without white feet.

LONGHAIR REX CAT

According to a 1994 German report, Eastern European breeders have recently created a long-haired version of the Rex Cat by crossing Rex Cats with Persians.

ORIENTAL LONGHAIR CAT

This is a recently developed, long-haired version of the Oriental Shorthair. Sometimes called the Mandarin Cat, it is a long-haired cat of Siamese body-type, but without the typical Siamese point-markings. The true source of the long-haired gene is not clear. By the early 1990s the new breed had been officially recognized by TICA in America, with other societies showing increasing interest. The colour forms are the same as for the Oriental Shorthair.

Note: Confusingly, in Australia 'Oriental Longhair' is an alternative name for the Balinese Cat.

PALOMINO CAT

A new, experimental breed from North America.

POODLE CAT

According to a 1994 report from Germany, a new type of Rex Cat has been developed by breeder Dr Rosemarie Wolf. Called the *Pudelkatzen,* or Poodle Cat, it was created by crossing Devon Rex with Scottish Fold to produce a breed with a lambswool coat and folded ears.

RACEKATTE OR RUGKATT

The Racekatte is a long-haired Danish breed, almost identical with the Siberian Forest Cat. Its Swedish equivalent is the *Rugkatt.*

SAFARI CAT

A new experimental breed.

SNOW CAT

Also known as the Alaskan Snow Cat. A new, experimental breed developed in the United States during the 1990s. Several breeders in Florida and Minnesota have been working towards producing a heavy-boned, thick-furred, silvery-coloured, round-headed cat, similar to the Siberian Forest Cat. This has been achieved by crossings between Somalis and Silver Persians. The early stages of this programme are still in progress at the time of writing.

STERLING CAT

This is a new name given to the long-established, silvery-coloured, Chinchilla Persian Cat, elevating it from a colour variant to a full breed. This move was proposed in the 1980s by the American breeder Jeannie Johnson and was recognized by TICA in 1994. The official show debut, using this name, was in New York in October 1995.

TRADITIONAL SIAMESE CAT

This is an alternative name for the recently re-created, old-style Siamese Cat. Because this is a new development, no agreement has yet been reached concerning the official title of this cat. At present it is known by many names, including Applehead Siamese, Applecat, Old-fashioned Siamese, Classic Siamese, Opal Cat and Thai Cat. In France this type of Siamese is called the *Thaï,* and in Germany the *Thaikatze.*

Appearance: A Siamese Cat with a well-balanced, solid form, lacking extreme elongation of the neck and body. The head is rounded instead of wedge-shaped and the ears only medium size.

History: During the past century the body shape of the Siamese has become increasingly exaggerated – more and more elongated, angular and slender, with a wedge-shaped head. In recent years this process has been taken to such lengths, and the Siamese show cats have become so extreme in type, that a number of breeders have felt the time was ripe for a return to something closer to the original Siamese, known so well from early, turn-of-the-century photographs.

In America a group was formed to promote this plan with careful breeding programmes. A statement made by this group in 1994 reads as follows:

'The Apple-head Siamese is now being recognized as a unique national cat breed named the Opal Cat. In short, the Opal Cat is a short-haired, American-style colorpoint as beautiful as the gem that inspired its name. Its sweet face is the setting for brilliant blue eyes that blaze with the stunning iridescent glow of precious blue opals. And, like the opal gem, the Opal Cat has a creamy lustrous coat that may be pointed in a wide range of delightful colors. Its body type is not Oriental. Rather, the Opal Cat has a body that uniquely reflects its American heritage.'

This revived form of the breed is also becoming popular in Europe where it is known as the Thai Cat. Breeders in Germany have also been re-creating the old-fashioned type of Siamese, with a rounder face and less elongated body. Because the increasing angularity of Siamese Cats in pedigree cat shows has led to criticisms from the German authorities, breeders there now fear that the more extreme forms of Siamese may eventually be banned, and they are trying to anticipate this by a voluntary return to the older type. Hence the re-introduction of the old-fashioned *Thaikatze*, or Thai Cat. It remains to be seen whether its popularity will increase to the point where it will eventually eclipse the exaggerated 'Modern Siamese', as some of its champions predict.

It is possible today to obtain two types of Traditional Siamese. The first is a 'reconstituted' cat, created by introducing stocky, short-haired cat elements into a strain of slender, modern Siamese, to modify the extreme angularity. The second type – the true classic Siamese – comes from purebred lines belonging to conservative breeders who have never succumbed to the extreme modernization of the breed and have kept their old lines unadulterated and pure. At first glance it is impossible to distinguish between these two types. Only an examination of breeders' records will give the answer.

Colour Forms: The Traditional breed is accepted only in traditional colours: Seal Point, Blue Point, Chocolate Point and Lilac Point.

Breed Clubs:

Fanciers of the Opal Cat of the United States (FOCUS). Publishes a quarterly magazine, *The Point of Focus.* Address: 1385 Hooper Avenue, Suite 280, Toms River, NJ 08753, USA.

Traditional Cat Association. Address: 1000 Pegasus Farms Lane, Alpharetta, GA 30201, USA.

Traditional Siamese. Address: 8752 Woodsman Court, Washington, MI 48094, USA.

Note: There is a breed publication called *Thai Line.* Address: P.O. Box 1106, Placentia, CA 92670, USA.

Victoria Rex Cat

In 1972 a kitten carrying the wavy-haired Rex gene was born to feral cats in the Victoria district of London. It was named Tuoh, and Peter Davis reported in the 1972 *Cats Annual* that hair samples from it showed incompatibility with Devon Rex. Nothing further is known about it.

COAT COLOURS AND PATTERNS

Many of the breeds of domestic cat have appeared in a large variety of colour forms and patterns. These increase in number, year by year, as breeders strive to develop new tones and variants. Each of the main colours and patterns may be subdivided; for these, see the separate entries for each. Unfortunately, some confusion has been caused because different cat societies use slightly different names. Where this has occurred, the alternatives are given. For simplicity, all the terms that have been used in the past to describe the visual quality of the coats are listed here, without any attempt to separate colours from patterns:

Critics have occasionally complained that, when naming the various tones and shades of their animals, pedigree cat breeders have sometimes fallen prey to what might be termed optimistic exaggeration. Despite this, it cannot be overlooked that, through careful and lengthy breeding programmes, the world of pedigree cats has managed during the past century to develop many stunningly beautiful feline coats.

AGOUTI

COAT PATTERN. Agouti is the name given to a coat in which each individual hair is marked with bands of black, brown and yellow. The typical agouti pattern is seen most clearly on the ticked coat of the Abyssinian Cat. This is an 'all-agouti' cat, unlike the tabby, in which the agouti areas are interspersed with darker markings. Genetically, these dark patches are superimposed on the agouti hairs, the yellow bands on each hair being overlaid with darker pigment, creating what looks to the naked eye like an all-dark hair.

The name 'agouti' is borrowed from a large South American rodent which has a coat with a similar textural appearance to that of the Abyssinian Cat.

AUBURN

COAT COLOUR. As a cat colour, this is rarely encountered, except in the case of the Turkish Van Cat, where it is used to describe the colour of the darker extremities.

BI-COLOUR

COAT PATTERN. In a general sense, any cat with a boldly patched coat of two colours is a Bi-colour Cat, but in practice the term is restricted to those that show a pattern of white plus another colour; for example: white and black, white and blue, white and orange, or white and cream. Most of the white colouring appears on the lower surfaces of the cat and there is typically a 'two-tone' face.

Such patterns are most common in non-pedigree cats such as household pets or ferals, but they are also accepted in some pedigree breeds. In earlier days, this acceptance was limited because it was felt that a bi-colour coat made a pure-bred animal look like a 'moggie'. The prejudice was overcome only if the coat pattern was attractively balanced in a special way. This might involve symmetry of markings, distribution of colour, or ratio of white to colour. For example, the American Cat Fanciers' Association requires that the white areas of the coat must amount to between one-third and one-half of the overall surface, and the coloured portion from two-thirds to one-half.

In earlier days any cat exhibiting a bold black and white coat pattern was referred to as a 'Magpie Cat'. In the United States, Bi-colour (spelt Bi-color) Cats are sometimes called 'Parti-colored Cats'. The terms 'Piebald' and 'Pied', commonly used with other animals, are rarely employed when referring to the coat patterns of cats.

Championship status for Bi-colour Cats was not gained until 1966. After a few years it was felt that the official standards set for the bi-colour pattern were too strict (they demanded perfect symmetry of markings, for example) and, in 1971, they were relaxed.

This coat pattern occurs in both short and long-haired versions, and in the following breeds: American Shorthair, British Shorthair, Cornish Rex, Cymric, Devon Rex, European Shorthair, Exotic Shorthair, Japanese Bobtail, Maine Coon, Manx, Persian and Scottish Fold.

BLACK

COAT COLOUR. The ideal black coat is so intensely black that it completely masks any other pigment or pattern. Inferior black coats may reveal, in bright light, a brown tinge or a faint tabby pattern.

An alternative name for black, sometimes used by American breeders in certain cases, is Ebony.

Variants of this colour include the following: (1) Black Smoke; (2) Black and White; (3) Van Black and White; (4) Black, Red and White (= Tricolour).

BLOTCHED TABBY

COAT PATTERN. This pattern is often referred to as the 'Classic Tabby', or 'Marbled Tabby'. In place of the dark, narrow streaks typical of the Mackerel Tabby, there are broader bands arranged in whorls and spirals on the sides of the body. At the centre of this pattern there is usually an oyster-shaped patch surrounded by one or more lines. This region of the Blotched Tabby pattern is sometimes referred to as the 'bull's-eye'.

The blotched markings of this type of tabby vary from cat to cat and sometimes become so extensive and fused with one another that the cat appears to be generally very dark-coated.

The Blotched Tabby pattern is more recent that the ancient Mackerel Tabby pattern, arising in Europe between 500 and 800 years ago and spreading outwards around the globe. Roger Tabor has christened this cat 'The British Imperial Cat', because 'it spread around the world in the wake of British colonialization . . . The initial waves of British settlers sailing to America in the 17th century, Canada in the 18th and Australia in the 19th took with them the cats that reflected the proportion of blotched tabbies in Britain at the time . . . In countries without British settlement, such as Egypt and Thailand, the numbers of blotched tabbies are minimal.'

BLUE

COAT COLOUR. Essentially, this is a dilution of a black coat. The so-called 'blue' in reality varies between pale grey and slate grey. There are many pattern variants of this colour among modern pedigree cats, including the following: (1) Blue Chinchilla Silver; (2) Blue Cream Smoke; (3) Blue, Cream and White (Dilute Tricolour); (4) Blue Silver Tabby; (5) Blue Silver Patched Tabby; (6) Blue Silver Tabby and White; (7) Blue Smoke; (8) Blue Tabby; (9) Blue Tabby and White; (10) Blue Patched Tabby; (11) Blue Patched Tabby and White; (12) Blue Tortie; (13) Blue and White (Bi-colour); (14) Van Blue and White.

Four breeds of blue cat are officially recognized today: the Chartreux, Korat, Russian Blue and British Blue (see British Shorthair Cat). Although these breeds are all treated separately today, in earlier times there was confusion between the Chartreux, the Russian Blue and the British Blue. It was believed by some authorities that the distinctions between them were not at all clear. Early authors often refer to a blue breed known as the Maltese Cat, which was said to be the ancestor of both the Russian Blue and the Chartreux. Other authors claim that, at one stage, there was no difference between the Chartreux and the British Blue. Whether these beliefs are valid or not, the four 'blues' have certainly diverged since then, and are now distinct breeds in their own right.

BLUE-CREAM

COAT PATTERN. This is the dilute form of the tortoiseshell pattern, with blue replacing the black, and cream replacing the red. According to geneticist Roy Robinson, European and American ideals for this coat pattern differ slightly: 'In Britain, the colours of the blue-cream should be softly intermingled whereas in the USA preference is given to those cats with segregated patches of blue and cream.'

Variants include the following: (1) Blue-Cream Shaded; (2) Blue-Cream Smoke; (3) Blue-Cream and White; (4) Blue-Cream Point; (5) Blue-Cream Lynx Point; (6) Parti-colour Blue-Cream; (7) Van Blue-Cream and White.

BRONZE

COAT COLOUR. A warm, coppery brown ground colour, lightening to tawny buff. The term 'bronze' is applied to one of the coat colours of the spotted Egyptian Mau.

BROWN

COAT COLOUR. There are two kinds of brown colour in the coats of domestic cats. First, there is the natural brown that exists as part of the pattern of the wild tabby. Second, there is a domestic brown resulting from a mutated brown gene that reduces the strength of black pigment and increases the strength of brown pigment. Breeders have been able to vary the quality of this domestic brown – from dark red-browns to light golden-browns – by manipulating other genes that modify the darkness and lightness of colours.

CALICO

COAT PATTERN. An American name for a Tortoiseshell and White Cat. Like the Tortoiseshell Cat, it is sex-linked and nearly always female. Males do occur occasionally but are extremely rare.

For most Americans, the Calico Cat and the Tortie and White are one and the same, but for some there are subtle distinctions between the two. Writing in 1989, Dennis Kelsey-Wood describes the Calico Cat coat as 'white with unbrindled patches of black and red. As a preferred minimum, the cat should have white feet, legs, underside, chest and muzzle . . . Once a cat has more than half of its body total in white, then it is a calico.' He explains that, with less white, a cat may be classified as either tortie and white or as calico, depending on how the white patches are distributed. In the calico, the lower parts of the cat should be predominantly white, as if the animal had stepped in a pail of milk.

Calico Cats were first taken seriously in the world of pedigree cat shows in the late 1950s. Since then, a number of variant forms have been developed including the following: (1) Cinnamon-Cream Calico; (2) Dilute Calico (= white with unbrindled blue and cream); (3) Fawn-Cream Calico; (4) Lavender-Cream Calico; (5) Van Calico (white with black and red confined to the extremities); (6) Cinnamon-Cream Van Calico; (7) Dilute Van Calico (white with blue and cream confined to the extremities); (8) Fawn-Cream Van Calico; (9) Lavender-Cream Van Calico.

Specialist Club:
Calico Cat Registry International. Address: P.O. Box 944, Morongo Valley, CA 92256, USA.

CAMEO

COAT COLOUR. An American name for a cat with a coat that is made up of hairs which are white with red tips. There are three types: Smoke, Shaded and Shell, according to the extent of the tipping. The Smoke variety is deeply tipped, the Shaded is moderately tipped and the Shell is lightly tipped. When the cat is still, its coat appears to be the colour of the tips of the hairs, but when it moves, the white bases of the hairs are revealed, so that its coat colour seems to change.

Modern variants include the following: (1) Shaded Cameo (= Red Shaded); (2) Cream Shaded Cameo; (3) Shell Cameo (= Red Chinchilla); (4) Cream Shell Cameo; (5) Smoke Cameo (= Red Smoke); (6) Dilute Smoke Cameo (= Cream Smoke); (7) Red Smoke Cameo; (8) Tabby Cameo; (9) Dilute Tabby Cameo; (10) Tabby and White Cameo.

Specialist Club:
Cameo Cat Club of America. Address: 1800 West Ardel, Kuna, ID 83634, USA.

CARAMEL

COAT COLOUR. This term is employed differently by different cat organizations. It can refer either to a cat with a reddish-brown coat, in which case it is the same as a Cinnamon Cat, or it can apply to a cat with a bluish-fawn coat.

CHAMPAGNE

COAT COLOUR. An American name for a buff-cream coat. It is used to denote one of the dilute version of the sable brown Burmese Cat, whose coat is described as 'warm honey beige, shading to a pale gold tan underside'. Its nearest British equivalent is chocolate.

CHARCOAL

COAT COLOUR. A dark grey coat, caused by a slight dilution of black.

CHESTNUT

COAT COLOUR. A rich chestnut brown coat, similar to chocolate. It is used today in the United States in connection with the Oriental Shorthair.

The following variants have been recorded: (1) Chestnut Silver; (2) Chestnut Silver Tabby; (3) Chestnut Smoke; (4) Chestnut Tabby; (5) Chestnut Tortie.

CHINCHILLA

COAT PATTERN. A Chinchilla Cat has a translucent silvery coat of a special kind. Each individual hair is white with a black tip. To put it another way, a Chinchilla Cat is a white cat ticked with black. The correct eye-colour to accompany this coat pattern is green or blue-green. Some silver-coloured cats have a mixture of all-white and all-black hairs, but those are not true Chinchillas.

The name was borrowed from the silvery-grey South American rodent called the Chinchilla. The first Chinchilla class at a major cat show appeared in 1894 at the Crystal Palace Show. The earliest Chinchilla Cat Club was formed in 1901 in a London suburb. In those days the typical Chinchilla Cat was much darker than its modern equivalent. As breeders moved more and more towards a paler version, the original form had to be given a new name: Shaded Silver.

Pedigree breeds that appear in the Chinchilla colour include American Curl, American Shorthair, American Wirehair, Cornish Rex, Devon Rex, Exotic, Maine Coon, Manx, Norwegian Forest Cat, Persian and Scottish Fold.

The first recorded Chinchilla Cat was a female called Chinnie, born at a vicarage near Wakefield in England in 1882. She was sold to a breeder for a guinea (21 shillings, or £1.05) and became what Frances Simpson called ' The Mother of Chinchillas'.

Perhaps the most internationally famous of all Chinchillas was Solomon, the Persian Cat that was lovingly caressed by the fiendish master-criminal Blofeld in the James Bond films *You Only Live Twice* (1967), *On Her Majesty's Secret Service* (1969) and *Diamonds are Forever* (1971).

Several colour variants of the Chinchilla Cat's silver coat have been developed in recent years, including: Blue Chinchilla Silver; Chinchilla Golden (for details, see entry); Chinchilla Shaded Tortoiseshell (= Shell Tortoiseshell); Dilute Chinchilla Shaded Tortoiseshell; Red Chinchilla.

Breed Clubs:

The Chinchilla, Silver Tabby and Smoke Cat Society, established in 1908. Issues a glossy quarterly Journal. Address: Lucky-Lite Farm, 219 Catherington Lane, Catherington, Waterlooville, Hants, PO8 0TB, England.

The United Chinchilla Association. Address: 35 Colebrook Avenue, West Ealing, London, W13 8JZ, England.

CHINCHILLA GOLDEN

COAT COLOUR. There appear to be two ways in which the golden sheen is created. One authority describes the coat as differing from the typical Chinchilla in having the tips of the white hairs dark brown instead of black. A second authority describes the coat as having an undercoat of rich, warm, cream-coloured hairs with black tips. Either way, the overall effect is that of a luxurious, shimmering golden fur. When they first appeared in Chinchilla Persian litters, these golden cats were called 'Brownies' and were discarded as unwanted variants. Eventually some breeders decided to retain them and develop them as a separate colour form. They were officially recognized as such by the CFA in America in 1977.

Pedigree breeds that appear in the Chinchilla Golden colour include American Curl, Exotic, Norwegian Forest and Persian.

CHINTZ

COAT PATTERN. According to Frances Simpson in her classic, turn-of-the-century study of cats, *The Book of the Cat* (1903), 'Chintz Cat' was the 'old-fashioned', northern name for the Tortoiseshell-and-White Persian. The modern American equivalent is 'Calico Cat'.

CHOCOLATE

COAT COLOUR. A medium to pale brown coat, this is a milk-chocolate colour that is paler than seal. In the United States, in the Burmese and Tonkinese breeds, the chocolate colour is given the special name of 'champagne'.

The following variants have been listed: (1) Chocolate Shaded; (2) Chocolate Silver; (3) Chocolate Smoke; (4) Chocolate Tortie; (5) Chocolate Tortie Shaded; (6) Chocolate Tortie Smoke; (7) Chocolate Point; (8) Chocolate Lynx Point; (9) Chocolate Tortie Point; (10) Chocolate Tortie Lynx Point.

CINNAMON

COAT COLOUR. A reddish brown coat. An alternative name for this colour is Sorrel. Variants that have been recorded include the following: (1) Cinnamon Shaded; (2) Cinnamon Silver; (3) Cinnamon Silver Tabby; (4) Cinnamon Smoke; (5) Cinnamon Tabby; (6) Cinnamon Tortie; (7) Cinnamon Tortie Shaded; (8) Cinnamon Tortie Smoke; (9) Cinnamon-Cream Calico; (10) Cinnamon-Cream Van Calico.

CLASSIC TABBY

COAT PATTERN. This is another name for the 'Blotched Tabby', and is sometimes also referred to as the Marbled Tabby. On the flanks of the cat, the dark markings of this tabby pattern are arranged in whorls and spirals, with a central, oyster-shaped patch. This contrasts with the thinner lines of the Mackerel Tabby.

(For further details see Blotched Tabby.)

COLOURPOINT

COAT PATTERN. The typical Siamese coat pattern, namely a pale ground colour with dark extremities. This pattern is temperature-dependent, the extremities, which are colder, growing darker as the animal matures, while the warmer regions remain pale. If an extremity is injured or infected and that part of the cat's body becomes abnormally hot, pale hair will grow there as a consequence.

In the course of cross-breeding, this Siamese coat pattern has been injected into other breeds. Today, colourpoint breeds include the following:

1 SIAMESE (and Somali)

2 COLOURPOINT SHORTHAIR (= New Colour Siamese)

3 COLOURPOINT BRITISH SHORTHAIR (British Shorthair with Siamese points)

4 COLOURPOINT EUROPEAN SHORTHAIR (European Shorthair with Siamese points)

5 HIMALAYAN (= Colourpoint Longhair; Colourpoint Persian; Pointed Persian)

6 BALINESE (= Longhair Siamese; Oriental Longhair)

7 JAVANESE (Longhair Siamese with unusual points-colours, in some countries)

8 TONKINESE (= Golden Siamese)

9 BIRMAN (Longhair Siamese markings, but with white feet)

10 RAGDOLL (Longhair Siamese markings, plus variable amounts of white)

11 RAGAMUFFIN (as for Ragdoll, but with unusual points-colours)

12 SNOWSHOE (Siamese with the addition of white spotting on the feet and face)

In recent years many minor colour variants of the colourpoint coat pattern have been developed, including the following: (1) Blue Point; (2) Blue Lynx Point; (3) Blue-Cream Point; (4) Blue-Cream Lynx Point; (5) Chocolate Point; (6) Chocolate Lynx Point; (7) Chocolate Tortoiseshell Point; (8) Chocolate Tortoiseshell Lynx Point; (9) Cream Point; (10) Cream Lynx Point; (11) Flame Point; (12) Lilac Point; (13) Lilac Lynx Point; (14) Lilac-Cream Point; (15) Lilac-Cream Lynx Point; (16) Red Point; (17) Red Lynx Point; (18) Seal Point; (19) Seal Lynx Point; (20) Seal Tortoiseshell Point; (21) Seal Tortoiseshell Lynx Point; (22) Tortoiseshell Point; (23) Tortoiseshell Lynx Point.

CREAM

COAT COLOUR. A cream coat is a dilution of red. Its precise tone varies slightly from breed to breed – from buff cream to pale pink cream to cool cream. It is known in both long-haired and short-haired forms. The palest of the creams is usually preferred because it decreases the chances of any tabby markings showing through the cream ground.

This is one of the older colour forms, one of the first 'exotic' colours of the early pedigree Persian Cats. Writing in 1903, Frances Simpson comments: 'This may be said to be the very latest of Persian breeds, and one which bids fair to become very fashionable.'

In more recent times, a number of variants have been recorded, including the following: (1) Cream Point; (2) Cream Shaded Cameo; (3) Cream Shell Cameo; (4) Cream Silver; (5) Cream Silver Tabby; (6) Cream Smoke; (7) Cream Tabby; (8) Cream Tabby and White; (9) Cream and White (= Bi-colour); (10) Dilute Blue, Cream and White (= Dilute Tricolour); (11) Fawn Cream; (12) Lavender Cream; (13) Van Cream and Tabby and White.

DILUTE

COAT PATTERN. The term 'dilute' is used in the names of certain pedigree colour patterns, when they appear in a paler version.

Many of the subtle, modern coat colours created by breeders are the result of a dilution gene working on a darker colour. If the mutant gene 'd' is present, it reduces the strength of a particular colour. In this way black become blue, red becomes cream and chocolate becomes lilac. Such animals are referred to simply as red, cream, or lilac, but if the colours being diluted exist as a pattern, such as tortoiseshell, rather than as a single colour, then the cat is named as a 'dilute tortoiseshell'.

Examples of the use of this term include the following: (1) Dilute Cameo; (2) Dilute Cameo Smoke; (3) Dilute Cameo Tabby; (4) Dilute Tortoiseshell; (5) Dilute Shaded Tortoiseshell; (6) Dilute Chinchilla Shaded Tortoiseshell; (7) Dilute Tricolour (blue + cream + white); (8) Van Dilute Calico (white with blue and cream extremities).

EBONY

COAT COLOUR. An alternative name for black, used in America for certain types of 'modified black' in the Oriental Shorthair category.

The following variants have been recorded: (1) Ebony Silver (undercoat white with a mantle of black tipping); (2) Ebony Silver Tabby (ground colour pale clear silver; markings dense black); (3) Ebony Smoke (white undercoat, deeply tipped with black); (4) Ebony Tabby (ground colour coppery brown; markings dense black); (5) Ebony Tortoiseshell (black mottled or patched with red and/or cream).

FAWN

COAT COLOUR. A light, pinkish-cream coat. This is a dilution of cinnamon and has been described by one authority as a pale, warm colour, a 'light lavender with pale cocoa overtones'.

It has been recorded in the following variant forms: (1) Fawn Shaded; (2) Fawn Smoke; (3) Fawn Silver; (4) Fawn Silver Tabby; (5) Fawn Tabby; (6) Fawn-Cream; (7) Fawn-Cream Shaded; (8) Fawn-Cream smoke; (9) Fawn-Cream Calico; (10) Fawn-Cream Van Calico.

FLAME POINT

COAT COLOUR. Flame point is an alternative name for red point. The term 'flame' is only used instead of red when it occurs in a colourpoint pattern. One variant has been recorded: in America, a cat with extremities showing red and orange tabby markings is sometimes called a Flame Lynx Point.

FROST

COAT COLOUR. Frost Point is an American name for Lilac Point.

GINGER

COAT COLOUR. Ginger is the popular term for the coat colour that geneticists used to call 'yellow', but now call 'orange'. To confuse matters further, pedigree cat breeders call it 'red', and storytellers call it 'marmalade'. The ginger gene has the effect of eliminating all black and brown pigment from the hairs of the cat.

When present, the ginger colour is always attached to a tabby pattern, so that the full name for a ginger cat should be 'a ginger tabby'.

Ginger is a sex-linked character and nearly all ginger cats are male. When females do occasionally occur, they are usually sterile.

GOLDEN

COAT COLOUR. A golden sheen can be created in one of two ways. In one form there are brown-tipped white hairs. In the other there are black-tipped golden hairs.

There are three variants: the Chinchilla Golden, the slightly darker Shaded Golden and the Golden Tabby.

Golden Persians used to be known as 'Brownies', when they first appeared in litters of silver kittens, in the 1920s. At first they were rejected, but later were prized and developed. The first recorded Golden was a kitten called 'Bracken', who was registered as a Sable Chinchilla in 1925.

GREY

COAT COLOUR. In domestic cats, the grey colour is a dilution of black. Although grey is a common enough colour among pedigree cats, the word is almost taboo. By a harmless conspiracy of mutual deception, all cat breeders refer to their conspicuously pure grey cats as 'blue'. Thus we have the Russian Blue and the British Blue, and the many blue variants of other breeds.

This convention is rarely broken, although there was once a coat pattern referred to as the 'Grey-spotted Tabby'. Even this usage now seems to have vanished and a quick check through the index of a recent volume describing the various cat breeds reveals the following number of times that the words blue and grey are mentioned: Blue: 86 times; Grey: 0.

HARLEQUIN

COAT PATTERN. A term that is occasionally used to describe the coat of a bi-colour cat which has more white than non-white fur. Technically, to be a Harlequin coat the pattern must be 50–75 per cent White and 50–25 per cent Coloured.

LAVENDER

COAT COLOUR. This pinkish-grey colour is a diluted form of chocolate. In America, the name lavender is preferred for some breeds, while lilac is used for others, but the two colours are essentially the same. In Britain, lavender is not employed in pedigree descriptions.

Variants of the colour include the following: (1) Lavender Cream; (2) Lavender Cream Calico; (3) Lavender Cream Van Calico; (4) Lavender Cream Shaded; (5) Lavender Cream Smoke; (6) Lavender Shaded; (7) Lavender Silver; (8) Lavender Silver Tabby; (9) Lavender Smoke; (10) Lavender Tabby.

LILAC

COAT COLOUR. Lilac is the name given to the dilute version of brown or chocolate. It bears the same relationship to brown that blue does to black.

Lilac has been described variously as pinkish dove-grey, as warm lavender with a pinkish tone, or (rather differently) as frost grey. Its appeal lies in the fact that it is a warmer, softer shade of blue.

In the United States, with some breeds, the name lavender is used in place of lilac, but this is not done in Britain.

LILAC-CREAM

COAT PATTERN. The lilac-cream combination is a diluted form of tortoiseshell. A 'Lilac-cream Point Cat' is a colourpoint cat with a white body and lilac points with patches of cream.

LYNX

COAT PATTERN. In the world of pedigree cats the term 'lynx' is applied specifically to the points of the colourpoint coat pattern. In the original version of the colourpoint coat, first seen in the earliest Siamese Cats, the points were always 'seal' coloured – very dark brown. As the years passed and new variants were produced, a number of different types of dark point appeared. Among these was a tabby-patterned point. In Britain this was given the obvious name of Tabby Pointed coat, but in the United States the more glamorous name of Lynx Point was preferred.

Colour variants of Lynx Points listed by American breeders include the following: (1) Blue-Cream Lynx Point; (2) Blue Lynx Point; (3) Chocolate Lynx Point; (4) Chocolate-Tortie Lynx Point; (5) Cream Lynx Point; (6) Lilac-Cream Lynx Point; (7) Lilac Lynx Point; (8) Red Lynx Point; (9) Seal Lynx Point; (10) Seal-Tortie Lynx Point; (11) Tortie Lynx Point.

MACKEREL TABBY

COAT PATTERN. The Mackerel Tabby pattern is the one closest to the markings seen on the ancestral Wild Cat. It consists of dark streaks on a paler background. These streaks are long, thin, curving and largely vertical. They tend to break up into short bars and spots. It is these breaks that are thought to have been exploited and exaggerated by breeders to create the domestic spotted breeds. By contrast, those wishing to exhibit a champion Mackerel Tabby worked in the opposite direction, trying to make the streaks as long, fine and unbroken as possible. (See also the entry for Striped.)

MACULATE

COAT PATTERN. An alternative name for a spotted coat. The term comes from the Latin *macula,* meaning a spot.

MARBLED TABBY

COAT PATTERN. This is a rarely used, alternative name for the Blotched or Classic Tabby.

MASKED SILVER

COAT COLOUR. Writing about colour forms of Persian Cats in 1947, Milo Denlinger says: 'Masked silvers are a "new" variety, and at present very few are bred . . . The ideal masked silver is a very beautiful animal; in colouring or, I should say, marking, they should resemble the Siamese Cat; that is to say, they should have a black mask or face, black feet and legs. The body should be as pale a silver as possible . . . the eyes deep golden or copper.' Apart from the eye colour, it would appear from this description that the 'Masked Silver' was very similar to what is now known as the Himalayan Cat, or Colourpoint Persian.

In 1964 Jeanne Ramsdale adds this comment: 'About 1900 there was a colour of Persian called Masked Silver which is not seen any more. From their pictures, these cats seemed to resemble Silvers having black faces and legs, similar to the "points" of a Siamese.'

MINK

COAT COLOUR. American breeders specializing in the Tonkinese breed have introduced the name 'mink' into their coat colours. There are the following variants of mink: (1) Blue Mink (soft, blue-grey with darker slate-blue points); (2) Champagne Mink (beige or buff-cream with medium brown points); (3) Honey Mink (ruddy brown with darker brown points); (4) Natural Mink (warm brown with darker brown points); (5) Platinum Mink (pale silvery-grey with darker grey points).

ORANGE

COAT COLOUR. 'Orange' is the geneticist's name for the coat colour that is called 'red' by cat breeders, 'ginger' by the general public, and 'marmalade' by story-tellers. To confuse matters further, in the early days it was also called 'yellow'. Geneticist Roy Robinson describes the orange gene in the following way: 'The recognized symbol for the gene is "O". The action of the "O" gene is to eliminate all melanic pigment (black and brown) from the hair fibres.'

In earlier days, the term 'orange' was also applied to various pedigree cats by breeders, before they switched to the official term 'red'. Some examples of early 'orange' cats were: Orange Tabby Short-hair (1887); Orange Persian (1903); Orange and White Persian (1903); Orange and Cream Persian (1907). (For further details see Ginger and Red.)

PARTI-COLOUR

COAT PATTERN. A term sometimes applied to those cats which have more than one colour. Some American authorities group bi-colours, tortoiseshells and calicos together under the general heading Parti-color. It is a rarely used term today, but the following variants can be found among the lists of pedigree colour forms: (1) Parti-colour Blue-Cream; (2) Parti-colour Silver; (3) Parti-colour Smoke; (4) Van Parti-colour Tabby and White.

PATCHED TABBY (TORBIE)

COAT PATTERN. This is the two-tone version of the tabby pattern, also known as the Tortoiseshell Tabby, or Torbie. The standard colouring is Brown Tabby/Red Tabby. The dilute version is Blue Tabby/Cream Tabby.

Colour variants include the following: (1) Blue Patched Tabby; (2) Blue Patched Tabby and White; (3) Blue Silver Patched Tabby; (4) Brown Patched Tabby; (5) Brown Patched Tabby and White; (6) Patched Tabby and White; (7) Dilute Patched Tabby and White; (8) Silver Patched Tabby; (9) Silver Patched Tabby and White.

PEWTER

COAT COLOUR. Pewter is the name sometimes used to describe a Blue-Silver Tabby coat. It lacks the rich warmth of the Blue Tabby.

PIEBALD

COAT PATTERN. The term Piebald or Pied is not commonly used today for cats, but was mentioned by Dechambre in 1957, as follows: 'By a pied cat is meant any cat with large patches of colour on a white background . . . Although extremely interesting, this variety has not so far been precisely selected and it is not admitted as a special breed at exhibitions.'

Later, in 1970, Claire Necker uses the term Piebald in the following way: *'White Spotting (Piebald)* The degree of white spotting ranges from a few white hairs on the throat to a completely white cat.' She goes on to explain how the white areas tend to favour the frontal parts of the cat's body and its undersides.

In the past, piebald cats have sometimes been referred to as 'Magpie Cats', but today they are more often called Bi-colours. (For further details see Bi-colour.)

PLATINUM

COAT COLOUR. An American name for the pale grey/fawn of one of the dilute colours of the Burmese Cat. The full description of the coat is as follows: 'a pale silvery gray with pale fawn undertones, shading almost imperceptibly to a slightly lighter hue on the underparts.' It is similar to the colour called lilac in Britain.

RED

COAT COLOUR. Red is the cat breeder's name for the colour that geneticists call orange. All the various 'red-tone' colours, such as yellow, marmalade, orange and red, are controlled by a single sex-linked gene, designated 'O' (for orange). The effect of this gene is to convert all black pigment to orange. This means that it converts an ordinary tabby pattern into orange tabby. In earlier days this always gave rise to the familiar 'ginger cat', but years of pedigree selective breeding have improved on the colour quality of that animal, creating a deeper, more luxurious red. This is done in several ways. First, there are 'rufous polygenes' that can be added genetically to strengthen the coat's redness. Second, the tabby contrast-markings can be minimized by careful breeding programmes. Third, the blotched (or classic) tabby patches can be selectively bred in such a way that they spread and congeal into extensive red zones. The combined effect of these changes is to produce an evenly spread, 'de-tabbied', intensified red that now graces some of the most appealing of all modern pedigree cats.

The following variant forms of red have been listed by pedigree breeders: (1) Red Chinchilla (= Shell Cameo); (2) Red Shaded (= Shaded Cameo); (3) Red Silver; (4) Red Smoke Cameo (= Cameo); (5) Red Tabby; (6) Red Tabby and White; (7) Red (Flame) Lynx Point; (8) Van Red and White; (9) Black, Red and Blue (= Tricolour).

RUDDY

COAT COLOUR. This was the name given to the coat colour of the original form of the Abyssinian Cat. It is a reddish-brown, burnt sienna, ticked coat reminiscent of the coats of several species of wild cat. The ticking is in bands of darker brown or black. During the early breeding history of the Abyssinian Cat, this was the only colour form known and it was some years before it was joined by a red variant and then, much later, by other variant forms. But for most people, it is the original, ruddy coat that is synonymous with this particular breed, a fact which explains why, in Europe, the coat name 'usual' is employed instead of 'ruddy'.

SABLE

COAT COLOUR. Frances Simpson introduced the term 'sable' into cat colours in 1903: 'With the "sable" cat, be it understood, I have no fault to find; I can forgive him even his white chin, because he is such a magnificent animal; but he is not a tabby, and should not be shown as such.'

A different description appears in 1957, when Dechambre defines it as 'a variety which has been created in America, where it is known as the Burmese. It is better to call them Zibelines or Sables, because of their coat, and to distinguish them from the true Burmese. These cats without doubt derive from the crossing of a Siamese with one or two more breeds . . . It is a short-haired cat of self colour, chocolate brown, with green eyes and a long tail.'

Today, the term Sable Cat is not used as a breed name; the Burmese is still called the Burmese. The original colour form of this breed – the dark brown – is, however, called a 'Sable Burmese' in the United States (in contrast to Europe, where it is known simply as a 'Brown Burmese').

SEAL POINT

COAT PATTERN. This is the original Siamese Cat colouring, with a fawn to cream body and the dark extremities a deep seal brown. It was first recognized in 1871 and remained the only Siamese colour form until the 1930s, when other extremity-colours were introduced.

Seal variants (recognized in 1966) include: (1) Seal Lynx Point (the seal brown on the extremities shows a tabby pattern); (2) Seal Tortie Point (the seal brown on the extremities shows a tortoiseshell pattern); (3) Seal Tortie Tabby Point (a combination of the previous two patterns).

SELF-COLOURED

COAT PATTERN. This type of coat was accurately defined as long ago as 1895, by Rush Huidekoper: 'The Self-coloured cats are those which are entirely of one solid colour, which may vary its hue or tint, but must not have any intermixture of white or of any other colour. The Self-coloured Cats are the Black, the Blue, the Red and the Yellow.'

Since then other self-colours have been added to that list, but the definition remains unaltered. (An alternative name for 'selfs' is 'solids'.)

SEPIA

COAT COLOUR. A colour name that is rarely used for cats. It is mostly applied to the Singapura Cat, whose coat is described as follows: 'Sepia Agouti only . . . dark brown ticking on a warm old ivory ground colour.'

SHADED

COAT PATTERN. A shaded coat is one that is made up of pale hairs each of which has a dark tip. The darkened portion of the tip reaches a *moderate* distance down the length of the hair. In the Shell Pattern, the darkened portion is very restricted. In the Smoke Pattern, the darkened portion reaches much further down the length of each hair. In other words, the Shaded Pattern is intermediate, between the Shell and the Smoke Patterns, in its visual effect.

There are the following colour variants of this pattern: (1) Shaded Blue; (2) Shaded Blue-Cream; (3) Shaded Blue Silver; (4) Shaded Cameo; (5) Shaded Cream Cameo; (6) Shaded Chinchilla Tortoiseshell (= Shell Tortoiseshell); (7) Dilute Shaded Chinchilla Tortoiseshell (= Dilute Shell Tortoiseshell); (8) Shaded Chocolate; (9) Shaded Chocolate Tortoiseshell; (10) Shaded Cinnamon; (11) Shaded Cinnamon Tortoiseshell; (12) Shaded Fawn; (13) Shaded Fawn-Cream; (14) Shaded Golden (see separate entry for details); (15) Shaded Lavender; (16) Shaded Red (= Shaded Cameo); (17) Shaded Silver (see entry below for details); (17) Shaded Tortoiseshell; (18) Dilute Shaded Tortoiseshell.

SHADED GOLDEN

COAT COLOUR. On a cat with a Shaded Golden coat, each hair is apricot or pale brown with a dark brown tip. This is the darker version of the Chinchilla Golden, just as the Shaded Silver (see entry) is the darker version of the typical Chinchilla.

Shaded Golden cats exist in both long and short-haired versions, as Shaded Golden Persians and Shaded Golden Exotics. They are also seen in two other breeds: The American Curl and the Norwegian Forest Cat.

SHADED SILVER

COAT COLOUR. On a cat with a Shaded Silver coat, each individual hair is silvery-grey with a black tip. The overall effect is of a light grey cat with a shimmering silvery texture.

Originally there was much confusion between Shaded Silver and Chinchilla. In the 19th century Chinchillas were slightly darker than they are today and it was almost impossible to distinguish between the two forms. They were sometimes lumped together as 'silvers'. But then, as the years passed, the Chinchilla cats became paler and paler, each hair becoming pure white with a dark tip. As a result, today it is easy to tell Shaded Silver cats from Chinchillas.

Shaded Silver cats exist in both long and short-haired versions, as Shaded Silver Persians and Shaded Silver Exotics. They are now also seen in the following breeds: American Curl, American Shorthair, American Wirehair, Maine Coon, Manx, Norwegian Forest, Cornish Rex, Devon Rex and Scottish Fold.

SHELL

COAT PATTERN. When a coat is made up of pale hairs with dark tips it is called either a Shell, Shaded or Smoke Pattern. The shell version has a very restricted darkening of the tip – less than the other two. Today a shell pattern is very similar to a 'shaded chinchilla'.

The following pedigree colour variants of this pattern have been recorded: (1) Shell Cameo (= Red Chinchilla); (2) Cream Shell Cameo; (3) Shell Tortoiseshell (= Shaded Chinchilla Tortoiseshell); (4) Dilute Shell Tortoiseshell (= Dilute Shaded Chinchilla Tortoiseshell).

SILVER

COAT COLOUR. The silver effect is created by a coat of hairs each of which is pale at the base and dark at the tip. (See also Chinchilla.)

Modern variants of this colour include: (1) Blue Silver; (2) Blue Silver Tabby; (3) Blue Silver Tabby and White; (4) Blue Silver Patched Tabby; (5) Blue Chinchilla Silver; (6) Blue Shaded Silver; (7) Chestnut Silver; (8) Chestnut Silver Tabby; (9) Chinchilla Silver; (10) Chocolate Silver; (11) Chocolate Silver Tabby; (12) Cinnamon Silver; (13) Cinnamon Silver Tabby; (14) Cream Silver (= Dilute Cameo); (15) Cream Silver Tabby; (16) Ebony Silver; (17) Ebony Silver Tabby; (18) Fawn Silver; (19) Fawn Silver Tabby; (20) Lavender Silver; (21) Lavender Silver Tabby; (22) Parti-colour Silver; (23) Red Silver (= Cameo); (24) Shaded Silver; (25) Silver Tabby; (26) Silver Patched Tabby; (27) Silver Tabby and White.

SMOKE

COAT COLOUR. Smoke is a coat pattern that is similar to Chinchilla (see separate entry), but whereas each Chinchilla hair is pale along its length except for a dark tip, a Smoke hair is pale at the base and then gradually darkens towards the tip. In other words, a greater proportion of each Smoke hair is dark. The effect of this is to make the cat literally change colour as it becomes active. A Black Smoke Persian, for example, will appear jet black when lying down in a relaxed posture, but when it jumps up and starts to move, its coat will shift to reveal the pale under-coat.

Persian Cats with a Smoke coat pattern were originally ignored and were placed in the 'any other colour' category at the first cat shows, but by 1893 Smoke Persians had already been given their own separate class.

Today the following 24 smoke colour variants are recognized: (1) Black Smoke (= Ebony Smoke); (2) Blue Smoke; (3) Blue-Cream Smoke; (4) Cameo Smoke; (5) Dilute Cameo Smoke (= Cream Smoke); (6) Chestnut Smoke; (7) Chocolate Smoke; (8) Chocolate Tortoiseshell Smoke; (9) Cinnamon Smoke; (10) Cinnamon Tortoiseshell Smoke; (11) Cream Smoke; (12) Ebony Smoke (= Black Smoke); (13) Fawn Smoke (14) Fawn-Cream Smoke; (15) Lavender Smoke; (16) Lavender Cream Smoke; (17) Particolour Smoke; (18) Red (= Cameo) Smoke; (19) Smoke-and-White Smoke; (20) Tortoiseshell Smoke; (21) Van-Smoke-and-White Smoke; (22) Smoke and White; (23) Black Smoke and White; (24) Van Smoke and White.

These colours are distributed among the various breeds as follows (according to American CFA listings):

AMERICAN CURL: Black, Blue, Red, Chocolate, Lavender, Cream, Tortie, Chocolate Tortie, Blue-Cream.

AMERICAN SHORTHAIR: Black, Blue, Red, Tortie, Blue-Cream, Smoke-and-White.

AMERICAN WIREHAIR: Black, Blue, Cameo.

BRITISH SHORTHAIR: Black, Blue.

EXOTIC: Black, Blue, Red, Cream, Tortie, Blue-Cream, Smoke-and-White, Van-Smoke-and-White.

MAINE COON: Black, Blue, Red, Tortie, Blue-Cream, Smoke-and-White.

MANX: Black, Blue.

Norwegian Forest: Black, Blue, Red, Cream, Tortie, Blue-Cream.

Oriental Longhair: Black (Ebony), Blue, Red, Lavender, Cream, Fawn, Cinnamon, Parti-colour, Chestnut.

Oriental Shorthair: Black (Ebony), Blue, Red, Lavender, Cream, Fawn, Cinnamon, Parti-colour, Chestnut.

Persian: Black, Blue, Red, Cream, Tortie, Blue-Cream, Smoke-and-White, Van-Smoke-and-White.

Scottish Fold: Black, Blue, Red.

Turkish Angora: Black, Blue.

Specialist Club:

Smoke Cat Society. Address: 36 Alden Avenue, Morley, Leeds, England.

Solid

Coat Pattern. An alternative name for self-coloured, meaning a cat whose coat is all of one, single colour, without any markings. (For further details see Self-coloured.)

Sorrel

Coat Colour. Described as 'brownish orange to light brown', this colour term is used exclusively by British breeders of Abyssinian and Somali Cats. The agouti coat of the sorrel variants of these breeds is officially given as 'base colour – copper red; ticking colour – chocolate'. The Silver Sorrel variant is given as 'base colour – silver peach; ticking colour – chocolate'.

In America the name 'red' is used in place of sorrel, but the matter is complicated by the fact that genetically there are two types of 'red' Abyssinian and Somali Cats which are being developed at present, in attempts to obtain deeper shades.

Spotted

Coat Pattern. The origin of the spotted coats seen in domestic cats is not clearly understood. It may have been developed by gradually modifying mackerel tabby streaks, making them more and more fragmented, into small blobs and finally into spots, by selective breeding. Or it may have been developed by utilizing a new, spotted mutation. Geneticists favour the first of these two explanations because, although the pedigree mackerel tabby is chosen for its long, unbroken streaks and stripes, stray non-pedigree mackerel tabbies frequently show much shorter and more broken streaks and stripes. By using such non-pedigree animals, those shorter marks could soon be rounded off into elegant, circular spots.

Striped

Coat Pattern. A coat with dark lines. Among domestic cats the striped pattern appears only on the Mackerel Tabby coat. This is the ancient form of tabby pattern and was once common over the whole range of the domestic cat. However, in medieval Europe a new form of tabby pattern arose, now called the Blotched, Marbled or Classic Tabby. It made its first appearance somewhere between 500 and 800 years ago and it then proceeded to spread and spread, dominating and displacing the Mackerel or Striped Tabby in more and more regions. Today the striped tabby pattern has become rare in Europe, but it is still encountered quite commonly among feral domestic cats further east.

It has been suggested that the striped tabby coat provides better camouflage in rural settings and that the blotched pattern blends in better in the urban environment, and that this may account for the modern differences in distribution of the two types. (See also Mackerel Tabby and Blotched Tabby.)

TABBY

COAT PATTERN. The history of the tabby pattern is complicated. The modern domestic cat originally appears to have developed from the African Wild Cat *(Felis sylvestris lybica)* in ancient Egypt. When this early domesticated cat was brought to ancient Greece and Rome by Phoenician traders, it spread across the European continent and, in so doing, hybridized freely with the local European Wild Cat *(Felis sylvestris sylvestris)*.

The coat pattern of both the African and the European races can best be described as suppressed, weak or washed-out tabby. The pattern is there, but not impressive. This is undoubtedly what the original domestic cats looked like and wall paintings confirm that three to four thousand years ago the Egyptian cats had light or broken stripes. But when this type of cat, transported abroad, began to hybridize with its European counterparts, the result was a full-tabby cat.

Tests have since shown that when the weak-tabby European and African Wild Cats are experimentally crossed with one another, the hybrid kittens develop coat patterns which are much closer to the full-tabby pattern of modern domestic cats than they are to the markings of either of their parents. This, it seems, is how the history of the tabby began.

The first cats of this type were what is called today the Mackerel Tabby, covered with thin, dark lines. Some of these lines break up into dashes or spots, but the overall effect is of a tigerish striping. To begin with, this was the only such pattern in existence, but then a new mutation arose. A Blotched Tabby arrived on the scene. On this animal the markings were much bolder and more complex; the narrow striping survived only in certain areas.

It is believed that these Blotched Tabbies arose first in Britain, in medieval or even Elizabethan times. The Elizabethan era was a time of great British expansion and it is thought that, in the guise of ships' cats, they were scattered from the British Isles all over the globe in a comparatively short space of time. With the growth of the British Empire in the Victorian era, they spread still further.

For some reason that is not fully understood, the Blotched Tabby was a winner. Perhaps the gene for this pattern was linked to an unusual level of aggressiveness or assertiveness, with the result that these cats soon managed to oust most other colour forms whenever there was a dispute over territory or females. Perhaps they were simply more healthy or more fertile. Whatever the reason, this new pattern began to dominate. The earlier striped tabby went into a rapid decline. Today it has become quite rare, while the Blotched Tabby is the most common form of all. It would not be too far from the truth, as cat authority Roger Tabor put it, to christen this most successful of all domestic felines 'the British Imperial Cat'.

Looking at the great variation in cat coat colours today, the first impression is that tabbies are now only one small part of the general spectrum of available patterns and hues. Genetically, the truth is rather different, because in reality *all* domestic cats are tabbies. If they do not appear to be so, it is because the tabby pattern is masked by the other non-tabby colours. In the absence of these masking colours, the cat's coat is seen as a mixture of banded (agouti) hairs and black hairs. The black hairs are arranged in patches, and it is this arrangement that we call 'tabby'. In addition to the two types mentioned already, there are three others that can be seen today.

The five types are as follows:

MACKEREL TABBY: The patches are mostly in narrow streaks. This is the ancient type of tabby pattern, close to that seen in the ancestral wild cat species. (See entry for Mackerel Tabby.)

BLOTCHED TABBY: The patches are in the form of large smudges. Among domestic cats this is the most common form of tabby marking and is therefore referred to as the 'Classic Tabby Pattern'. This name is somewhat inappropriate because, with the Mackerel Pattern being closer to the wild feline condition, it could be argued that the more ancient pattern should be given the name of 'Classic'. (See entry for Blotched Tabby.)

SPOTTED TABBY: In a few breeds the dark patches are formed into small spots. For most people, such animals would simply be described as 'Spotted Cats' rather than 'Spotted Tabbies'. It is not known whether the spots develop from broken Mackerel Tabby streaks, or from a separate mutation. (See entry for Spotted.)

TICKED TABBY: This is the Abyssinian form of tabby marking, with very faint markings on a generally ticked coat.

PATCHED TABBY: This is the two-toned tabby, or Tortoiseshell Tabby, sometimes called the Torbie. In the typical form, there are separate patches of brown tabby and red tabby on the same animal. (See entry for Patched Tabby.)

Pedigree cat breeders have been busy and today there are many colour variants of these basic tabby patterns, including the following (some of which are simply alternative names for the same variant): (1) Blue Tabby; (2) Blue Patched Tabby; (3) Blue Silver Patched Tabby; (4) Blue Silver Tabby; (5) Brown Tabby; (6) Brown Patched Tabby; (7) Cameo Tabby; (8) Dilute Cameo Tabby; (9) Chestnut Tabby; (10) Chestnut Silver Tabby; (11) Chocolate Silver Tabby; (12) Cinnamon Tabby; (13) Cinnamon Silver Tabby; (14) Cream Tabby; (15) Cream Silver Tabby; (16) Ebony Tabby; (17) Fawn Tabby; (18) Fawn Silver Tabby; (19) Lavender Tabby; (20) Lavender Silver Tabby; (21) Red Tabby; (22) Silver Tabby; (23) Silver Patched Tabby.

In some tabby cats, there are areas of pure white in addition to the tabby zones: (24) Tabby and White; (25) Patched Tabby and White (= Torbie and White = Brown Tabby/Red Tabby/White); (26) Dilute Patched Tabby and White (= Blue Tabby/Cream Tabby/White); (27) Blue Tabby and White; (28) Blue Patched Tabby and White (= Dilute Patched Tabby and White); (29) Blue Silver Tabby and White; (30) Brown Tabby and White; (31) Brown Patched Tabby and White; (32) Cameo Tabby and White; (33) Cream Tabby and White; (34) Red Tabby and White; (35) Silver Tabby and White; (36) Silver Patched Tabby and White.

In some tabby cats, the coloured portions are restricted to the extremities of an otherwise white cat. This is known as the 'Van Tabby Pattern': (37) Van Tabby; (38) Van Tabby and White; (39) Van Cream Tabby and White; (40) Van Parti-colour Tabby and White; (41) Van Red Tabby and White.

TICKED

COAT PATTERN. An alternative name for the agouti coat, in which each hair is banded with black, brown and yellow. This is the typical coat pattern of the Abyssinian, the Somali, the Wild Abyssinian, the Singapura and the Ceylon.

TORBIE

COAT PATTERN. A commonly used abbreviation of tabby tortoiseshell. In this version of the tortoiseshell coat, the black areas are replaced by dark tabby patterning. Also known as a patched tabby.

TORTIE

COAT PATTERN. A commonly used abbreviation of tortoiseshell.

TORTOISESHELL

COAT PATTERN. Any domestic cat with a coat pattern that appears to be black, red and cream. On closer scrutiny, it becomes clear that the coat is, in reality, black plus orange tabby. The lighter, orange tabby areas, being two-toned, create the overall impression of a three-coloured cat. It is nearly always female; when male, it is sterile.

The chances of finding a male tortoiseshell cat have been calculated at about 200 to one. What makes the sex distribution of these cats so odd is that normally only a female kitten can display black patches inherited from one parent and red tabby patches inherited from the other. This is because the genes controlling these particular colour forms are both carried on the X chromosomes, the red gene on one and the non-red gene on the other. The catch is that only females have two X chromosomes, so only females can display the 'red plus non-red' tortoise-shell combination. Males have instead one X chromosome and one small Y chromosome, which means that on their single X they carry either the red *or* the non-red gene, but cannot have both. So they are either all-over red tabby or all-over black.

If this is the case, it is hard to see, at first glance, how male tortoiseshells can exist at all. The answer is that occasionally there is a minor genetic error and a male cat develops with the genetic combination XXY. The double X gives it a chance to be red and black, while the Y chromosome gives it male characteristics. It does, however, have a problem because its masculinity leaves a lot to be desired. To start with, it is sterile. Also its behaviour is extremely odd. It acts like a masculinized female rather than a true male.

One particular male tortoiseshell cat that was observed in a colony of cats revealed a strange personality. It was nonchalant in its dealings with other cats, disdainfully ignoring the usual status battles, which were nearly always between males or between females – there was little social fighting across the genders. Perhaps because the tortoiseshell male cat was neither fully male nor fully female, it did not feel the need to compete in these single-sex pecking-order disputes.

In other respects it was also peculiar. It did not start to spray urine at the age when any typical male would have done so. It did not court or attempt to mate with females on heat, even though it appeared to be anatomically well equipped to do so. It did, however, allow young tom-cats to mount and attempt to mate with it.

When it had grown older it did show a little interest in females and even deigned to mate with a few, though never with much enthusiasm. It also sprayed urine in a desultory fashion, but never behaved like a full-blooded tom at any stage. Once, it was experimentally isolated with a highly sexed female and was observed to mate several times, but the female failed to become pregnant, confirming the typical male tortoiseshell infertility.

So, although it is not true to say that *all* tortoiseshell cats are female, it is true to say that they are all feminine – even the rare males. And it is probably true to add that no tortoiseshell cat has ever fathered a litter of kittens.

There is one compensation, however, for the unfortunate tortoiseshell toms. Their great rarity has given them a special value in times past, so that they have often escaped the indifference and persecution that has befallen the commonplace moggies. In Celtic countries it was always considered a good omen if one of these cats decided to settle in the home. In England there was a belief that warts could be removed simply by rubbing them with the tail of a tortoiseshell tom during the month of May. And Japanese fishermen would pay huge sums for a tortoiseshell tom, to keep as a ship's cat, for it was thought it would protect the crew from the ghosts of their ancestors and the vessel itself from storms.

So, although these cats may be doomed to a disappointing sex life, in other respects they have fared rather well.

There are many colour variants of this coat pattern, which occurs in both short and long-haired versions. These variants including the following: (1) Blue Tortoiseshell; (2) Chestnut Tortoiseshell; (3) Chinchilla Shaded Tortoiseshell (= Shell Tortoiseshell); (4) Chocolate Tortoiseshell; (5) Chocolate Tortoiseshell Point; (6) Chocolate Tortoiseshell Lynx Point; (7) Chocolate Tortoiseshell Shaded; (8) Chocolate Tortoiseshell Smoke; (9) Cinnamon Tortoiseshell; (10) Cinnamon Tortoiseshell Smoke; (11) Dilute Tortoiseshell; (12) Dilute Chinchilla Shaded Tortoiseshell (= Dilute Shell Tortoiseshell); (13) Dilute Shaded Tortoiseshell; (14) Ebony Tortoiseshell; (15) Lilac Tortoiseshell; (16) Seal Tortoiseshell; (17) Shaded Tortoiseshell; (18) Shell Tortoiseshell; (19) Smoke Tortoiseshell; (20) Tortoiseshell Point; (21) Tortoiseshell Lynx Point; (22) Tortoiseshell and White.

Folklore: According to the ancient Khmers of South-east Asia, the first tortoiseshell cat was created in a magical ritual performed by a wise old man. During the course of the ritual, the cat sprang from the menstrual blood of a young goddess born of a lotus flower.

Tricolour

Coat Pattern. This term was first introduced by Leslie Williams in 1907 when she referred to the 'Tortoiseshell and White, or Tricolour Persians'. Since then the Tortie and White Cat has been given the modern name of Calico Cat, but the title of 'tricolour' has found a new use in connection with the Japanese Bobtail Cat, where the following versions have been recorded:

(1) Tricolour (= black, red and white – the traditional Mi-Ke version); (2) Dilute Tricolour (= blue, cream and white); (3) Patched Tabby and White (= brown tabby, red tabby and white); (4) Dilute Patched Tabby and White (= blue tabby, cream tabby and white).

Usual

Coat Colour. The word 'Usual' has become a technical term in the world of pedigree cats, where it refers to the traditional coat colour of a particular breed – the one that was present with the original specimens when the breed began, before modern trends began to add all kind of variations. It is a term favoured for a few breeds by the GCCF in Britain, but which is rarely used elsewhere. For example, the rich golden-brown colour of the typical, original Abyssinian Cat is called 'Usual' by the GCCF, but 'Ruddy' by feline organizations in Europe and America.

Van

Coat Pattern. The Van pattern, as seen on the Turkish Van Cat, consists of a white body with coloured areas confined to the head and tail. The original, typical colouring of the extremities was auburn, but in recent years other colour forms have been developed. (See Turkish Van Cat.)

White

Coat Colour. The pure white cat has long been a favourite of the show bench, but, surprisingly, this colour was originally preferred for functional rather than aesthetic reasons.

Writing in 1874, Gordon Stables comments: 'Millers often prefer them as hunters to black cats, thinking, perhaps with reason, that they are not so easily seen among the bags [of white flour].'

All-white cats usually have either golden or blue eyes, and it is well known that many of these animals, especially the blue-eyed ones, suffer from deafness. A survey carried out by two geneticists in 1971 revealed the following figures. Of 185 white cats examined, 25 per cent had golden eyes and normal hearing; 7 per cent had golden eyes and were deaf; 31 per cent had blue eyes and normal hearing; and 37 per cent had blue eyes and were deaf.

Many cats are only partially white. This is the result of a 'white-spotting gene' that masks the cat's true colour. It usually appears in irregular patches, but generally favouring the lower regions of the body. There are special names given to the different degrees of white-masking:

1 A cat with white paws is said to be 'mitted'.
2 A cat with a white patch on its chest is said to have a 'locket'.
3 A cat with several small, white belly-patches is said to have 'buttons'.
4 A cat with roughly half its body surface white is said to be 'bi-colour'.
5 A cat with a predominantly white coat and a few colour-patches is a 'harlequin'.
6 A cat with a white coat except for colouring on the tail and head is a 'Van'.
7 A black cat with white legs, underside and chest is called a 'tuxedo cat'.
8 A black and white cat is sometimes called a 'jellicle cat'.

There are many pedigree colour forms that include areas of white: (1) Black and White (Bi-colour); (2) Black Smoke and White; (3) Black, Red and White (Tricolour); (4) Blue and White (Bi-colour); (5) Blue-Cream and White; (6) Blue Tabby and White; (7) Blue Patched Tabby and White; (8) Blue Silver Tabby and White; (9) Blue, Cream and White (Dilute Tricolour); (10) Brown Tabby and White; (11) Brown Patched Tabby and White; (12) Cameo and White; (13) Cream and White (Bi-colour); (14) Cream Tabby and White; (15) Patched Tabby and White (Torbie and White); (16) Red Tabby and White; (17) Silver Tabby and White; (18) Silver Patched Tabby and White; (19) Smoke and White; (20) Tabby and White; (21) Tortie and White; (22) Van Black and White; (23) Van Blue and White; (24) Van Blue-Cream and White; (25) Van Cream Tabby and White; (26) Van Parti-colour and White; (27) Van Red and White; (28) Van Red Tabby and White; (29) Van Smoke and White; (30) Van Tabby and White.

YELLOW

COAT COLOUR. An early name for 'orange', which is the geneticist's name for the colour of a ginger cat. To cat-breeders this colour is now known as red. To storytellers it is usually 'marmalade'. See also Ginger.

MODERN CAT SOCIETIES

Modern cat societies include the following, in alphabetical order. (Only national societies are listed here. For specific breed clubs, see the breeds in question.)

The American Association of Cat Enthusiasts (AACE). Organizes shows at which exhibitors can compete with breeds that are not accepted by the large organizations. Address: P.O. Box 213, Pine Brook, NJ 07058, USA. Tel: 201-335 6717.

The American Cat Association (ACA). 8101 Katherine Avenue, Panorama City, CA 91402, USA. Tel: 818-782 6080 or 818-781 5656. The ACA is the oldest feline registry in the United States, having been active since 1899.

American Cat Council (ACC). Address: P.O. Box 662, Pasadena, CA 91102, USA. A small organization based on the West Coast of the United States which follows exhibition rules similar to those of the GCCF in Britain (with exhibitors vacating the hall during judging).

American Cat Fanciers' Association (ACFA). Address: P.O. Box 203, Point Lookout, MO 65726, USA. Tel: 417-334 5430. An international organization with affiliations in Canada and Japan. It publishes a monthly news bulletin.

Association Internationale Féline (AIF). Address: 38 Avenue du Président-Wilson, 75116 Paris, France. Tel: 45 53 71 48.

Association Nationale des Cercles Félins Français (ANCFF). Address: 7 Rue Chaptal, 75009 Paris, France. Tel: 48 78 43 54.

Association Nationale Féline (ANF). Address: Km 1 – Route de Montner, 66310 Estagel, France. Tel: 68 29 15 91.

Australian Cat Federation (ACF) Address: P.O. Box 40752, Casuarina, NT 0811, Australia.

Austrian Feline Fanciers Alliance (AFFA). Address: Postfach 75, 1172 Wien, Austria. Tel: 02 22/4 57 00 43.

Canadian Cat Association (CCA). The only national cat organization in Canada. It publishes a bilingual (French and English) quarterly newsletter: *Chats Canada*. Address: 83 Kennedy Road, South Unit 1805, Brampton, Ontario, L6W 3P3, Canada. Tel: 905-459 1481.

Cat Action Trust (CAT). Address: The Crippets, Jordans, Beaconsfield, Bucks, England.

The Cat Association of Britain (CA). Formed in 1983 as an alternative to the GCCF, it became a member of FIFe in 1990. Address: Mill House, Letcombe Regis, Oxfordshire, OX12 9JD, England. Tel: 01235-766543.

Cat Club de Belgique (CCB). Address: 33 Rue Duquesnoy, B-1000, Brussels, Belgium.

Cat Club de Espagne (CCE). Address: 60 Olivido, Barcelona, 26, Spain.

The Cat Fanciers' Association (CFA). The biggest of the American organizations. With its affiliates, it produces more than 360 cat shows each year. It claims to be 'the largest cat registry in the world'. Like the ACFA it has affiliations in Canada and Japan. It publishes a yearbook and a bi-monthly newsletter called *Trend*. It has also produced a *CFA Cat Encyclopedia* giving details of the show Standards of all the 43 'official' breeds which it recognizes for competition. Address: P.O. Box 1005, Manasquan, NJ 08738-1005, USA. Tel: 908-528 9797. OR 1309 Allare Avenue, Ocean, New NJ, USA. Tel: 201-531 2390.

The Cat Fanciers Federation (CFF). Tel: 513-787 9009. A registering body that centres its activities in the North-east of the USA. It publishes a *CFF Newsletter* and a *CFF Yearbook*. Address: 9509 Montgomery Road, Cincinnati, OH 45242, USA. Tel: 513-984 1841. OR P.O. Box 661, Gratis OH 45330.

Cat Lovers of America (CLA). Issues a quarterly *Cat Lovers* magazine and a monthly *Bulletin*. Address: P.O. Box 5050, El Toro, CA 92630-9982, USA.

Cats Protection League (CPL). Address: 17 Kings Road, Horsham, West Sussex, RH13 5PN, England. Tel: 01403-61947.

Cat Survival Trust (CST). Address: Marlind Centre, Codicote Road, Welwyn, Herts., AL6 9TV, England. Tel: 01438-716873 or 01438-716478.

Chovatelu Drobneho Zvirectva. Address: Hermanova 6, 170 000 Prague 7, Czechoslovakia.

Club Félin Français (CFF). Address: 15 bis, Avenue du Parc, 78150 Le Chesnay, France. Tel: 39 54 37 85.

Co-ordinating Cat Council of Australia (CCCA). Address: P.O. Box 404, Dickson, ACT 2602, Australia.

Crown Cat Fanciers' Federation (CROWN or CCFF). Organized cat shows in eastern USA and western Canada. (Now disbanded.) Address: P.O. Box 34, Nazareth, KY 40048, USA.

Deutscher Edelkatzenzuchter – Verband (DEKZV). Address: 48 Friedrichstrasse, D-6200, Wiesbaden, Germany.

Fauna Cat Lovers' Association. Address: 129041, Moscow 68, Prospect Mira, USSR.

Fédération Féline Française (FFF). Address: 75 Rue Decaen, 75012 Paris, France. Tel: 46 28 26 09.

Federation Feline Helvetique (FFH). Address: Via Quiete 15, CH-6962, Viganello, Switzerland.

Federation Feline Italienne (FFI) Address: 20 Via Principi d'Acaja, 1-10138, Torino, Italy.

Fédération Internationale Féline (FIFe). Established in 1949, this has become the largest feline organization in the world, with affiliated societies throughout Europe and beyond. Its aim is to be considered as the United Nations of the pedigree cat world and, to that end, it has established a federation of 31 nations, with a member association in each. Notable exceptions are the United States, Canada, Australia, New Zealand and Japan. The members of the Federation agree to follow common rules concerning breeds, showing and judging. FIFe acknowledges three official languages: English, French and German. It has been estimated that it now unites over 150,000 pedigree-cat breeders. Address: Boerhaavelaan 23, NL-5644 BB, Eindhoven, Holland or 33 Rue Duquesnoy, B-1000, Brussels, Belgium or Friedrichstrasse 48, 6200 Wiesbaden, Germany.

Felikat Mundikat. Address: Rotterdamse Rijweg 94, NL-3042, AR Rotterdam, Holland.

Feline Advisory Bureau (FAB). Address: 350 Upper Richmond Road, Putney, London, SW15 6TL, England. Tel: 0181-789 9553.

Friends of the Cat (FOTC). Address: P.O. Box 52429, Saxonwold 2132, South Africa.

Governing Council of Associated Cat Clubs of South Africa (GCACC). Address: P.O. Box 532, Florida, Transvaal, South Africa.

The Governing Council of the Cat Fancy (GCCF). Founded in 1910, this major cat organization now has over 100 affiliated clubs. Address: 4-6, Penel Orlieu, Bridgwater, Somerset, TA6 3PG, England. Tel: 01278-427575.

The Independent Cat Association (ICA). Address: 211 East Oliver (Suite 201), Burbank, CA 91502, USA.

Independent Feline Alliance (IFA). Formed in 1994 as an 'alternative show system' with the motto 'Equal Opportunities for all Cats', it includes special classes for household pets and even disabled cats. Address: Gremora, Shepeau Stow, Whaplode Drove, Spalding, Lincs., PE12 0TU, England.

The Independent Pet Cat Society (IPCS). Formed in 1985. Address: 109 Locksway Road, Milton, Southsea, Hants, PO4 8JW, England.

The International Cat Association (TICA). Formed in 1979, TICA organizes cat shows throughout the USA, with affiliates in Canada and Japan, and claims to have created the largest genetically based cat registry in the world. It produces a *TICA Yearbook* and a twice-monthly newsletter called *TICA Trend*. Address: P.O. Box 2684, Harlingen, TX 78551, USA. and 134 Avenue de Paris, 78740 Vaux-sur-Seine, France. Tel: 210-428 8046.

Landsforeningen Felis Danica. Address: Tranehusene 44, DK-2620, Albertslund, Denmark.

Loisirs Félins Français (LFF). Address: 8, Rue du Parc, 78980 Paris, France Tel: 34 78 05 51.

Lukz. Address: Csetneki v 13, 11-1113, Budapest, Hungary.

National Cat Club. Address: The Laurels, Chesham Lane, Wendover, Bucks, England.

National Cat Fanciers' Association (NCFA). Now disbanded. Address: 20305 W. Burt Road, Brant, MI 48164, USA.

New Zealand Cat Fancy (NZCFa). Address: P.O. Box 3167, Richmond, Nelson, New Zealand.

New Zealand Cat Federation (NZCFe). Address: 20 Warren Kelly Street, Richmond, Nelson, New Zealand. Tel: 054-46721.

Norske Rasekattklubbers Riksforbund (NNR). Address: Nordane Valkyriegate 9, N-Olso 3, Norway.

Oevek. K.K.O. Address: Spaunstrasse 40, A-4020 Linz, Austria.

Royal Austrian Cat Club. Address: Postfach 75, 1172 Wien, Austria. Tel: 02 22/4 09-48 69.

Société Centrale Féline de France (SCFF). Address: 24 Rue de Nantes, 75019 Paris, France. Tel: 40 35 18 04.

South African Cat Register. Address: P.O. Box 4382, Randberg, Transvaal 2125, South Africa.

Suomen Rotukisshayhdistysten Keskusliitto r.v. (SRK). Address: Raappavuorenrinne 1 D 59, SF-01620 Vantaa 62, Finland.

Sveriges Raskattklubbars Riksforbund (SVERAK). Address: PL 4094 A, S-524 00, Herrljunga, Sweden.

United Cat Federation (UCF). A medium-sized organization centred on the West Coast of the USA. Address: 6621 Thornwood Street, San Diego, CA 92111, USA.

United Feline Organization (UFO). Address: P.O. Box 770578, Coral Springs, FL 33077, USA.Tel: 305-726-9556.

World Cat Federation. Address: Hubertstr. 280, D-45307, Essen, Germany. Tel: 02 01-55 07 55.

INDEX

Pictures can be found on pages shown in bold

ACKNOWLEDGEMENTS

The publisher thanks the photographers and organisations for their kind permission to reproduce the following photographs in this book:

1 Larry Johnson; 2–6 Adriano Bacchella; 28 Marc Henrie; 31 Animals Unlimited; 33 Bob Schwartz; 35 Adriano Bacchella; 37 NHPA/Gerard Lacz; 40 Adriano Bacchella; 41–44 Marc Henrie; 47 Adriano Bacchella; 48 NHPA/Gerard Lacz; 49 Anthony Verlag/Prenzel-Anthony; 51–54 Marc Henrie; 57 Bruce Coleman/Kim Taylor; 58 Ardea London/Yan Arthur–Bertrand; 61 Marc Henrie; 62 Animals Unlimited; 65 NHPA/Henry Ausloos; 66 Chanan; 69 Spectrum; 72 Animals Unlimited; 76 Chanan; 78 Marc Henrie; 83 Adriano Bacchella; 84–91 Chanan; 92 Marc Henrie; 96 Chanan; 98 Marc Henrie; 101 Ardea London/John Daniels; 106 Chanan;108 Bob Schwartz; 111 Animals Unlimited; 114 Bruce Coleman/Hans Reinhard; 116 Chanan; 119 Jacana/Axel; 120 Animals Unlimited; 123–124 Chanan; 127 Marc Henrie; 128 NHPA/Henry Ausloos; 130 Marc Henrie; 135 Ardea London/Yann Arthur-Bertrand; 136 Bob Schwartz; 137 Marc Henrie; 141 Bob Schwartz; 143 Marc Henrie; 144 Chanan; 145–154 Marc Henrie; 157 NHPA/Gerard Lacz; 158 Chanan; 159 Marc Henrie; 160 Bob Schwartz; 162 Bruce Coleman/Werner Layer; 163–165 Chanan; 166–168 Marc Henrie; 170 Jacana/Axel; 171–173 Chanan; 175 Adriano Bacchella; 177 NHPA/Gerard Lacz; 179 Chanan; 180–184 Marc Henrie; 187 Animals Unlimited; 190 Dr. Truda Straede; 192 Bob Schwartz; 195 Marc Henrie; 196 Bob Schwartz; 198 Animals Unlimited; 202 Jacana/Axel; 204–206 Marc Henrie; 207 Bob Schwartz; 209–210 Chanan; 212 Alan Robinson; 214 Tetsu Yamazaki; 216–218 Chanan; 219 David Brinicombe; 221–225 Chanan.